THE EVERYTHING®
GUIDE TO
OVERCOMING PTSD

Dear Reader,

Have you experienced a traumatic event that seems to have permanently transformed your life? Do casual reminders of what you experienced force you to relive what happened? Are you constantly checking and rechecking your surroundings for possible threats because you are afraid of becoming a victim again? And are these symptoms damaging the quality of your life and your relationships with the people around you?

The devastating symptoms experienced by people with Post-Traumatic Stress Disorder (PTSD) can seem overwhelming. But help is available. PTSD is becoming increasingly recognized as a disorder that can alter the minds and bodies of its sufferers. Whether this is due to lack of understanding of what is happening in their minds or because they are afraid of being labeled "crazy," far too many of those sufferers fail to get the help they need. It is important to realize that PTSD symptoms will not go away over time.

By writing this book, I hope to provide you with a better understanding of PTSD and how it affects you, and give you an arsenal of resources for finding help. Above all else, remember that there *is* hope for recovering, and there are people out there who can help you achieve that goal.

Romeo Vitelli, PhD

Welcome to the EVERYTHING® Series!

These handy, accessible books give you all you need to tackle a difficult project, gain a new hobby, comprehend a fascinating topic, prepare for an exam, or even brush up on something you learned back in school but have since forgotten.

You can choose to read an Everything® book from cover to cover or just pick out the information you want from our four useful boxes: e-questions, e-facts, e-alerts, and e-ssentials.

We give you everything you need to know on the subject, but throw in a lot of fun stuff along the way, too.

We now have more than 400 Everything® books in print, spanning such wide-ranging categories as weddings, pregnancy, cooking, music instruction, foreign language, crafts, pets, New Age, and so much more. When you're done reading them all, you can finally say you know Everything®!

QUESTION

Answers to
common questions

FACT

Important snippets
of information

ALERT

Urgent
warnings

ESSENTIAL

Quick
handy tips

PUBLISHER Karen Cooper

MANAGING EDITOR, EVERYTHING® SERIES Lisa Laing

COPY CHIEF Casey Ebert

ASSISTANT PRODUCTION EDITOR Alex Guarco

ACQUISITIONS EDITOR Eileen Mullan

DEVELOPMENT EDITOR Eileen Mullan

EVERYTHING® SERIES COVER DESIGNER Erin Alexander

Visit the entire Everything® series at *www.everything.com*

THE EVERYTHING®
GUIDE TO OVERCOMING PTSD

Simple, effective techniques for healing and recovery

Romeo Vitelli, PhD

Avon, Massachusetts

An Everything® Series Book.
Everything® and everything.com® are registered trademarks of F+W Media, Inc.

Published by
Adams Media, a division of F+W Media, Inc.
57 Littlefield Street, Avon, MA 02322. U.S.A.
www.adamsmedia.com

ISBN 10: 1-4405-7462-6
ISBN 13: 978-1-4405-7462-7
eISBN 10: 1-4405-7463-4
eISBN 13: 978-1-4405-7463-4

Printed in the United States of America.

10 9 8 7 6 5 4 3 2 1

Library of Congress Cataloging-in-Publication Data
Vitelli, Romeo, author.
The everything guide to overcoming PTSD / Romeo Vitelli.
    pages cm. -- (An everything series book)
    Includes bibliographical references and index.
    ISBN-13: 978-1-4405-7462-7 (pb)
    ISBN-10: 1-4405-7462-6 (pb)
    ISBN-13: 978-1-4405-7463-4 (ebook)
    ISBN-10: 1-4405-7463-4 (ebook)
    1. Post-traumatic stress disorder--Popular works. I. Title.
    RC552.P67V58 2014
    616.85'21--dc23
                                    2014002371

Cover images © Piotr Krześlak/123RF.

This book is available at quantity discounts for bulk purchases.
For information, please call 1-800-289-0963.

Contents

Top 10 Ways to Cope with PTSD **10**

Introduction **11**

1 The Basics of PTSD / 13

Definition of PTSD **14**

Who Gets PTSD? **17**

How Common Is PTSD? **17**

PTSD Facts **19**

PTSD in Different Forms **22**

2 History of PTSD / 27

Soldier's Heart **28**

Shell Shock **30**

Combat Fatigue **34**

The Fight for PTSD's Recognition **36**

PTSD Today **38**

3 PTSD and the Brain / 41

Stress and the Body **42**

How Trauma Affects the Brain **46**

Are Some People More Vulnerable to Trauma? **51**

Other Factors Linked to PTSD Vulnerability **54**

Is There a PTSD Gene? **55**

4 Symptoms of PTSD / 59

General Symptoms of PTSD **60**

Responding to Disasters **65**

Thoughts and Behaviors **68**

Symptoms That Confuse **69**

Can It Be More Than One? **70**

5 Comparing PTSD to Other Disorders / 75

Acute Stress Disorder **76**

Anxiety Disorders **77**

Obsessive-Compulsive Disorder (OCD) **78**

Depression **80**

Personality Disorders **81**

Traumatic Brain Injury **82**

Conversion Disorder **84**

6 Who PTSD Affects / 87

Types of Traumatic Events **88**

Important Factors **89**

Famous People Who Developed PTSD **91**

Isn't Everyone a Little Different? **94**

Natural Disasters **97**

PTSD in Wartime **98**

Refugees and PTSD **98**

Personal Trauma **99**

PTSD and Sexual Abuse **100**

7 **Special Populations and PTSD / 101**

PTSD in Veterans **102**

PTSD in Children **105**

Risk Factors in Children **110**

PTSD in Victims of Violence **111**

PTSD and Traumatic Brain Injury **113**

8 **The Role of PTSD in Building Relationships / 117**

Impact of Trauma **118**

When Parents Have the Disorder **121**

Social Relationships **124**

Professional Relationships **125**

Romantic Relationships **127**

Why Are You in This Relationship? **128**

9 **PTSD Paired with Other Disorders / 131**

Trauma and Your Health **132**

PTSD and Substance Abuse **133**

Mood Disorders **135**

Anxiety Disorders **137**

PTSD and Infection Resistance **138**

Cardiovascular Disease **140**

Chronic Pain **141**

10 **Can PTSD Be Prevented? / 145**

Immediate Help **146**

Critical Incident Stress Debriefing **151**

Psychological First Aid **153**

Forming Social Support Networks **159**

Using Online Resources **160**

11 **If Someone You Love Has PTSD / 163**

Being Supportive **164**

When to Intervene **165**

Expressing Your Concerns **167**

Dealing with Denial and Confusion **168**

What Should You Say? **169**

What Should You Do? **170**

What If Your Child Has PTSD? **173**

12 **Treatment for PTSD / 175**

Treatment Basics **176**

When Is Treatment Necessary? **177**

Where to Go for Help **179**

Finding Information **180**

Sifting Through Information **182**

Is It Working? **183**

Group Support **184**

Treating PTSD in Children **188**

13 **Therapy Options for PTSD / 191**

Psychotherapy **192**

Acute Post-Traumatic Interventions **193**

Drug Therapy **195**

Cognitive-Behavioral Therapy **199**

Does EMDR Help? **203**

Counseling/Psychotherapy **204**

14 **The Family and PTSD / 211**

PTSD Symptoms in the Family **212**

Characteristics of the Family System **213**

Creating Social Support Networks **214**

Defusing Stress **216**

Learning to Cope in the Present **217**

Family and Couples Therapy **218**

15 **Handling the Symptoms / 223**

Learning to Cope **224**

Controlling Stress **225**

Dealing with Flashbacks **227**

Coping with Reminders **228**

Confronting Triggers **231**

Learning Hope **235**

16 **What Is Resilience? / 237**

Research on Resilience **238**

Why Are Some People More Resilient? **239**

Can Resilience Be Learned? **242**

Is Resilience Enough? **246**

Incorporating Resilience Into Everyday Life **248**

Resilience in the Workplace **252**

Resilience and Aging **253**

17 **When PTSD Goes Untreated: How Not to Cope / 255**

PTSD Does Not Just Go Away **256**

Self-Medication **257**

Emotional Numbing **258**

Short-Term Consequences **259**

Long-Term Consequences **262**

18 **Where to Go from Here / 265**

Living Life with PTSD **267**

Moving On **268**

Gaining Control **269**

Easing the Destructive Impact **271**

Learning to Cope in the Future **273**

Appendix A: DSM-5 Criteria for PTSD Diagnosis **275**

Appendix B: PTSD Checklist (PCL) **283**

Appendix C: Useful PTSD Resources **289**

Appendix D: Suggested Reading **293**

Index **295**

Dedication

To my parents, Attilio and Anna Maria.
And also to the countless health professionals, families, and volunteers
helping people with trauma move on with their lives.

Acknowledgments

I would just like to extend my appreciation to everyone
involved in this project.

Top 10 Ways to Cope with PTSD

1. Learn all you can about the different symptoms of PTSD. Understanding what is happening to you can help you better cope with what is happening.

2. Identify the different emotional states you are experiencing. Try to understand why you are feeling angry, anxious, or depressed and what is triggering these emotions in you.

3. Learn about the different triggers that can lead to flashbacks and unpleasant memories. These can include certain sights, sounds, and even odors that you have learned to associate with traumatic memories.

4. Keep track of important anniversary dates. Your symptoms are more likely to flare up at certain times and places that are more likely to remind you of what you experienced.

5. Don't be afraid to share your feelings with others. Isolating yourself from the important people in your life means depriving yourself of valuable support.

6. Learn about relaxation and stress management techniques that can help you control panic and anxiety attacks. Make certain that you pace yourself to keep stress from building up in your daily life.

7. Learn about grounding techniques that can help you root yourself in the present. These are especially important during flashbacks or when the intrusive memories are overwhelming you.

8. Learn about sleep hygiene and how to get to sleep at night naturally and without relying on sleep medications.

9. Establish realistic life plans for yourself and don't become pessimistic if you aren't recovering as quickly as you would like. There is no fixed timetable and everyone is different.

10. Maintain strong social support networks. That can include family members, friends, coworkers, therapists, community workers, fellow trauma survivors, and volunteers. Learn to depend on them and to offer help to others as they need it.

Introduction

IF YOU HAPPEN TO be a fan of the *Beetle Bailey* comic strip, you likely noticed something odd that happened to Beetle in early 2013. Running steadily since 1950, the comic strip by Mort Walker—which features the misadventures of a rather unmotivated army private and his perennial clashes with his arch-nemesis, Sergeant Snorkel—has usually focused on the funny side of life in the U.S. Armed Forces. In June, though, the three-panel strip featured Beetle in bed having a series of nightmares relating to his experiences in the army. In the third panel, Bailey is wide awake with the message, "Post-Traumatic Stress Can Affect Any Soldier."

This installment of the comic strip was run by Mort Walker to help kick off a public service campaign that wanted to call attention to the epidemic of post-traumatic stress among the men and women in the U.S. Armed Forces. Beginning in the month of June, which is Post-Traumatic Stress Disorder (PTSD) Awareness Month, the campaign highlighted the critical need for soldiers with PTSD and traumatic brain injury (TBI) symptoms to come forward and seek treatment.

In recent years, treating PTSD in returning veterans has posed major challenges for mental health professionals. The surge in new cases threatens to overwhelm available health services even though many veterans refuse to seek help. With an estimated 19 percent of the 1.6 million members of the U.S. Armed Services deployed to Iraq and Afghanistan in the past five years reporting mental health symptoms, finding better treatment options has become more crucial than ever.

But PTSD doesn't just affect soldiers. According to a 2009 study by the World Health Organization examining trauma in twenty-one countries, a substantial minority of the people responding to the study reported experiencing a traumatic event, whether through exposure to war, a serious accident, trauma involving a loved one, or through witnessing or becoming a victim of violence. The National Comorbidity Survey estimated that in the

United States alone, the lifetime prevalence of PTSD is 6.8 percent. That figure is substantially higher for women (9.7 percent) than men (3.6 percent) reflecting the impact of domestic violence and sexual abuse.

For people dealing with PTSD, the temptation to "tough it out" and not seek treatment can be hard to resist, especially considering the stigma that is often associated with any form of psychiatric problem. But the symptoms rarely go away on their own, and untreated PTSD can lead to a wide range of problems including substance abuse, depression, medically unexplained physical problems, and even suicide.

The following chapters will explain the definition of PTSD, introduce the most common symptoms linked to the PTSD diagnosis, and discuss the most effective treatment methods that have been developed to date. Please note that this book is *not* intended as an aid to help you diagnose yourself. If you suspect that you or a loved one is experiencing PTSD symptoms, the Appendix section will provide you with possible resources to get the proper treatment. While seeking help can be a frightening prospect, especially for someone who has never attended counseling before, the resources in this book can assist you in achieving that goal. Just remember that the right help is out there.

CHAPTER 1

The Basics of PTSD

Most everyone has experienced stressful situations in their lives, but sometimes these events can have a lasting impact on a person's mental and physical well-being. According to the fifth edition of the *Diagnostic and Statistical Manual of Mental Disorders* (DSM-5) released in early 2013, Post-Traumatic Stress Disorder (PTSD) is defined as "the development of characteristic symptoms following exposure to one or more traumatic events." The DSM-5 goes on to define a traumatic event as occurring when a person "experienced, witnessed, or was confronted with an event or events that involved actual or threatened death or serious injury, or a threat to the physical integrity of self or others." Though most people who experience traumatic events will not develop PTSD, there is no way to predict who will develop symptoms and who will not.

Definition of PTSD

The three major features that characterize PTSD are the re-experiencing of the traumatic event through dream and/or waking thoughts; emotional numbing to other life experiences and relationships; and symptoms of autonomic instability, depression, and cognitive difficulties (such as poor memory or concentration). In people with PTSD, autonomic instability can include physiological signs of high stress including rapid heartbeat, excessive sweating, and high or low blood pressure. Though some degree of acute stress is often found in people experiencing traumatic events, a diagnosis of PTSD typically requires that symptoms last longer than one month and that they are severe enough to interfere with occupational or social functioning.

FACT

It is important to draw a clear distinction between words such as "traumatic" and "stressful," which are often treated interchangeably. Though there can be some overlap between how people respond to traumatic events and highly stressful situations, they are not the same thing. Everyone faces everyday hassles and life-changing events such as unemployment, but survivors and families of survivors know that traumatic stress is very different.

The full DSM-5 diagnostic criteria are included in Appendix A for your reference along with a widely used PTSD diagnostic checklist in Appendix B, but these are **not** intended for self-diagnosis. While you may recognize many of the symptoms in yourself or someone you care about, a proper diagnosis should only be completed by a trained professional who has experience dealing with cases of PTSD.

Alternative Definition

As an alternative to the DSM-5 criteria, the International Statistical Classification of Diseases and Related Health Problems (ICD-10), defines PTSD as:

- Exposure to a stressful event or situation (either short or long lasting) of an exceptionally threatening or catastrophic nature that is likely to cause pervasive distress in almost anyone.
- Persistent remembering or "reliving" the stressor by intrusive flash-backs, vivid memories, recurring dreams, or by experiencing distress when exposed to circumstances resembling or associated with the stressor.
- Actual or preferred avoidance of circumstances resembling or associated with the stressor (not present before exposure to the stressor).
- Either:

  1. Inability to recall, either partially or completely, some important aspects of the period of exposure to the stressor
  2. Persistent symptoms of increased psychological sensitivity and arousal (not present before exposure to the stressor) shown by any two of the following: difficulty in falling or staying asleep; irritability or outbursts of anger; difficulty in concentrating; hypervigilance (extreme sensitivity to one's surroundings, i.e., compulsive scanning of the environment for potential threats); or exaggerated startle response

Much like the DSM-5 criteria, the ICD-10 guidelines are only regarded as applicable if the symptoms arise within six months of a *severe* traumatic event. Since there are a number of other psychological or medical conditions that can mimic some of the symptoms of PTSD (which will be covered in a later chapter), clinical diagnosis needs to be left up to a qualified mental health professional. It is also possible for post-traumatic symptoms to arise much later than six months, even decades later, if the PTSD sufferer experiences a situation similar enough to the initial event to trigger PTSD flashbacks. Such cases tend to be rare and harder to treat as a result.

How PTSD Appears

How PTSD appears in an individual varies widely across sufferers, ranging from primarily fear-based responses (including being prone to flashbacks) and behavioral symptoms, to symptoms very similar to chronic depression. "Classic" PTSD can present with multiple symptoms. Some

PTSD sufferers may deliberately conceal many of the symptoms they are experiencing to avoid being labeled as "crazy."

FACT

If you feel that you are experiencing some or all of the symptoms being described in this chapter, it is important to seek out a qualified mental health professional as soon as possible.

When diagnosing PTSD in children younger than six years old, many of the diagnostic criteria are the same as they for adults and older children, except that traumatic exposure can also include learning that the traumatic event occurred to a parent or caregiver. Symptoms including flashbacks, avoidance of people, places, and objects that act as reminders, and blunted emotion or inability to feel positive emotions are also common in young children with PTSD. While children may not be able to articulate what is happening to them, PTSD symptoms can come out in how they play or in the form of frequent nightmares (whether or not the nightmares relate to the trauma).

Traumatized children are also prone to angry outbursts and even extreme temper tantrums along with hypervigilance (advanced state of sensory sensitivity), concentration problems, and sleep disturbances. Again, these symptoms need to have a disruptive effect in how the child relates to parents, teachers, or children their own age for a diagnosis of PTSD. Also, the effects of other medical conditions (including Attention-Deficit Hyperactivity Disorder or Autism) need to be ruled out by a qualified professional.

ALERT

Appendix C contains resources including national organizations dedicated to making PTSD resources available to the general public. While not every organization will have a local chapter near you, these resources can recommend professionals and volunteers that you can contact. Your family doctor can also be a good person to put you in touch with available resources in your own neighborhood.

Who Gets PTSD?

PTSD can occur in people facing potentially life-threatening situations and can overwhelm their natural ability to cope. This may include people surviving natural disasters such as the 2004 Indian Ocean tsunami and the effects of Hurricane Katrina in 2005, war veterans, peace officers, victims of domestic or sexual assault, accident victims, and victims of violence. Though not everyone who has encountered these traumatic events will develop PTSD, there is no way of predicting who will develop symptoms and how those symptoms will appear to other people.

As the definition of PTSD has broadened in recent years, the likelihood of being diagnosed has increased as well. While it is possible to be diagnosed with PTSD based on secondary trauma (e.g., learning that a loved one has died unexpectedly or learning about traumatic events experienced by a friend or loved one), these cases are often controversial.

Still, the potential for PTSD exists in anyone who has been touched by a traumatic event, whether directly or indirectly. As you will see in later sections, the effects of trauma can even be passed on from parents to their children, and dealing with PTSD is as much a burden for family members and friends as it is for survivors themselves.

How Common Is PTSD?

Developing PTSD symptoms is far more common than most people realize. According to the National Comorbidity Survey, more than 60.7 percent of men and 51.2 percent of women reported having experienced at least one traumatic event in their lifetime. Many of the survey respondents reported experiencing two or more such events (56.3 percent of men and 48.6 percent of women). The most frequently reported traumas were:

1. Witnessing someone being badly injured or killed (35.6 percent of men and 14.5 percent of women)
2. Fire, flood, or other natural disasters (18.9 percent of men and 15.2 percent of women)
3. Life-threatening accidents (25 percent of men and 13.8 percent of women)

There are also significant differences in the types of traumatic events experienced by men and women. Men are more likely to experience combat, being physically assaulted, being threatened with a weapon, or being kidnapped or held hostage. Women, on the other hand, are far more likely than men to experience rape, sexual molestation, childhood neglect, and domestic violence.

Military veterans remain the most widely recognized group with respect to being diagnosed with PTSD. According to the U.S. Department of Veterans Affairs, an estimated 830,000 Vietnam veterans suffer from PTSD symptoms. That only applies to veterans who have been formally diagnosed with PTSD. In recent surveys, as many as four out of five veterans report one or more PTSD symptoms even decades after their war experience ended. Other occupational groups including police officers and firefighters have also been identified as being likely to experience traumatic events that could produce PTSD although available statistics are still scarce.

FACT

Even people in occupations where there is a high risk of death or serious injury (such as construction work) can have an increased risk of developing PTSD, especially since many of these industries fail to provide mental health resources for workers experiencing job-related trauma. Some companies provide lists of health-care professionals for employees needing physical or mental health treatment. You can do your own research as well.

Additional factors that can increase the likelihood of developing PTSD include age and prior history of traumatic exposure. Overall, younger people are more likely than older adults to experience traumatic events. A 1998 study suggested that people in the 16–20-year-old age bracket are most vulnerable. History of prior exposure to trauma also significantly increases likelihood of developing PTSD both in civilians and in the military.

Still, whatever the nature of the traumatic event that leads up to the development of PTSD, the end result is remarkably similar, whether in returning military veterans, victims of sexual assault, or survivors of childhood sexual abuse. Ultimately, PTSD occurs because people have been wounded beyond their ability to heal themselves.

PTSD Facts

Anyone can get PTSD. Despite the stigma that can get attached to developing symptoms of a mental disorder, everyone is vulnerable to experiencing a potentially traumatic event at some point in their lives. The risk for PTSD increases sharply if the traumatic event is sudden and unpredictable, lasts a long time (or seems to), involves a very real threat of sexual abuse or physical injury, appears likely to happen again, and involves more than one type of threatening event.

FACT

Children are especially vulnerable to PTSD since the trauma occurs in the early years while the personality is still forming and abuse coming from trusted family members is far more devastating than what they might experience from strangers. Trauma can also lead to long-term personality problems in children with a lack of trust or empathy becoming part of their basic personality structure.

People vary widely in how they respond to trauma and individual factors seem to play a significant role in whether PTSD develops. This can include history of prior victimization (which can make people more vulnerable to new trauma), negative personality factors such as pessimism or depression, mental health problems, and even biological differences. Females seem more vulnerable to PTSD than males, possibly due to a greater likelihood of being able to express emotions without seeming "weak." That also makes them more likely to respond successfully to treatment.

There seems to be a range of protective factors that can reduce or prevent post-traumatic stress. These can include having a basic sense of humor, the ability to express emotion to others (again more common in females than in males), the ability to tolerate distress, self-esteem, creativity, problem-solving skills, and basic resilience (this will be covered in a later chapter). Though these are all important factors, they are also things that can be learned and developed, either before the traumatic event occurs or afterward in the form of treatment. Ironically, traumatic events can also become learning experiences since they can lead people to develop those skills that can protect them in the future.

A strong social support network of family and friends is also important in protecting against traumatic stress. People who are socially isolated are also more vulnerable to developing PTSD. Children particularly need warm, loving adults in a secure and predictable setting to help counteract the effects of trauma. This kind of support can help them develop trust and learn to express emotions safely. On the other hand, negative family environments can make adults and children more vulnerable to developing PTSD due to the lack of emotional support and added stress that can exhaust essential resources needed to cope with trauma.

Parents with PTSD can often pass their trauma on to their children by raising them to share their hypervigilance and pessimism about the world. In that way, PTSD can create a legacy of fear that can potentially be passed on for generations.

The effects of PTSD can also be made worse by what the sufferer experiences *after* the traumatic event occurs. These risk factors can include:

- **Lack of emotional support**—Not everyone feels comfortable discussing their feelings or the emotional impact of a traumatic event. The feeling of being shut out of the lives of other people who might be reluctant to provide support due to their own unwillingness to deal with the traumatic event can worsen the impact of trauma.

- **Refusal to believe or support the victim**—This is a common experience for victims of sexual abuse or domestic violence. Forcing victims to feel shame by placing the blame on them rather than on the victimizer occurs quite frequently, especially in families that "close ranks" against the victim for pressing criminal charges in the first place. Whether the victim is accused of lying or of exaggerating the abuse, the trauma is often magnified as a result.

- **Secondary victimization**—Though support agencies and professionals are meant to provide help for victims of traumatic events, they can often aggravate the trauma due to bureaucratic inertia or even accusing the victim of lying. In the case of sexual assault victims, dealing with skeptical police and defense attorneys attempting to shred their credibility can often be as traumatic as the initial violence. People who have experienced trauma following a serious automobile accident or natural disaster often encounter problems filing insurance claims and insurance medical examiners telling them that their problems are all in their heads.

- **Total silence**—In many cultures, domestic and sexual abuse are deemed to be too shameful to discuss openly or out of fear of legal consequences. Children who have been abused can be told to keep quiet to avoid having the offender (often a trusted family member) being sent to prison.
- **Lack of treatment**—Not every community will have trauma services readily available within easy reach of the trauma sufferer's home. People who have been traumatized may often find themselves being placed on lengthy waiting lists or being forced to travel long distances to get the help they need. While health services are becoming more available for victims interacting with counselors using telecommunications, this is still in development in most places.
- **Ineffective coping strategies**—Many people lack the effective resources they need to cope with an unexpected trauma. When devastating events occur out of the blue, trauma sufferers may attempt to deal with their emotional issues on their own or else resort to potentially destructive coping methods ranging from substance abuse to self-cutting.

There is no typical PTSD patient and no fixed pattern of recovery. Along the way, there will be setbacks, unexpected problems, and breakdowns in the treatment process. People with PTSD can find themselves stuck at some point and symptoms will often persist for many years. As they learn new coping skills, symptoms can become more manageable, but rarely disappear completely.

Unfortunately, many trauma survivors often resort to unhealthy ways of coping that may relieve symptoms of distress to some extent, but are often likely to lead to health problems in future. These can include drinking, drug use (including abuse of prescription drugs), cigarette smoking, overeating, and unsafe sex. Treatment can help survivors find alternative ways of coping that can help them live longer and more productive lives.

PTSD in Different Forms

What are some of the consequences of unresolved PTSD? Though people can often successfully hide their symptoms for a certain amount of time, they will come out eventually and in ways that can be potentially destructive to the sufferer and the people around them. Potential problems associated with untreated PTSD include:

Suicide

When the pain becomes overwhelming, giving in to despair becomes all too common. While depression remains the most common psychological problem linked to attempted and completed suicide, PTSD sufferers remain at high risk. Though exact statistics linking PTSD to suicide in the general population remain scarce, suicide statistics for returning U.S. veterans are grim. In 2009 alone, the suicide rate among male veterans using Veterans Administration services was 38.3 per 100,000 and 12.8 per 100,000 in females. This was substantially higher than the suicide rate seen in the general U.S. population (19.4 per 100,000 for males and 4.9 per 100,000 for females). Though there does not appear to be a clear correlation between combat exposure and suicide, the highest relative suicide rate has been seen in veterans who have been repeatedly wounded whether or not they received a formal diagnosis of PTSD.

Suicide attempts among rape victims is ten times higher than nonvictims and similar trends are noted among incest and domestic violence victims, which demonstrates the impact that trauma can have on later suicide. A National Comorbidity Survey study showed that PTSD was significantly associated with suicide ideation and attempts. Studies also showed that the relationship between suicide and PTSD remained strong even when controlling for the effects of physical illness and other mental disorders. While not all PTSD sufferers will commit suicide, family members and friends must recognize that the risk is there and that getting them into treatment is potentially lifesaving.

Warning Signs of Suicide

Some of the warning signs suggesting that someone is considering suicide can include:

- Sudden neglect of personal appearance, including unexplained weight gain or loss.
- Sudden changes in appetite (eating too much or too little) or sleeping patterns.
- Expressing feelings of hopelessness or helplessness.
- Mood changes or angry outbursts.
- Visible fatigue or loss of interest in activities that used to be enjoyable.
- Sudden personality changes, including becoming more unpredictable.
- Self-destructive thoughts or behavior. Engaging in risky behaviors.
- Substance abuse, especially if they are drinking or using drugs more than usual.
- Neglecting responsibilities such as attending classes or going to work.
- Giving away prized possessions or otherwise showing signs of putting their affairs in order.
- Previous suicide attempts.

Ironically, some people considering suicide can seem quite cheerful in the days leading up to their death (they think their problems are over, after all). Though some people can commit suicide without showing any of these classic warning signs, leaving friends and family members devastated, staying alert can often mean the difference between life and death. While people planning suicide may not be open about their intentions, persuading them to get help from the nearest hospital emergency department or personal physician can help save their lives. Keeping a suicidal person alive can be emotionally draining, and family and friends often require emotional support themselves, as a result.

Deliberate Self-Injury

Not every attempt at self-harm involves intentionally trying to commit suicide. Trauma survivors of all ages, particularly survivors of childhood trauma, can carry out different kinds of self-injury including self-cutting, head-banging, swallowing foreign objects, self-mutilation, hair pulling, poking sharp objects into themselves, or refusing treatment for pain problems. While not necessarily considered a form of self-injury, trauma survivors who become thrill-seekers and take unnecessary risks to personal safety may also be regarded as being self-destructive.

There can be different reasons for self-injury, including a need to convert emotional pain into physical pain, as punishment for perceived offenses, to relieve stress through stress-induced analgesia, to contain aggressive thoughts, to gain attention from family members or health professionals, or even as a way of feeling alive. Though people who engage in self-injury may deny intending to commit suicide, recent research suggests that self-injury may be a risk factor for suicide. Family members and friends who see this kind of behavior in trauma survivors should notify health authorities immediately.

Re-Victimization

People who have been traumatized once have an increased risk of experiencing new traumatic events in future. Lingering trauma can reduce the body's ability to cope with new traumas as they are experienced and the impact, even if not as severe as previous traumatic experiences, can add to the total emotional damage that trauma survivors experience. Military veterans facing trauma in the field can often find themselves becoming emotionally numb to being re-exposed to the same situation time and again. Victims of childhood sexual abuse or domestic violence often encounter similar traumatic events over time that can make the trauma far harder to treat. They can also develop problems with poor self-esteem and the attitude that they "deserve" to be victimized.

Intergenerational Transmission of Trauma

People with PTSD are often capable of passing their trauma on to family members. The children of Holocaust survivors are referred to as the "Second Generation" due to growing up with their parents' stories of the traumatic events they experienced. The children experience their own trauma at hearing the stories and dealing with the emotional consequences. Although they often learn to be more resilient to encountering trauma in their own lives,

Holocaust survivors and their children develop a second generation "complex," according to psychologists who treat this group, that can lead to problems in self-esteem, identity, and pessimism about the world.

In the same way, children of PTSD sufferers can often experience secondary trauma due to parental stories about the trauma they had experienced directly. Though learning about these events can help bolster the child's ability to cope, parents with PTSD need to be aware of the potential damage that can occur as well. The legacy resulting from chronic problems such as physical and sexual abuse can continue for generations.

Sexual Problems

Many of the symptoms associated with PTSD can lead to a loss of sexual intimacy. This can include the inability to trust, emotional detachment or numbing, survivor guilt, depression, anger, poor self-esteem, and generalized anxiety. People whose trauma involves sexual abuse often experience flashbacks associated with sexual acts and can need extensive counseling to be able to resolve their sexual issues. Some survivors can often use highly sexualized relationships as a way of coping with trauma, which can result in additional problems, e.g., sexually transmitted diseases and unwanted pregnancies. There can also be a "flip-flopping" in trauma victims who find themselves wishing for sexual intimacy and emotional closeness, but being repulsed by it as well. Partners of people with PTSD experiencing sexual problems need to recognize the nature of the problem and not take rejection personally.

Substance Abuse

The strong relationship between PTSD and substance abuse has been recognized by researchers for decades. Studies about men and women receiving inpatient and outpatient substance abuse treatment have found a high prevalence of PTSD symptoms (as high as 80 percent in one study of women receiving treatment for substance abuse problems). In adolescents being treated for substance abuse, females were far more likely than males to have a history of PTSD symptoms.

As for the question of why substance abuse is so common in trauma sufferers, researchers have proposed a self-medication hypothesis in which trauma sufferers deliberately resort to drugs or alcohol to numb the emotional problems they are experiencing. While the self-medication hypothesis is still controversial, especially in explaining away the whole spectrum of addictive disorders, trauma alone does appear to play a strong role in developing later drug or alcohol problems. At the same time, people with substance abuse problems can also be at higher risk for developing PTSD so the relationship is not entirely one-way.

CHAPTER 2

History of PTSD

Though literary descriptions of the emotional problems associated with PTSD date back thousands of years (including the *Iliad* and the *Odyssey*), recognition of the emotional and physical problems associated with post-traumatic stress is surprisingly recent. It fact, it took the outbreak of the American Civil War in 1861 before doctors began to discover the powerful effect that trauma has on the body.

Soldier's Heart

Early reports of what doctors would eventually call "irritable heart syndrome" or "soldier's heart" began in 1862, when physicians began noting unusual symptoms among the soldiers receiving medical care. Along with battlefield injuries and diseases such as malaria, dysentery, and typhoid, army physicians also observed severe heart palpitations in the soldiers who had survived combat. According to one physician, Alfred Stille, the soldiers themselves attributed the strange symptoms to the rigorous campaigning, including long marches with heavy backpacks. Based on his own observations, Stille reported to his colleagues that the palpitations were due to extreme exhaustion.

Other physicians reported on the "cardiac muscular exhaustion" seen in soldiers and expanded on what Stille was observing. Henry Hartshorne described what he was seeing as exhaustion. Specific symptoms included a rapid, feeble pulse rate, an abnormally fast heart rate (even when the soldier was at rest), and breathing problems. Hartshorne argued that the symptoms were caused by overexertion, lack of rest, and poor nutrition, though he was careful to distinguish the new syndrome from ordinary nervous exhaustion.

The name most commonly associated with the irritable heart syndrome seen in soldiers was Jacob Mendes Da Costa who was the first physician to link the symptoms he was observing to psychological factors. The condition he described is often called Da Costa's Syndrome in his honor. Da Costa reported in 1867 to the U.S. Sanitary Commission that he regarded the condition he was seeing in patients as a "cardiac neurosis," since "the mass of cardiac disorder is not organic, but functional." Since there were no physical signs of actual heart disease involved, the symptoms themselves represented the condition he needed to treat.

Along with the heart symptoms, soldiers were also describing "jerking during sleep," disturbed sleep, and nightmares. While Da Costa was careful not to label the new syndrome as being a mental disorder, he did insist that the condition was not easily faked (even then, military authorities were wary of possible malingerers). He also acknowledged that the condition was being seen more frequently in soldiers as the war dragged on. Treatment with conventional heart medications such as digitalis showed little real effect.

Soldier's Heart in Civilians

After the war ended, Da Costa continued writing about the condition, which he saw in civilian patients as well. He maintained that the symptoms could be caused by any significant strain, which, among other things, could mean emotional shock. Many of the case histories he presented described how his syndrome could develop even in nonsoldiers. In an 1874 medical journal, Da Costa wrote:

We can understand how even mental emotion, acting through the nervous system on the nerves of the heart, may produce real trouble, and how the worry of life, and strain on the feelings, when long kept up, may give rise to conditions which, in figurative language, we call "heart-weary," and "heart-sick," and which, not as a figure of speech, but in truth, may be the beginning of actual cardiac malady.

Da Costa also suggested that irritable heart symptoms could be caused by anything that resulted in overexertion of the heart including sexual disorders, abuse of tea or coffee, irregularity or excess in eating or drinking or, "long matrimonial engagements." In other words, virtually anything that caused nervous irritability could cause irritable heart syndrome. For treatment, Da Costa recommended rest above all else though he also advocated medication (especially digitalis for the heart). Despite the lack of real evidence that irritable heart syndrome actually involved heart disease, Da Costa based his ideas about the syndrome on patients becoming "heart-weary" due to chronic overexertion.

Though Da Costa and his colleagues came close to realizing the role that traumatic stress could play on the body, they never quite managed to make that final connection. Physicians such as Da Costa mainly focused on the role that overexertion and fatigue had on the heart since these were things they could observe directly. Acknowledging the role of psychic factors that could only be inferred likely seemed a step backward. Da Costa described the rigors of combat that soldiers faced as well as lack of sleep, poor nutrition, and exposure to disease. All of these were potential factors for irritable heart syndrome as far as he was concerned. That soldiers were also constantly afraid was something he failed to mention in his writings.

Whether because he did not want irritable heart patients accused of cowardice or he simply refused to consider other factors besides over-work, Da Costa never wavered in regarding fatigue as the culprit. And fatigue was certainly a problem in nineteenth-century medicine. In an era before labor legislation or safety regulations, many workers were obliged to work long hours under unsafe conditions we nowadays see only in Third World factories. That many of these workers also developed irritable heart symptoms seemed to prove Da Costa's hypothesis about over-work being the culprit.

As the memory of the Civil War faded and new wars arose, irritable heart syndrome would give way to new diagnoses as physicians recognized that it was not a heart syndrome at all. As cardiologist James Mackenzie pointed out in 1916, such cases were not heart-related, but were actually due to emotional exhaustion. That the horrors of war take a terrible toll on soldiers and civilians caught in the crossfire seems obvious enough. Recognizing that constant threat of death could lead to legitimate medical conditions rather than the type of symptoms associated with cowardice would take much longer.

Shell Shock

With the outbreak of World War I in 1914, the Great War that raged from 1914 to 1918 added a new dimension to warfare with modern artillery raining down on troops as they dug into their trenches. An estimated 10 percent of all troops deployed were killed (compared to 4.5 percent in World War II) with countless more being severely wounded. With the modern way of fighting wars came a new awareness of how troops were being affected. While troops of previous wars had presented symptoms of the extreme stress they were facing (e.g., soldier's heart), it was in 1915 that a British medical officer named Charles Myers was the first to use the term "shell shock" in a medical journal to describe the impact of battle on even experienced soldiers who displayed a range of bizarre symptoms that medical doctors on both sides of the conflict couldn't figure out how to treat.

Trauma on the Front Lines

Shell shock was just one of the diagnoses that a soldier experiencing medical problems received during World War I. Doctors tended to classify shell shock under the general category of "war neuroses" (which basically meant any nonphysical problem that prevented soldiers from fighting). Other diagnoses that traumatized soldiers could be given included hysteria, neurasthenia (nervous exhaustion), and "disordered action of the heart." Shell shock was considered to be the most serious diagnosis and, as you might guess from the name, tended to be reserved for soldiers who had been exposed to heavy artillery.

Shell shock got its name from the assumption that the symptoms being reported by soldiers were being caused by brain damage resulting from exposure to vibrations from explosions. Since the explosions could also result in soldiers receiving brain concussions or other forms of Traumatic Brain Injury, many of the symptoms seen in cases of shell shock were similar enough to what would be seen in brain damage for military physicians to assume that the brain damage hypothesis was correct.

Still, while many cases involved soldiers who had faced the heat of battle, symptoms were also being found in soldiers who had never been deployed in the field. For the ones who had never faced battle or had no obvious injuries, accusations of cowardice were all too common. Soldiers sent to hospitals for treatment were overcome with shame over their lack of bravery, with four out of five soldiers being unable to return to fighting afterward. Often urged to face their trauma in a "manly way," soldiers rarely received sympathy from commanding officers or fellow soldiers. A distinction was usually made between the symptoms reported by common soldiers and what officers developed, and the different ranks would typically be sent to different hospitals.

Given the high casualty rates that were occurring during the war and the need for soldiers to fight, the priority was given to treatment methods that would get soldiers back into action. Different therapists advocated radically different approaches, ranging from simple talking cures to "torpillage" or electroshock therapy (especially popular in the French army). Advocated by Clovis Vincent, a French neurologist, for use with cases of hysterical paralysis, the treatment involved Vincent applying a sharp current to the patient's body to provoke involuntary movement. The treatment fell out of favor after a soldier received a court-martial for punching Vincent. A similar approach was followed for the treatment of German soldiers and was known as the "Kaufman Cure," named after its primary exponent, Fritz Kaufman. The treatment involved "surprise" methods including shock and physical intimidation and resulted in the deaths of an estimated twenty patients.

On and Off the Battlefield

As Ben Shephard reported in his book, *A War of Nerves: Soldiers and Psychiatrists, 1914–1994*, a British army directive was issued in 1915, stating that, "Shell shock and shell concussion cases should have the letter 'W' prefixed to the report of the casualty, if it were due to the enemy; in that case the patient would be entitled to rank as 'wounded' and to wear on his arm a 'wound stripe.' If, however, the man's breakdown did not follow a shell explosion, it was not thought to be 'due to the enemy,' and he was to be labeled 'Shell-shock' or 'S' (for sickness) and was not entitled to a wound stripe or a pension."

By 1917, all British cases of shell shock were separated into "commotional cases" (due to physical causes) and "emotional" cases, who were increasingly kept in their units unless the cases were extreme. The treatment of shell shock cases in their units by counselors (not necessarily medical) gave rise to the *PIE principles* for treating shell shock cases. Treatment focused on *Proximity* to the fighting, *Immediate* treatment (as soon as possible), and the *Expectation* that shell-shocked soldiers would be returned to active service following treatment. These same principles would be adopted in American and Commonwealth armies following the war (although their effectiveness in preventing PTSD has since come into question).

The shell shock diagnosis did not prove popular with the upper echelons of the British military and was abandoned in 1918. All too frequently, shell-shocked soldiers faced military tribunals and could be executed for cowardice. In fact, 306 British and Commonwealth soldiers were executed on a variety of military charges ranging from cowardice to desertion. Although some of the soldiers had been previously treated for shell shock, it may never be known how many of the executed soldiers (some as young as sixteen) were suffering from psychological trauma resulting from their combat experiences.

The circumstances in their offenses may have varied, but the end result was the same: a brief trial (often as short as twenty minutes) with no appeal and subsequent execution at dawn by firing squad. When public criticism arose back in England, the British commanders defended the executions by emphasizing the necessity of enforcing discipline and downplaying the possibility that any of the soldiers could have been suffering from a psychiatric illness. In many cases, families of executed soldiers were not told of the circumstances of how their loved ones had died although word usually leaked out. The stigma of cowardice would remain for more than ninety years until a blanket pardon was issued for the 306 executed soldiers in 2006. While the pardon did not annul the actual sentences, some closure was provided for surviving family members. By comparison, Germany only executed twenty-five soldiers during the war and had pardoned them all within a decade after the war ended.

After the End of World War I

The use of the term "shell shock" fell into disrepute over the course of the war and was formally dropped as a diagnosis by 1918. By the end of World War I, the British army alone had dealt with approximately 80,000 cases of shell shock. The problems did not end in 1918 as Allied governments were faced with the monumental task of reintegrating so many psychologically disabled soldiers into a society for which they were unprepared. A British royal commission published a report in 1922 laying out guidelines for dealing with shell-shocked solders but the stigma surrounding combat stress remained. Germany faced the same problem with its returning veterans. The resources of the impoverished Weimar Republic were strained to the breaking point trying to deal with them all.

Did Adolf Hitler suffer from PTSD?
While he was never formally diagnosed during his lifetime, most accounts of Adolf Hitler's life suggest that his entire personality changed as a result of his experiences during World War I. Along with being wounded in combat, his military experiences and the impact of what he had endured would be featured in many of his speeches as well as his political writings. He also displayed some classic PTSD-like symptoms and often required heavy medication for pain and emotional problems. Many of his fellow Nazis were recruited from former soldiers who had similar experiences. Whether PTSD played a role in his later political career is something historians are still debating.

Combat Fatigue

In the years following World War I, an overwhelming number of former soldiers found their lives shattered by the war and were committed to psychiatric hospitals. Many of them were classified as "incurable" though doctors wavered about their official diagnosis. Though the patients and people close to them thought they were shell-shocked, post-war governments were reluctant to recognize that their mental illness was war-related. These patients would often stay in the hospital for years and even decades since they often failed to respond to standard treatment. They were also largely forgotten since "war neurosis" tended to be viewed as a problem only in wartime. It would take decades for mental health professionals to recognize that traumatic stress could occur following any kind of disaster, whether natural or human-made.

PTSD in World War II

In 1941, while World War II was underway in Europe, Abram Kardiner published the first book on traumatic stress to be released in the United States. Now recognized as a classic, Kardiner's book provided the first symptom list for what would become known as PTSD (including many of the symptoms in the checklist provided in Appendix B). Though Kardiner had studied under Freud, he formed his own ideas about trauma that were very different than the Freudian theories that were popular in Europe. According to Kardiner, traumatic events led to extreme levels of excitement that people were unable to overcome. It was the feeling of losing control and being unable to adapt to what was happening that people found so crippling.

ESSENTIAL

Two of the most famous incidents of World War II involving soldiers suffering from traumatic stress occurred in August of 1943 during the Sicily Campaign. General George S. Patton reportedly slapped two soldiers under his command who were showing signs of combat fatigue, but no visible injuries. In addition to slapping the soldiers, General Patton then threatened army hospital staff with a pistol and ordered them not to admit the soldiers whom he accused of cowardice. Though reports of the incidents were suppressed out of loyalty to the general, word eventually reached Dwight D. Eisenhower, who arranged for Patton to be removed from command for over a year. While General Patton later apologized for his actions, public demands for his firing and questions about how sincere the apology really was dogged him for years afterward.

As the United States entered World War II and thousands of American soldiers went overseas, learning how to treat traumatic stress became more important than ever. Studies of how American soldiers responded to brutal military campaigns and the psychiatric symptoms that many soldiers developed afterward were carefully studied. Though there was no separate category for traumatic problems, soldiers were usually treated as close to the front lines as possible to get them back to their units. Only the most severe cases were sent to hospitals and desertion became a common problem. Military commanders were reluctant to accept that trauma was a legitimate condition and soldiers suspected of malingering were treated harshly.

With the end of World War II, interest in war neurosis faded again despite veterans with lingering post-traumatic problems having trouble becoming reintegrated into society. A 1955 Veterans Administration report on war neuroses identified many of the same symptoms described by Kardiner and later researchers but veterans were usually diagnosed as suffering from other, more recognized, conditions. Based on research looking at war veterans, the American Psychiatric Association created the first *Diagnostic and Statistical Manual of Mental Disorders* in 1952 with disease classifications already being used by the U.S. military. Both the DSM-I and the DSM-II, which came out in 1968, were widely criticized for problems with classifying mental illness and did little to help mental health professionals understand the role of traumatic stress in disease.

FACT

After the war, mental health professionals were faced with the thousands of Holocaust survivors who had been liberated from Nazi death camps. Many of them were displaying symptoms of trauma more severe than anything the doctors had ever seen before. In recognition of what they were seeing, the doctors suggested that the survivors were displaying a radical new psychiatric disorder, which they christened, "concentration camp syndrome." That civilians exposed to severe traumatic stress could also develop the sort of problems usually seen in soldiers was something that would take years to be recognized.

The Fight for PTSD's Recognition

Not until 1980, when the American Psychiatric Association put together the third version of the DSM, did Post-Traumatic Stress Disorder finally become recognized as a formal diagnosis. Though the DSM-I had contained a similar diagnosis known as "gross stress reaction," it was only seen as a temporary condition and the next version of the DSM dropped it completely. Instead, the DSM-II listed "transient situational disturbance," which was completely useless in explaining what was happening in returning war veterans. Everything changed with the DSM-III and the new PTSD diagnosis. Though most of the diagnostic criteria are similar to what we see in PTSD sufferers today, it was a radical change from previous versions of the DSM.

PTSD Becomes Mainstream

It was the Vietnam War that first brought PTSD to public attention. Beginning in the early 1960s and ending with the final withdrawal of American troops in 1973, the war would claim thousands of lives and leave hundreds of other soldiers with long-term medical problems. Frequent news stories of mental health problems in soldiers stationed in Vietnam and after they returned home, including suicide, substance abuse, and bizarre acts of violence, fostered the idea of Vietnam veterans being mentally unstable. While psychologists and psychiatrists dealing with veterans tried to diagnose their patients using earlier versions of the DSM, the lack of a proper diagnosis made treatment harder than it needed to be.

As antiwar activists and advocates for returning veterans began publicizing the condition faced by many returning veterans, a psychiatrist named Chaim Shatan first coined the term "post-Vietnam syndrome" in 1972 as part of a feature he wrote for the *New York Times*. According to Shatan, the syndrome he was seeing in returning veterans was caused by a "delayed massive trauma," which produced the bizarre symptoms they were displaying. The condition formed an officially unrecognized mental disorder for which sufferers needed real treatment. Shatan and other activists organized formal panels at different psychiatric conventions and pushed for its inclusion in the new DSM that was in the planning stage at that time.

Though recognizing that the mental health of returning soldiers was a hot political issue, psychiatrists in charge of organizing the new DSM, including Dr. Robert Spitzer, were skeptical about the existence of an unrecognized mental disorder. Shatan responded by organizing his own working group to develop information on the disease, which was expanded to include traumatic stress experienced after natural disasters and other high-stress events. Collecting reports on natural and human-made disasters as well as case histories taken from Vietnam veterans, Shatan and his colleagues proposed that the new diagnosis be known as "catastrophic stress disorder."

Conservative psychiatrists fought against the new diagnosis on the grounds that existing disorders such as depression, panic disorder, and schizophrenia already included many of the symptoms involved. By 1978, the working group presented a final proposal recommending that the new disorder, renamed as Post-Traumatic Stress Disorder, be included in the DSM-III. Despite opposition following accusations that the new diagnosis was driven by politics, the working group's proposal was accepted and PTSD became an officially recognized diagnosis.

Though adopting the new diagnosis would take time and cause major changes in organizations such as the Veterans Administration, it also had major financial consequences as well. Veterans denied benefits in the years before the PTSD diagnosis was recognized would demand retroactive compensation while veterans from earlier wars denounced the new diagnosis as unnecessary and political. It would take time to demonstrate that PTSD was a legitimate diagnosis in its own right, and the criteria for diagnosis would change and expand over time, but the battle for recognition would be won.

PTSD Today

As the neuropsychiatrist Nancy Andreasen once wrote, PTSD is a "disorder that has long been recognized in clinical psychiatry but for which official recognition has been minimal, late in arriving, and long overdue." While restricted to military veterans, much of the scientific research into post-traumatic stress focuses on veterans of the Vietnam (and now the Gulf) war and the Veterans Administration is still the largest source of PTSD research funds in the world. But that is slowly changing as the World Health Organization is adopting guidelines for treating PTSD in countries across the globe and providing support for victims following wide-scale disasters. The classic PTSD symptoms have been identified in survivors of natural disasters, refugees, assault victims, and survivors of accidents occurring in or out of the home.

FACT

Following the 2011 earthquake and tsunami in Japan, hundreds of workers at the Fukushima Daiichi nuclear plant remained at work to contain potential contamination from three damaged nuclear reactors. Along with the potential health dangers they faced from being exposed to dangerous levels of radiation, researchers have found significant signs of post-traumatic stress as well. Based on their responses to clinical surveys, about 47 percent of workers at the Daiichi plant are reporting psychological distress with 30 percent showing signs of PTSD.

While the PTSD diagnosis is widely accepted, making treatment available to all the people who need it is a far greater challenge. While the World Health Organization estimates that 3.6 percent of the world's population suffers from some form of PTSD (with enormous variations across different countries), making mental health care available to the ones who need it is a critical challenge that has still not been met.

CHAPTER 3

PTSD and the Brain

One of the primary features associated with PTSD is the acute stress involved in dealing with the psychological and biological challenges of stressful events. While everybody experiences stress from time to time in their daily lives, extreme stress can lead to long-term psychological and physical damage.

Stress and the Body

The modern medical concept of stress began in the 1920s when physiologist Walter Cannon first proposed that stress occurred when the body's homeostasis was disrupted. While ordinarily our bodies are in a state of relative balance with the environment, being presented with a stressful situation disrupts that balance. At that point, the body draws on internal resources to become restabilized. For example, the sympathetic nervous system prepares the body to deal with the new challenge (which Cannon termed the "fight-or-flight response") with the adrenal medulla releasing a cascade of hormones leading to the secretion of catecholamine neurotransmitters. This prepares the body for a strong response to the stressful event.

FACT

Catecholamines are organic compounds produced in the nervous system that have a variety of different functions including acting as neurotransmitters and as hormones. In general, they prepare the body for physical activity (fight or flight) by speeding up heart rate, blood pressure, and acting on the sympathetic nervous system. The most common catecholamines are dopamine, norepinephrine, and epinephrine (adrenaline). Many popular stimulants work by mimicking catecholamine activity in the body.

It is this fight-or-flight response that represents the first stage of what Canadian physiologist Hans Selye termed the *general adaptation syndrome*, describing the short-term and long-term consequences of extreme stress. According to Selye, the syndrome has three main stages:

1. **Stage of alarm**—This is the fight-or-flight response in action with the body preparing to deal with extreme stress. This stage has two main components: the shock phase in which the body is first reacting to the stressful event, and the anti-shock phase during which the body reacts by increasing the capacity for coping with stress. Along with increased catecholamine production, the hypothalamus in the brain's limbic system secretes adrenocorticotropic hormone (ACTH), which then stimulates the adrenal glands above the kidneys.

The adrenal glands in turn generate cortisol to increase blood sugar production and aid in metabolizing fat, proteins, and carbohydrates. The pituitary gland releases the adrenocorticotropic hormone to modulate the stress response. This is all part of what is known as the hypothalamic-pituitary-adrenal (HPA) axis, which plays a central role in the body's response to environmental changes and maintaining homeostasis. During the alarm stage, the body becomes more resistant to severe changes such as blood loss, temperature extremes, and other environmental threats.

2. **Stage of resistance**—Once the body is prepared and the stressful event is recognized, resistance sets in as the body attempts to deal with the event as effectively as possible. While the body is in a state of resistance, the release of hormones intensifies the body's ability to cope and maintain the needed resources. The length of the stage of resistance is limited only by the internal resources that the body can provide to deal with the threat. While the body's capacity to handle stress can be considerable, a prolonged or severely threatening event can overwhelm the body's capacity to cope.

3. **Stage of exhaustion or recovery**—If the stressful event subsides and is successfully resolved, recovery sets in. During this time, the body restores homeostasis and compensates for the resources that were consumed. The length and extent of recovery depends on whether the resources consumed exceed the body's ability to recover.

Exhaustion

On the other hand, if the stressful situation is not resolved or if the resources consumed are greater than what the body can safely provide, then exhaustion sets in. All of the body's resources are used up and normal functioning is no longer possible. The body can signal that exhaustion is happening through increased sweating, rapid or shallow heart rate, increased blood pressure, etc. For long-term exhaustion, the body begins breaking down and a range of illnesses can set in, which include peptic ulcers, digestive problems such as diarrhea/constipation, depression or other mental illnesses, diabetes mellitus, and even cardiovascular problems.

Many of the symptoms associated with PTSD can be linked to acute exhaustion demonstrating that stress has overcome the body's natural ability to cope. This can include many of the autonomic and cognitive symptoms seen in PTSD sufferers but also in people with a number of other conditions. Again, a formal diagnosis of PTSD requires that these symptoms continue longer than a month and be severe enough to merit a formal diagnosis.

The PTSD symptoms that can appear are often linked to the type of stress that can trigger those symptoms in the first place. According to neuroendocrinologist Bruce McEwen, there are four types of stressors that can produce "wear and tear" on our ability to handle stress, especially in traumatic situations. These are:

- Repeated hits from multiple stressors, which, while relatively manageable individually, can overwhelm the body's ability to cope because normal coping responses are frequently and repeatedly activated which brings on exhaustion more rapidly.
- Lack of an adaptation response due to the presence of other health or mental health problems that reduce the body's ability to cope effectively. For that reason, people suffering from various types of chronic illness or even problems of old age may be less able to handle traumatic stress.
- Prolonged stress response where the duration, frequency, or intensity of the traumatic event persists beyond the body's ability to cope effectively. This is especially common for people living in war zones, domestic abuse victims, or people who have a realistic fear of being re-traumatized and who are unable to find a place of relative safety.
- Inadequate response in which the body fails to deliver the proper level of support for dealing with stress, i.e., the traumatic event becomes far greater than was originally expected.

McEwen argues that all of these stressors affect the brain, cardiovascular system, and metabolism of the body and overwhelm our natural capacity to deal with stress. Later researchers have also suggested that all four stressors can occur at the same time in many traumatic situations. Also, how a person responds to stress can result in the stressful situation actually becoming worse with time. This is especially true for people who resort to poor coping strategies such as substance abuse or social isolation.

Allostatic Load

Another term coined by McEwen to describe the cumulative damage that stress has on the body is allostatic load. Through frequent activation of the body's fight-or-flight response, allostatic load can damage the body in the long run. While the body needs to be able to adapt to deal with stress (a process known as allostasis), increased allostatic load can lead to the development of disease and a weakened immune system. Problems resulting from an increased allostatic load include:

- Repeated stress reactions to multiple novel stressors
- Failing to adapt to multiple stressors of the same kind
- Delayed shutdown leading to failing to turn off the stress response in time
- Hyperactivity of other systems as a result of compensation

QUESTION

Why are traumatic memories different from regular memories?
For most people, normal memories are formed when the brain codes those memories and stores them in specific brain regions so they can be retrieved later. Most memories tend to be quickly forgotten. Traumatic memories, however, tend to be linked to strong emotions such as fear or guilt. Many survivors find themselves replaying these memories in their heads over and over again which makes them more difficult to forget.

Allostatic load can be measured through careful physiological analysis to measure lifetime damage resulting from repeated stress. For people dealing with traumatic stress, the allostatic load will vary depending on whether the trauma is from a single event or multiple sources of trauma. For that reason, the allostatic load will be greater in survivors of prolonged traumatic exposure such as childhood abuse or long-term domestic abuse. Sustained stress and an inability to compensate for the effects of that chronic stress can lead to an allostatic state, i.e., elevated blood pressure, changes in body chemistry, and atrophy of brain structures, which can all lead to the body becoming more vulnerable to disease.

How Trauma Affects the Brain

In looking at the impact that PTSD has on the brain, it is important to understand the role that traumatic stress plays on the brain's biochemistry. During times of crisis, numerous different regions of the brain are activated at the same time and different neurotransmitters are released in the brain. Although the effect that stress has on the body has already been discussed in the previous section, research studies looking specifically at PTSD have found that responding to fear leads to the widespread release of norepinephrine in the brain. This release activates areas of the brain that dictate how we pay attention to potentially threatening events.

FACT

According to trauma researcher Chris Brewin and his colleagues, traumatic memories can be stored in different ways that make them both *verbally accessible* and *situationally accessible*. Verbally accessible memories involve information that is easily remembered such as where and when a traumatic event occurred and how survivors reacted. Situationally accessible memories are less easily recalled and can be linked to specific situational triggers such as certain sounds, smells, or images. They are also much richer in detail than verbally accessible memories. Dealing with traumatic memories often means coming to terms with situationally activated memories such as flashbacks and recognizing how certain triggers lead to vivid recall.

The Amygdala

The amygdala, an almond-shaped region of the brain linked to the body's threat response as well as controlling fear, is also activated.

What is norepinephrine?
Norepinephrine is a catecholamine that can function as either a neurotransmitter or a hormone. One of the most important functions of norepinephrine is to control heart activity, increase blood pressure, and generally prepare the body for a fight-or-flight response. Norepinephrine works by acting on different types of adrenergic receptors throughout the body but especially in the central nervous system. Many psychiatric medications act by increasing norepinephrine activity in the brain.

The amygdala also plays an important role in how the brain processes memories of threatening events. Research has already shown that doses of norepinephrine administered just after stressful events occur can enhance later recall of those events. There are other stress-induced neurotransmitters that can also boost memory, usually by increasing norepinephrine production in key regions of the brain. The "fear conditioning" seen in PTSD is also affected by the high levels of catecholamines and cortisol released during stress, which can also directly influence the amygdala. The amygdala also relays information to the brain's hypothalamus and other catecholamine regions creating a feedback loop to relay the stress exposure of other parts of the brain.

The Prefrontal Cortex

The next area of the brain that researchers have linked to stress and PTSD is the prefrontal cortex. Located in the forward part of the brain's frontal lobes, the prefrontal cortex is linked to processing complex behaviors, decision-making, and our basic personality. High levels of catecholamines and other stress-induced brain chemicals seem to have the opposite effect than on the amygdala. The prefrontal cortex plays an important role in planning, guiding, and organizing behavior, so why do higher levels of stress-released brain chemicals such as catecholamines reduce its functioning? According to one theory, the reduced functioning limits the ability of the prefrontal cortex to process irrelevant information that might distract the brain. Also, by reducing the prefrontal cortex's capacity to develop novel ways of responding, the brain and body can respond using survival strategies that are already in place and have become habitual (relying on fight-or-flight responses rather than trying a novel strategy that might be disastrous). There are also specialized brain receptors that help protect the prefrontal cortex under conditions of stress though they may not work as well under conditions of repeated traumatic events or long-term stress.

FACT

Cortisol is a steroid hormone produced in the adrenal cortex and is released whenever the body is exposed to acute stress. Often known as "the stress hormone," cortisol helps control blood pressure, maintain blood sugar levels, lower sensitivity to pain, and can also boost memory functioning. Higher-than-normal cortisol levels that persist over time due to prolonged stress can lead to reduced cognitive functioning, create blood sugar imbalances (high or low blood sugar), increase blood pressure, reduce bone density, and other symptoms linked to stress disorders.

As a summary, under conditions of extreme stress, the amygdala triggers the release of high levels of catecholamines and cortisol, which makes it more active while reducing the prefrontal cortex's control of the body's behavior as well as the ability to think and feel. It is this stimulation of the brain's amygdala and suppression of the prefrontal cortex that may lead to many of the common symptoms associated with PTSD, especially under situations of prolonged stress where the body has exhausted all internal resources.

Medical studies comparing PTSD patients with control subjects have found significant differences in norepinephrine levels and reduced brain receptors suggesting that the brain adapts to high levels of traumatic stress over time. In research studies using yohimbine, an antidepressant that increases postsynaptic release of norepinephrine, patients with PTSD experience significant increases in heart rate and subjective anxiety, while there is little effect on healthy subjects. PTSD patients taking yohimbine also experience a sharp increase in hypervigilance and intrusive memories. In combat veterans with PTSD, nearly 80 percent experience vivid memories of combat trauma while 40 percent experience full-blown flashbacks.

Serotonin

Along with norepinephrine, serotonin is another neurotransmitter that has been linked to depression and PTSD. Derived from tryptophan, serotonin is found in the central nervous systems of humans and animals and serotonergic neurons are found almost exclusively in the raphe nuclei of the brainstem and extend throughout the brain's limbic system and all parts of the cerebral cortex. That includes the prefrontal cortex, amygdala, and other parts of the brain associated with PTSD including the hippocampus. Serotonin appears to play a major role in how the brain controls emotional functioning including the regulation of mood, appetite, and sleep by way of the autonomic nervous system and hormonal production. For that reason, pharmaceutical companies have focused on serotonin production in developing different classes of antidepressant medication.

Researchers have also found that serotonin plays an important role in the functioning of the orbitofrontal cortex. This region of the brain controls the filtering, processing, and evaluating of social and emotional information. Along with evaluating social cues, the orbitofrontal cortex is involved in the processing of emotional memories and is likely important in emotional decision-making. Patients with damage to the orbitofrontal cortex develop problems with social decisions and often lose their emotional inhibitions, making them more impulsive and even potentially violent.

In studies of people with PTSD, researchers have reported changes in serotonin levels and how well the subjects perform on cognitive tasks sensitive to orbitofrontal cortex functioning. Brain-imaging studies of women with PTSD found decreased cerebral blood flow in the prefrontal and orbitofrontal cortex. Specific PTSD symptoms including greater impulsivity, enhanced emotional memories, and misinterpreting social cues are also seen in patients with orbitofrontal cortex damage. Serotonin also influences the amygdala and norepinephrine production, which can explain many of the other clinical symptoms seen in PTSD including hypervigilance and fear-related behaviors.

While research that links serotonin to PTSD is still in its early stages, studies have already found a strong link between serotonin functioning and aggression, suicide, and depression. The strongest evidence supporting the role of serotonin in PTSD comes from pharmacological studies using a specific class of antidepressants known as selective serotonin reuptake inhibitors (SSRIs) in treating patients with traumatic stress. Two medications approved for treatment of PTSD, paroxetine and sertraline, are both SSRIs, and large-scale studies have shown that both these medications can reduce PTSD symptoms. Another class of antidepressants, monoamine oxidase inhibitors (MAOIs), which prevent the breakdown of serotonin in the brain, has also been found to be beneficial.

Though the hypothalamic-pituitary-adrenal (HPA) axis and its role in the body's response to stress have already been covered, research has also found significant changes in HPA functioning in PTSD patients as well as abnormal cortisol levels, which can cause many of the cognitive problems these patients experience. Much of this research is still preliminary, however, and a clear link between HPA abnormalities and cognitive problems in PTSD patients has not been found so far.

DHEA

Another brain steroid, dehydroepiandrosterone (DHEA), which is produced by the adrenal gland along with cortisol, has been linked to serotonin functioning and appears to play a strong role in helping the body resist traumatic stress, possibly by boosting frontal lobe functioning. Combat veterans with PTSD have shown higher DHEA levels compared to veterans without PTSD and similar results have been found in Kosovo refugees. There appears to be a negative relationship between DHEA levels and avoidance/hyperarousal symptoms of PTSD, with low DHEA levels leading to greater vulnerability to developing post-traumatic stress. Activation of DHEA receptor sites in the amygdala has also been linked to the forming of fear-based memories.

Overall, research has shown that the brain's biochemistry and specifically neurotransmitters such as serotonin, norepinephrine, cortisol, and DHEA are strongly involved in the development of PTSD symptoms. These neurotransmitters act on different regions of the brain associated with decision-making, memory formation, emotional regulation, and problem-solving. Reduced serotonin and elevated levels of norepinephrine and cortisol all contribute to impaired functioning in the prefrontal cortex. This in turn would trigger the amygdala and other parts of the limbic system leaving them in a hyperactive state. As a result, PTSD patients then develop the hypervigilance, exaggerated startle response, reduced problem-solving ability, and other symptoms commonly resulting from post-traumatic stress.

But there is still much more that needs to be learned about PTSD and the brain. There are likely other neurotransmitters involved in mediating stress in the brain. Certainly other regions of the brain have been linked to how the brain mediates stress, including the hippocampus and anterior cingulate cortex. As well, the beneficial effects that SSRIs such as paroxetine have on PTSD symptoms are still not clearly understood since they affect many different regions of the brain in completely unexpected ways. While research into the complex relationship between brain functioning and PTSD is still underway, new lines of investigation are already promoting greater understanding of how the brain deals with trauma and more effective means of treating post-traumatic symptoms.

Are Some People More Vulnerable to Trauma?

There appear to be different factors that can increase the likelihood of developing PTSD symptoms. Despite enormous differences in how people respond to traumatic events, identifying specific risk factors can be difficult since not every trauma is going to affect people in the same way. Even research looking at how wide-scale disasters such as Hurricane Katrina in 2005 or the 2004 tsunami affected survivors can show huge differences in terms of the actual trauma that occurred.

FACT

In a 1993 study looking at the effect of Hurricane Hugo on adolescents in South Carolina, the single biggest factor predicting the later development of PTSD was previous experience with violence, i.e., whether they had witnessed or experienced violence directly. In another study looking at the same disaster, the degree of trauma appeared to be influenced by pre-existing financial, marital, and physical problems that made people more vulnerable to the effect of traumatic stress.

According to a 1996 Central Michigan University study examining PTSD symptoms found in 1,632 male and female Vietnam War veterans, there were significant sex differences in the specific factors linked to PTSD. For male veterans, previous trauma—whether in the form of exposure to previous accidents, assaults, or natural disasters—was the single greatest predictor of developing PTSD symptoms. Also, male veterans who were exposed to combat at a younger age displayed more symptoms. Other factors that appeared to play an indirect role included family instability and childhood antisocial behavior. For women veterans, family instability also played an indirect role.

In general, people with a history of early behavior problems including childhood hyperactivity, antisocial behavior, and general substance abuse problems are more likely to be diagnosed with PTSD following a traumatic event. Children who are neglected or subjected to sexual or physical violence (whether they are victimized themselves or witness it happening to others) are also more vulnerable.

According to the 1998 Adverse Childhood Experience Survey looking at 13,000 patients in a large health maintenance organization in the United States, experiencing one or more adverse events in childhood dramatically increased later health problems including depression, lung problems, and other lifestyle-related medical conditions. For the researchers, an "adverse childhood event" (ACE) was defined as an experience of any of the following before the age of eighteen:

- Recurrent physical abuse
- Recurrent emotional abuse
- Sexual abuse
- Family drug or alcohol abuse
- A family member in prison
- A family member with chronic mental illness (including suicide attempts)
- Seeing your mother being treated violently by a family member

A single ACE score was generated by assigning one point to each of the adverse childhood events. Compared to people with an ACE score of 0, people with a score of 4 or greater were 60 percent more likely to develop depression, 260 percent more likely to develop lung problems (likely due to smoking), and 250 percent more likely to have a sexually transmitted disease. Overall, childhood trauma has a long-lasting influence on health and coping and can also make people more vulnerable to later trauma.

Having previous problems with physical or mental health is a major risk factor for distress after a traumatic event. This can include having a prior history of depression, longstanding personality disorders, substance abuse problems, or other mental disorders.

Personality

There can also be tremendous individual differences in temperament, or innate personality factors such as being introverted or extroverted, that play a role in responding to traumatic stress. Researchers in the area of personality have identified five dimensions that can be used to describe human personality. Of the five personality dimensions (see following sidebar), neuroticism appears to be an important predictor of how people respond to stress. The emotional instability seen in highly neurotic people can make them more vulnerable to developing PTSD symptoms, especially in people who seem easily prone to depression, anger, or anxiety from an early age.

ESSENTIAL

The "Big Five" personality dimensions include: an openness to experience (inventive/curious vs. consistent/cautious), conscientiousness (efficient/organized vs. easy-going/careless), extraversion (outgoing/energetic vs. solitary/reserved), agreeableness (friendly/compassionate vs. analytical/detached), and neuroticism (sensitive/nervous vs. secure/confident). The Big Five Model has been supported by numerous research studies over the past five decades.

Neuroticism remains a strong predictor of who will develop PTSD following exposure to traumatic stress. A study by researchers at London's University College looked into the aftermath of a deadly London Metro fire in 1987. They found that neuroticism in survivors was strongly correlated with the acute distress they reported when asking for help afterward.

Children displaying "problem" temperaments such as chronic shyness, introversion, or proneness to depression or anxiety often show greater emotional problems later in life and it also seems to make them more vulnerable to the effects of traumatic events. Personality is also remarkably stable over time. For example, a person's personality at the age of thirty largely remains the same later in life. That includes traits such as neuroticism and anxiety as well as positive traits such as happiness and emotional well-being. Long-standing problems managing stress, guilt, or insecurity can often be seen in people who later develop PTSD.

Other Factors Linked to PTSD Vulnerability

Studies have also shown that differences in IQ scores and educational achievement can predict severity of PTSD symptoms. According to some studies, greater intelligence can help people compensate for traumatic events (though this remains controversial). More specific research looking at problem-solving, cognitive competency, or cognitive skills suggests that people with fewer intellectual resources are more likely to develop more severe symptoms.

Overall, pre-existing psychological and/or medical problems are going to have a significant impact on the body's ability to cope with traumatic stress. People with a history of depression or other issues that have already depleted available resources are going to be more vulnerable to severe traumatic events and lead to more serious PTSD symptoms. As well, people with greater intellectual and emotional resources such as problem-solving ability, strong family support networks, and a stable upbringing are going to be less likely to develop symptoms. Part of the reason for this long-term stability may be due to a strong genetic component to personality (more on that in the next section).

Ultimately, while risk factors can be identified, there is no real way of predicting ahead of time the extent and degree to which post-traumatic stress will occur since even people exposed to identical traumatic events such as natural disasters are not going to be affected in the same way.

Is There a PTSD Gene?

Numerous medical studies have suggested that genetic factors can play a role in how the body responds to the different neurotransmitters that have been linked to PTSD. For instance, healthy subjects who are homozygous carriers of the alpha2cDel322-325-AR adrenoreceptor gene show exaggerated total body effects of norepinephrine production and slower-than-normal return to baseline levels after taking norepinephrine agents such as yohimbine. While researchers have speculated that people carrying this particular genetic polymorphism may be more vulnerable to PTSD and depression, this remains controversial.

FACT

Most diploid genetic traits have two matching sets of chromosomes, known as *alleles*. One allele is inherited from the father and the other from the mother. If both alleles are the same, the trait is said to be *homozygous*, and *heterozygous* if they are different. In many genetic diseases, whether or not a child develops the disease can depend on whether or not both alleles are present. Hemophilia and cystic fibrosis are two examples of homozygous diseases.

Research has also shown a strong link between depression and genes coding for serotonin production and tryptophan production (serotonin is a biochemical product of tryptophan). A 2003 study has shown that stress can significantly increase the risk of depression in people carrying a specific version of the 5-HT transporter promoter gene. Another inhibitory neurotransmitter, gamma-aminobutyric acid (GABA) has also been implicated in cases of PTSD, and a recent study reported significant interactions between three polymorphisms in the GABA alpha-2 receptor gene and the severity of childhood trauma in predicting PTSD in adults.

There are numerous different mutations known to affect how the brain produces cortisol, DHEA, GABA, and other brain chemicals. Basic research will still be needed to identify these different gene markers and how they affect individual variation in the ways that people respond to traumatic stress. Understanding how the brain and body interact during life-threatening events will lead to better ways of preventing and treating PTSD symptoms.

There also appears to be a strong genetic component to basic aspects of personality such as temperament. Along with evidence of a physiological basis for personality differences including the amount of frontal lobe and limbic system activation, studies looking at common personality traits in fraternal and identical twins have found strong evidence of genetic similarities with estimates of genetic inheritance ranging from 50–65 percent for traits such as neuroticism. Since neuroticism is an important factor in developing PTSD symptoms, the likelihood of one or both twins being diagnosed with PTSD seems high.

FACT

A *polymorphism* is a natural variation in DNA sequences or chromosomes. The most common type of polymorphism is a variation of a single base pair, but can involve long stretches of DNA. Polymorphisms occur widely in any population and are usually harmless though there can be significant medical consequences depending on which version of the polymorphism is present in the body. Pharmaceutical companies have been focusing on polymorphism research to study the link between drug response and genetics.

A study conducted by the University of Oslo, published in 1993, found a higher prevalence for PTSD in identical twins than in fraternal twins with anxiety problems. A twin study of Vietnam veterans conducted by the St. Louis University Medical Center found similar results with greater likelihood of PTSD developing in identical twins than in fraternal twins. Studies have also shown similar results for developing major depression following stressful life events, suggesting that genetic factors can make people more vulnerable to traumatic life events.

Ultimately, the complex relationship between genetics and environmental factors will likely not be explained without a better understanding of how genes interact and change over time as a result of exposure to stress. Epigenetics is the study of how outside factors can change the way in which genes express themselves; researchers studying the role of epigenetics in

PTSD suggest that epigenetic changes in the HPA axis could be linked to greater vulnerability to traumatic stress, which could then be passed on to later generations. In mothers experiencing post-traumatic stress while pregnant, for example, changes in cortisol levels can result from hormonal changes, which can lead to a "re-programming" of how their offspring respond to cortisol production.

CHAPTER 4

Symptoms of PTSD

Traumatic events can occur anywhere and at any time. Though you can plan ahead and make preparations when possible, the risk of encountering a trauma-provoking situation will always be there. While not everyone will develop full-blown PTSD symptoms, exposure to trauma will often trigger a range of different responses depending on previous experience and the community support people receive. In the case of personal traumas such as exposure to violence or sexual abuse, the symptoms may often be masked by shame or feelings of guilt. As a result, the warning signs of trauma may go unnoticed by people close to the victim except for a general increase in visible distress and/or the development of psychological problems.

QUESTION

Can video games control traumatic symptoms?
A 2010 study by researchers at Oxford University looked at how effective certain video games were in helping people control traumatic flashbacks. The study compared people playing Tetris with people playing a popular video quiz game immediately after seeing a graphic film about automobile fatalities. Results showed that playing Tetris within six hours of seeing the film appeared to reduce traumatic flashbacks more than other games. According to the researchers, the results showed that intrusive flashbacks could be prevented by perceptual stimulation, which affects how well people remember upsetting information. While warning that the results are still experimental, the researchers suggest that video games can someday be part of a preventive treatment approach for trauma victims.

General Symptoms of PTSD

The symptoms of PTSD can vary widely, with some people displaying multiple symptoms from the very beginning and others experiencing a delayed effect that might only appear after decades. Even the symptoms and appearance of PTSD symptoms can vary widely from person to person, which makes diagnosis especially difficult since the symptoms can mask underlying emotional and physical problems that can make recovery more difficult.

In research studies of Vietnam veterans who returned home after being exposed to prolonged stress, many veterans showed repeated problems with stressors even after moving on with their lives. This included repeated problems with postwar adjustment such as divorce, unemployment, substance abuse, social isolation, and general loss of self-worth (all of which are stressful in their own right). Along with the complex nature of PTSD, they were also prone to developing later psychiatric problems and health issues that further reduced their ability to cope with stress.

In many ways, being subjected to intentional human-caused trauma is usually more far-reaching and harder to treat than trauma stemming from natural disasters or accidents. PTSD symptoms resulting from such trauma are often more complex and last longer for a number of reasons. Victims of sexual violence, for instance, are often forced to deal with feelings of shame or guilt as well as the secondary trauma of dealing with police and the courts. Human-made traumas can also cause victims to become mistrustful of fellow humans and often of themselves for not reacting better than they did. In trauma caused by natural disasters, on the other hand, being able to bond with fellow victims can have a therapeutic effect by allowing victims to band together to fight a common foe.

Looking Closer at PTSD Symptoms

Despite already covering the primary symptoms of PTSD, it is probably best to discuss the most common symptoms in greater detail:

1. **Re-experiencing the traumatic event**—Intrusive recollections of the traumatic event(s) can occur in any number of ways, whether in the form of thoughts, mental images, or waking dreams. These intrusive recollections are unwelcome, painful, and devastating at times and often force the victim to relive the traumatic experience that caused them. The emotional response to these intrusions can include disgust, guilt, sadness, or grief (often in the form of survivor guilt). Any sensory cue can remind victims of what they experienced, whether it is a familiar sound, smell, or image.

   At their most extreme, intrusions can take the form of flashbacks in which victims find themselves reliving the traumatic event, often to the point of being completely unaware of their current surroundings. In military veterans who have faced enemy fire, something as innocuous as a car backfiring can be enough to trigger a flashback that can blind them to whatever else is occurring. Flashbacks can also be triggered by insomnia, fatigue, excessive stress, or the effects of some recreational drugs. For PTSD sufferers prone to flashbacks, it is important to identify those specific triggers causing the flashback and be aware of them at all times.

2. **Negative cognitions and mood problems**—People with PTSD often develop negative attitudes about themselves, other people, or the future. Statements such as, "Nothing will ever change for me," "People can't be trusted," or "It was all my fault this happened" may become extremely common in trauma survivors. These negative cognitions are often accompanied by symptoms of depression including acute sadness, loss

of pleasure, loss of interest in activities that were formerly enjoyable, and becoming incapable of feeling positive emotions such as happiness, joy, or sexual pleasure. Many survivors can also develop physical problems including weight loss or weight gain due to changes in appetite, concentration and memory problems, and anger issues.

3. **Nightmares and sleep terrors**—Nightmares of the traumatic event are extremely common, especially in the early stages of recovery. Studies have shown that most trauma survivors report frequent nightmares (as high as 96 percent in some studies). Along with causing sleep problems, recurring traumatic nightmares also result in considerable emotional distress during the day and can make survivors terrified of going to sleep at night. About half of those who report nightmares describe them as direct replays of the traumatic event or having details that remind survivors of their experiences. Sleep lab research indicates that traumatic nightmares are more likely to occur early in the night during different stages of sleep.

ESSENTIAL

Sleep or night terrors usually occur within the first few hours of sleep, but can also occur during daytime naps. While similar to nightmares, night terrors are usually marked by sweating, rapid breathing, rapid heart rate, and physical thrashing, which can lead to injury. Though fairly rare (occurring in about 1 percent of adults and 1–6 percent of children), having PTSD can increase the risk of developing night terrors in addition to other sleep problems.

These nightmares not only cause survivors to relive their experiences at night, but they are often accompanied by gross body movements that can endanger themselves and others as well. Researchers have also speculated that nightmares and sleep problems may be a key factor in developing long-term PTSD symptoms and can persist even when other symptoms have been successfully treated. Different treatments for nightmares can include cognitive-behavioral therapy and breathing exercises to control feelings of anxiety.

4. **Sleep disruption**—In addition to nightmares, trauma survivors often experience disturbed sleep and insomnia, which can prevent them from getting enough sleep at night. Sleep problems can relate to nightmares, sleep apnea (more on this in a later chapter), emotional agitation, or physical restlessness. Along with feeling tired during the day, trauma survivors with sleep problems may find themselves having difficulty driving, operating heavy machinery, or being able to focus during business meetings or in a classroom. Prolonged insomnia can also lead to emotional issues including depression, irritability, and memory lapses.

5. **Arousal**—In many ways, the nervous system of PTSD sufferers has become extremely sensitized by trauma. As a result, the nervous system can overreact to even mild stressors leading to troubled sleep, anger outbursts, concentration or memory problems, and hypervigilance where sufferers are acutely scanning their surroundings for potential threats. Increased sensitivity can also lead to an exaggerated startle response where the PTSD sufferer seems easily "spooked" by any potentially threatening stimulus. This can lead to such things as jumping, flinching, or otherwise appearing tense when someone suddenly appears from behind. This is especially apparent when the situation where the stimulus occurs is similar to the traumatic event, e.g., drivers who have been in traumatic automobile accidents being easily startled by unexpected road mishaps. An overly sensitized nervous system can also have other indicators such as excessive sweating, rapid heartbeat, tight chest or stomach, etc.

6. **Avoidance and/or numbing**—Because trauma sufferers find intrusive reminders so unpleasant and painful, they often go to great lengths to avoid anything that might remind them of the trauma. If the traumatic event occurred in a specific location, they might avoid that location or anything similar to it. Someone who has been in a serious automobile accident might avoid the specific intersection where the accident occurred or else avoid driving on highways or under weather conditions similar to when the accident happened. Returning veterans can also refuse to return to active service since it might mean re-experiencing the conditions that they associate with previous traumatic events. PTSD sufferers often live their lives in active

denial, refusing to discuss or even acknowledge traumatic incidents in their past. In extreme cases, this can take the form of psychogenic amnesia with the memory of the traumatic incident being completely blocked out of conscious awareness.

QUESTION

How can I tell the difference between the symptoms of a severe anxiety attack and an actual heart attack?
Unfortunately, you can't. *Any* problems with hyperventilating, rapid breathing, or acute anxiety need to be looked at by a qualified professional. If you can't secure an immediate appointment with a family doctor or at a walk-in clinic, proceed to your nearest hospital emergency room. It is far better to be safe than sorry.

In dealing with painful memories, emotional numbing can also occur. That can involve suppressing all feelings, even positive ones, to avoid having to deal with the pain and trauma that traumatic memories can awaken. PTSD sufferers may avoid all pleasurable activities they used to enjoy including hobbies or relaxation. They can often be heard to say things like "I don't know how to have fun anymore" and become detached from their old lives. This also leads to becoming alienated or estranged from the people who were once important to them, whether due to the numbing itself or a sense that anyone who lacks their experiences could not possibly know how they really feel.

Because they are no longer comfortable in social gatherings, they often isolate themselves and show a restricted range of affect in their social interactions. This means an inability to show any type of strong emotion—no laughter, crying, or spontaneous expressions of love or intimacy. Since some work environments actually encourage suppressing emotions to some extent (including military or emergency service work), this may help conceal the emotional numbing that is readily apparent to friends and family members.

Trauma can also lead people to feel disconnected from their future and incapable of seeing themselves going on to have a happy life. Often referred to as a sense of a foreshortened future, PTSD sufferers may be extremely pessimistic about future prospects and have a "doomsday orientation," leaving them with the feeling that disaster is imminent. People who are unable to resolve their feelings about past traumatic events tend to be incapable of making future plans. In a real sense, blocking off the past means that the present and future are blocked off as well.

Responding to Disasters

For more wide-ranging traumatic events that can affect entire communities, such as a natural or human-made disaster, a PTSD response can be far more visible and immediate. According to the Institute of Medicine, the psychological responses to disaster can be classified into three broad categories of reactions: behavioral changes, distress responses, and psychiatric illness.

- Behavioral changes cover the wide range of different approaches that people take to get on with their lives after a disaster. After a disaster severely disrupts a community, people need to adapt and change their behaviors to survive and recover. Behavioral changes can be either adaptive, i.e., doing things that can improve the chances of survival such as cooperating with aid organizations and helping neighbors, or they can be maladaptive, which usually means negative behaviors such as reversion under stress (see next section).
- Distress responses include all the different ways people experience a disaster. This includes all the classic traumatic symptoms such as insomnia, feeling confused or distracted, emotional responses such as anxiety, fear, grief, and feeling helpless. There can also be positive emotions though, including hope, and a heightened sense of community and of spirituality. People from different cultures respond to traumatic events in different ways depending on what their cultural expectations are of how people should deal with a crisis. There can also be somatic reactions including headaches, abdominal pains, vomiting, double vision, or psychosomatic illness.
- Reactions to trauma can be so overwhelming that survivors develop various psychiatric disorders including PTSD, major depression, alcohol or drug use problems, or even psychotic disorders following extreme trauma.

In many cases, people can develop numerous different symptoms with periods of recovery, relapses, or rapid shifting between symptoms. For most people, the initial distress will subside over time, but for a large minority, problems such as PTSD will develop if they do not receive the proper help.

ALERT

Though the warning signs for traumatic stress will not always be visible, the possibility should always be considered. That applies to *all* survivors, not just the ones who are asking for help. Many trauma survivors may refuse to ask for help out of a fear of seeming "weak" or the belief that the symptoms will go away on their own. While this might be true, there are no guarantees, and ignoring warning signs can be extremely dangerous both for the survivors and for the people in their lives.

For mental health professionals and family members dealing with trauma survivors, specific warning signs to watch for in determining whether treatment is needed can include:

- Personal neglect of appearance or health, e.g., signs of poor sleep, poor nutrition, general distress
- Appearing disorganized in terms of behavior or how they communicate (bizarre speech or behavior)
- *Any* statement questioning whether they should keep on living ("What's the use of going on?")
- Bizarre ideas or an inability to face reality (holding out unrealistic hope that appears irrational)
- When family members or close friends insist "something is wrong" even when the survivor denies it
- Simple "gut feeling" (sometimes, intuition can be more valuable than relying on clear warning signs)

Though available resources may not be enough to provide help for everyone, there should always be care workers available to help as needed.

After the Earthquake

Mental health experts warn that the humanitarian crisis in Japan from the 2011 earthquake and tsunami is taking a heavy psychological toll on survivors. With an estimated 24,665 dead or missing, thousands remain homeless in makeshift camps with minimal resources available. Despondency and depression are becoming increasingly common as survivors recognize that their plight will likely continue for an indefinite period of time. According to one volunteer doctor at a shelter in the heavily affected Iwate Prefecture in an interview with local reporters, "For a lot of people who, up until this point, have been able to ignore reality and what actually happened, as they get back on their feet they realize that, for instance, their house is gone or their children are dead and they're being forced to confront these facts. A lot of them are extremely uncertain as to what they can do."

Despite a massive humanitarian relief effort to house, feed, and clothe survivors, there are few resources available for mental health services. Post-traumatic symptoms remain common, with many survivors finding themselves afraid to sleep at night out of fear of earthquakes. This fear is compounded by the hundreds of aftershocks recorded since March 11, 2011, and the nuclear crisis at the Fukushima reactor site. Survivors often report sleeping fully clothed and are easily startled by even routine noises in their environment.

While psychological counseling centers have been set up at many disaster evacuation sites, with posters describing possible symptoms of post-traumatic stress, there are an inadequate number of counselors to handle the number of survivors. Survivors often report being unable to find volunteer counselors when needed and are forced to cope on their own as a result.

Inadequate mental health services have been a common problem with other natural disasters in other countries around the Pacific Ring of Fire. The psychological aftermath of previous earthquakes, including the Kobe earthquake in 1995, the 2004 Indian Ocean earthquake and tsunami, and the 2008 earthquake in China's Sichuan Province have all left scars on survivors. Children and the elderly are particularly vulnerable to physical problems resulting from mental stress. To assist child evacuees, the Japanese government is working to reopen schools in areas affected by the tsunami. While teachers and school administers are aware of the psychological problems their children face, the road to recovery is likely to be long.

Thoughts and Behaviors

When people respond to a traumatic event, a range of pervasive thoughts and behaviors can occur that can be either adaptive or maladaptive depending on the prior experiences and inner resources of the people experiencing the event. These can include:

1. Depersonalization, i.e., feeling that you are having a dream or that the event is somehow not real. This is a common sensation during many extremely traumatic events. Following the 9/11 attacks in New York City, many survivors witnessing the collapse of the World Trade Center told reporters that what they were experiencing made them feel like they were "in a movie."

2. Guilt at being left relatively unharmed while others were injured or killed. "Survivor guilt" is frequently reported in survivors of combat, plane crashes, epidemics, natural disasters, or even after a loved one commits suicide. The sense of guilt for surviving when others perceived as "more deserving" of life did not is often reported by people experiencing PTSD. A more extreme form of survivor guilt was identified following World War II in people who survived concentration camps. The psychiatric symptoms reported by survivors was dubbed "concentration camp syndrome," though it is now recognized as a form of PTSD.

3. People who have lost a loved one under traumatic circumstances are especially prone to develop acute grief symptoms. These can include extreme sadness, difficulty maintaining a regular routine, concentration and memory problems, fatigue, sleep and eating problems, as well as anger issues. Survivor guilt is a common feature along with acute problems with stress and increased risk of suicide.

4. Learned helplessness is a psychological condition where people believe that any attempt at relieving stress is useless. First proposed by psychologist Martin Seligman as an explanation for depression and neurosis in humans and animals, learned helplessness is often displayed by long-time victims of domestic violence or sexual abuse. Though most commonly associated with major depression, learned helplessness may also be displayed by PTSD victims in the belief that no relief is possible for their symptoms, and they may make no effort to help themselves.

5. Extreme pessimism about the future and a general feeling that "nothing will ever get better." Along with giving in to despair, this also discourages people who have been traumatized from engaging in any positive actions to help themselves. Essentially a form of learned helplessness, pessimism can often lead to maladaptive behaviors that often make the situation worse.

Reversion under Stress

One maladaptive behavior pattern that is often encountered following a traumatic event is reversion under stress. People who have overcome problem behaviors in the past, such as drinking alcohol or smoking cigarettes, may find themselves with renewed cravings for these things as a source of comfort. In children who have been traumatized, reversion may take the form of bedwetting or thumb sucking, habits that had previously been overcome but which the child may find comforting. In the same way, "hidden" trauma victims who are unwilling or unable to admit to having been sexually or physically victimized may show signs of reversion without any apparent reason.

Other maladaptive reactions that will be discussed in later chapters include suicide attempts, self-harming behaviors (such as cutting or self-mutilation), drug or alcohol abuse, or adopting other high-risk behaviors that can mask self-destructive impulses.

Symptoms That Confuse

In the days and weeks immediately following a traumatic event, whether it involves an entire community or just a single individual, there are always going to be a wide range of potential psychological reactions to trauma. Depending on the inner resources of the trauma victim and the external resources made available in the short term, these reactions can run the gamut from anxiety, panic attacks, grief, depersonalization, to physical symptoms or depression. Though many of these symptoms might suggest future PTSD, most will eventually subside as people adapt to their circumstances and learn to rebuild their lives. Acute stress disorder, which will be discussed in the next chapter, can have many of the same features as PTSD but the symptoms are likely to subside after only a few weeks.

In many cases, the symptoms will often not require formal intervention by a treatment professional. With the emotional support provided by friends and family, people exposed to trauma can gain the reassurance they need to move on and heal themselves. If symptoms persist for longer than a few weeks or if they are severe enough to disrupt their ability to function, then a referral to a qualified professional is strongly advised.

Can It Be More Than One?

While the DSM-5 only acknowledges one PTSD, there can be sub-classifications depending on additional symptoms that may complicate the treatment process. Some of these complications have already been mentioned, including developmental regression, which can be severe enough for traumatized children to lose their ability to speak or walk. PTSD sufferers can also develop psychotic symptoms including pseudo-hallucinations, or the sensory experience of hearing one's own thoughts spoken in different voices, or severe paranoia. All of these symptoms can make the PTSD diagnosis especially difficult for professionals since they can resemble other psychiatric disorders such as schizophrenia.

Complex PTSD (C-PTSD)

Complex PTSD (C-PTSD) is defined as a psychological disorder resulting from prolonged exposure to long-term trauma, such as with victims of long-standing physical or sexual abuse. Most often seen in abused children but also in victims of chronic domestic abuse, C-PTSD has not been included in the DSM-5 although many advocates have suggested that it should be listed as a separate disorder. First described by psychiatrist Judith Herman, C-PTSD is typically distinguished from classic PTSD in that the abuse causing the trauma persists over long periods of time, often for decades.

Along with other PTSD symptoms, C-PTSD sufferers lose all sense of safety or even ability to form emotional attachments due to a betrayal of trust. One of the critical elements discussed in the C-PTSD clinical literature focuses on the vulnerability of C-PTSD victims to being re-victimized, whether by the original abuser or through new relationships. Treatment is often difficult and deals with helping victims learn to develop trust and a sense of safety.

FACT

Some researchers have proposed a separate diagnosis for children who have been exposed to multiple traumas. This new diagnosis is known as developmental trauma disorder (DTD), although it has still not been formally recognized as a separate condition. Similar to C-PTSD, DTD symptoms are especially harmful in younger children whose brains are still developing. As a result, traumatized children are more likely to have long-term physical and emotional problems that can take a lifetime to resolve. Though still controversial, DTD is becoming increasingly recognized and new treatments are being developed.

Continuous Traumatic Stress (CTS)

A second suggested diagnosis, continuous traumatic stress (CTS), which was first proposed by Gillian Straker, is often seen in countries where the ever-present threat of arrest or violence exists on a relatively permanent basis. While Straker and her colleagues did not consider CTS to represent a full-blown psychiatric disorder such as C-PTSD (except in the most extreme cases), treating CTS often poses unique challenges to therapists. People experiencing CTS are usually more preoccupied with the possibility of future traumatic events than by what happened to them in the past. For them, staying vigilant is a healthy way of responding to what they must face although they need to learn to tell the difference between *realistic* and *imagined* threats to their safety.

Rumors about potential threats are increasingly common among survivors, and cases of panic, and even mass hysteria, have been known to strike as people respond to these rumors. For example, following the outbreak of cholera among Haitian refugees coping with the deadly 2010 earthquake, rumors that the outbreak was caused by "black magic" led to riots that claimed twelve lives.

When counseling people experiencing CTS, therapists need to help them recognize the difference between real and imaginary threats. While people living in high-risk settings should stay alert, they also need to keep their natural caution from slipping over into paranoia. Though many people experiencing these kinds of repeated traumas will have enough resilience to avoid developing full-blown trauma symptoms, coping with CTS often depends on how or where the trauma takes place. This includes war zones where the threat of physical attack remains very real and a state of "permanent emergency" exists. Soldiers, UN peacekeepers, relief agency workers, people in refugee camps, and even civilians living in these war zones often experience CTS on a daily basis.

FACT

Since these permanent emergencies can last for decades in some places, providing any kind of help is difficult. Examples include countries such as Syria and Libya, and any place where gang violence is a daily reality. Since the threat of attack never really goes away, people experiencing CTS need to learn to live with that continuous feeling of danger for as long as they remain in that environment.

According to Ignacio Martin-Baro, a social psychologist and Jesuit priest whose work with victims of repression in El Salvador was tragically ended in 1989 when he and his coworkers were massacred by the Salvadoran Army, there are four basic responses in people living in chronic fear:

1. A sensation of vulnerability
2. Exacerbated alertness
3. A sense of impotence or loss of control (learned helplessness)
4. An altered sense of reality, making it impossible to objectively validate one's own experiences or knowledge

He also suggested that people living under continual fear often become desensitized to violence, increasingly rigid and conservative in their beliefs, paranoid, and obsessed with revenge. That pent-up anger, combined with the frequent rumors that helped reinforce paranoid fears, helps explain why rioting and vigilante justice often breaks out in these communities.

Ultimately, while there can be different post-traumatic reactions depending on the nature and persistence of the traumatic event, exactly how those symptoms will emerge in people can vary for a range of different reasons. As well, the symptoms seen in PTSD can be very similar to other psychiatric disorders (which was why people with PTSD were so often misdiagnosed in the years prior to the diagnosis being officially recognized).

CHAPTER 5

Comparing PTSD to Other Disorders

Given the complex nature of PTSD symptoms and the similar symptoms seen in other mental disorders, self-diagnosis can be especially dangerous. Self-diagnosis can lead to a delay in people receiving the help that they need. If you believe that you are experiencing PTSD-like symptoms, proper diagnosis should always be left up to qualified professionals. Don't be afraid to seek the help of a medical professional.

Acute Stress Disorder

Essentially, acute stress disorder represents the early stage immediately following exposure to a traumatic event. First described by physiologist Walter Cannon in 1920 as "acute stress reaction," the disorder represents the mind and body reacting to an immediate threatening event which triggers the body's fight-or-flight response. While acute stress is a natural reaction to trauma, developing symptoms that last longer than a few days usually suggests that a referral to a treatment professional is warranted.

According to the DSM-5, persistent post-traumatic symptoms lasting from three days to one month following traumatic exposure can meet the criteria for a diagnosis. The clinical presentation for acute stress disorder can vary depending on the person but usually involves re-experiencing or emotionally reacting to the traumatic event in some way. This can include recurring dreams, flashbacks, thoughts, illusions, or distress on encountering reminders of the traumatic event. Psychological withdrawal, whether mentally in the form of depersonalization (see sidebar) or physically through active avoidance of anything that reminds the person of the trauma is also common. Catastrophic or negative thoughts, guilt, panic attacks, and hypervigilance are also common. The symptoms will often change over time and people experiencing trauma can often display a range of different reactions depending on individual circumstances.

FACT

Depersonalization essentially involves feeling detached from reality, as if you are watching yourself act with no ability to control what is happening. Many people reporting depersonalization say that it is like living in a dream. While it can happen to anyone to some degree, chronic depersonalization is most often seen in people who have experienced severe trauma or who are extremely stressed for a long period of time. It can also be seen in people with neurological conditions such as migraines or epilepsy.

To be diagnosed with acute stress disorder, there needs to be a clear connection between the symptoms and the traumatic event. The symptoms also need to be distressing enough to interfere with normal functioning, whether vocationally (either through regular work or participating in post-event relief efforts), socially (how people interact with each other), or recreationally.

Symptoms also cannot be linked to other possible causes such as substance abuse or pre-existing psychiatric problems. If the symptoms persist for longer than one month, then the diagnosis changes to PTSD although most people with acute stress disorder usually find their symptoms subsiding within a few weeks. With acute stress disorder, treatment usually focuses on helping patients learn to cope with their symptoms and preventing the development of full-blown PTSD.

In general, women are more likely to develop acute stress disorder than men though that can often vary in terms of the nature of the traumatic event that is experienced. For example, women are more likely to be sexually victimized than men are. Individual factors such as previous psychiatric history, neuroticism, and a general tendency to avoid unpleasant situations can also play a role in developing symptoms. The single greatest risk factor is history of exposure to previous traumas.

Anxiety Disorders

Anxiety disorders include different conditions sharing symptoms such as fear and anxiety and related behavior problems. According to the DSM-5, fear is the emotional response to real or perceived imminent threat while anxiety is anticipation of a future threat. Though both terms are treated as being identical, there are important differences since fear is usually associated with the physical symptoms relating to fight-or-flight (rapid heart rate, sweating, etc.), thoughts of being in immediate danger, and an acute desire to escape from whatever is causing the fear response. Anxiety is usually more associated with hypervigilance over perceived threats and being in a state of continuous tension over future dangers.

The term "anxiety disorder" covers a number of different conditions with similar features and often requires a professional to make a proper diagnosis. These conditions can include:

- Phobias concerning specific objects or situations. This can include *agoraphobia*, or a fear of open spaces, *claustrophobia*, or a fear of closed spaces, etc.

- Social anxiety (including "selective mutism" where people are too afraid to speak in social settings) and generalized fear
- Panic disorder involving recurring and unexpected panic attacks
- Separation anxiety disorder when individuals become separated from people to whom they are attached
- Generalized anxiety disorder is seen in individuals experiencing intense and uncontrollable worry about a range of different events or activities in their lives

A panic attack is one specific example of a fear response including autonomic symptoms such as intense fear, hyperventilation, nausea, faintness, trembling, and chest pains. People experiencing panic attacks often feel as if they are about to die and the symptoms can often be confused with a heart attack. Panic attacks usually respond to treatment, including antidepressant medication and cognitive-behavioral therapy.

Anxiety or panic attacks can be triggered by any perceived threat, whether that threat is exaggerated or not. While everyone experiences fear at some point in their lives, anxiety disorder symptoms are recognized when they are more extreme than the situation that provoked them usually warrants or if they persist over time. For a formal diagnosis, the symptoms also need to be severe enough to disrupt an individual's life in some way. Since anxiety disorder symptoms are similar to many PTSD symptoms, recognizing the difference can be difficult although PTSD symptoms are usually associated with a specific traumatic event.

Obsessive-Compulsive Disorder (OCD)

Another condition that can often be confused with PTSD is obsessive-compulsive disorder (OCD), which involves having intrusive thoughts or fixations. These fixations can include a tendency to overestimate threats, being intolerant of uncertainty, an inflated sense of responsibility, perfectionism, and the need to control unwanted thoughts. OCD symptoms can include:

- Obsessions that are repetitive or persistent thoughts, mental images, or urges to engage in some behavior they consider unpleasant or involuntary.
- Compulsions, i.e., repetitive behaviors (such as frequent hand-washing) or mental acts (counting, repeating words silently) that people feel compelled to carry out in response to an obsession or depending on rigidly enforced rules. This can take the form of daily rituals such as not leaving the house without checking and rechecking to ensure the front door is locked. In many cases, the rituals are repeated until the OCD patient is certain they have been done "just right."

ESSENTIAL

Not everyone displaying perfectionistic tendencies necessarily has OCD. The term "obsessive-compulsive" is commonly used to describe people who seem preoccupied with getting things right or practice nervous rituals, but people with Asperger's disorder, ADHD, or a similar condition may also have symptoms that resemble OCD in many ways. A proper diagnosis should always be made by a qualified mental health professional.

People with OCD often have good insight into the irrational nature of their beliefs, but often find themselves experiencing obsessive thoughts and engaging in daily rituals whether they want to or not. While not the same thing as obsessive-compulsive personality disorder (OCPD), where individuals have a longstanding pattern of excessive rigid thinking or perfectionism, OCD is often linked to chronic anxiety or depression.

Although PTSD sufferers often experience intrusive thoughts much like OCD patients, there is an important difference: The intrusive thoughts are typically linked to a specific traumatic event. PTSD symptoms such as hypervigilance and paranoia about safety can lead to behaviors that resemble some of the compulsive behaviors seen in OCD. Since it is possible for individuals to be diagnosed with OCD and an anxiety disorder (there is often an overlap between the symptoms seen in the two patient populations), there is still a potential for misdiagnosis in PTSD cases.

Depression

While everyone feels depressed at some point in their lives, being diagnosed with a depressive disorder usually means that the depression is severe enough to make you incapable of functioning normally. There are a number of different possible depressive disorders depending on the nature and pattern of the symptoms being reported. According to the DSM-5, a diagnosis of major depressive disorder requires either a severely depressed mood or loss of interest or pleasure accompanied by symptoms such as weight loss, too much or too little sleep, restlessness or agitation, fatigue, feelings of worthlessness, concentration problems, or recurring thoughts of death.

Severe depression is often seen as a stand-alone condition, but it can also be linked to different medical conditions or be part of a broader psychiatric condition. Since individuals experiencing PTSD or severe grief can develop some or all of the symptoms seen in major depression, therapists dealing with PTSD cases showing depressive symptoms need to be careful in recognizing that there are important differences. In major depression, the symptoms usually come on for no apparent reason, unlike the depression following a traumatic event.

QUESTION

What is persistent depressive disorder (PDD)?
Persistent depressive disorder is a mood disorder with many of the same symptoms and features as major depression, but is usually less severe and longer lasting. Formerly called dysthymia or chronic depression, it was renamed persistent depressive disorder in the latest version of the DSM. People with persistent depressive disorder can be prone to "double depression," in which they develop major depression along with their persistent depressive symptoms.

For PTSD sufferers, experiencing grief due to traumatic loss, and feelings of sadness are also likely to come in waves (often called the "pangs of grief") that will slowly subside over time. Feelings of grief and loss are usually accompanied by thoughts and reminders about who or what has been lost. Suicidal thoughts or ideas should be carefully investigated, whether due to PTSD or major depression. Depression can last for a few weeks or for years depending on the causes and the type of treatment received. As we will see in coming chapters, medication and psychotherapy can be beneficial for PTSD much as it is with major depression.

Personality Disorders

According to the definition provided in the DSM-5, a personality disorder is an "enduring pattern of inner experience ad behavior that deviates markedly from the expectations of the individual's culture, is pervasive and inflexible, has an onset in adolescence or early adulthood, is stable over time, and leads to distress or impairment." There are a wide range of personality disorders with different symptoms and patterns of behavior. People with personality disorders can appear odd or eccentric, antisocial, erratic, or even borderline psychotic depending on the symptoms they are showing.

FACT

According to a 2009 survey by the World Health Organization, about 6 percent of the world's population meets the criteria for a personality disorder as listed in the DSM-IV. Other surveys provide slightly different percentages, though the estimates range from 1–10 percent, depending on the diagnosis and level of severity. For most personality disorders, men are more likely to be diagnosed than women.

Though personality disorder symptoms are usually very different from the symptoms seen in PTSD, people dealing with trauma can often show the kind of interpersonal problems that would be associated with long-term personality problems. People with personality disorders are often more vulnerable to the effects of traumatic stress and their symptoms often worsen as a result of added stress. If they were socially isolated or showing borderline psychotic symptoms before the trauma occurred, that pattern of symptoms can become more severe afterward. Individuals with a history of explosive rage or antisocial behavior are a source of special concern, particularly in terms of safety issues for workers dealing with them.

Traumatic Brain Injury

The brain is the most complex organ in the human body, with billions of neurons and long axon fibers carrying messages to every part of the body. Though the brain is protected by the thick bone of the skull and three protective membranes as well as meninges containing cerebrospinal fluid, it can still be damaged by a strong enough external force. Despite the brain's amazing capacity for recovering from even severe damage, traumatic brain injury (TBI) is a major cause of death and disability worldwide. The extent of the damage that occurs in TBI depends on the severity and location of the injury, the nature of the injury (whether or not the injury penetrated the skull), and the extent of the brain tissue that was damaged. TBI can be either *open*, resulting from the skull and protective membranes being penetrated by a sharp object (such as a bullet wound), or *closed*, resulting from a blow to the head, severe rotational force, or acceleration-deceleration trauma (such as in an automobile accident).

Medical experts dealing with TBI typically use the following classification system:

- Minimal TBI is defined as a loss or alteration of consciousness of less than thirty minutes, *post-traumatic amnesia* (loss of memory following the accident) of less than twenty-four hours, neurological deficits that are usually short-term in nature, and minimal signs of coma.
- Moderate TBI involves a loss of consciousness of more than thirty minutes and/or post-traumatic amnesia of greater than twenty-four hours with moderate signs of coma (reduced awareness and response on admission to hospital).
- Severe TBI includes all the moderate TBI criteria as well as strong signs of coma upon admission to hospital. People with severe TBI are more likely to have sustained profound brain damage.

The severity of the injury does not necessarily relate to the severity of the brain damage that occurs. Older people appear more vulnerable to TBI and even relatively mild cases of brain injury can have long-term consequences. For moderate and severe TBI, extensive occupational therapy and rehabilitation are often required to help patients recover.

In any traumatic event, the possibility of TBI should always be considered, whether it is a bomb blast, a physical assault, or even the effects of concussion resulting from acceleration or deceleration following a vehicle accident. Since the type of traumatic event that produces TBI can also result in PTSD, the symptoms can often occur together and, at times, the exact nature and cause of the symptoms can be difficult to determine. Many of the symptoms often seen in TBI, which can mimic PTSD symptoms, include: irritability, concentration problems, fatigue, sleep problems, impulsivity, alexithymia (see following sidebar), and personality changes.

Even relatively minor concussions can result in lingering symptoms that can persist for months and as long as a year following injury. These symptoms can include headaches, sensitivity to light and sound, memory and concentration problems, fatigue, dizziness, and irritability. The DSM-5 and ICD-10 have both set out criteria for postconcussive syndrome (also called postconcussional disorder), and an estimated 38 percent of all people experiencing some form of brain injury will develop symptoms to some extent although they usually go away on their own in time.

FACT

Alexithymia refers to the inability to recognize or describe emotions. People with alexithymia often have significant problems in social settings due to their lack of emotional awareness, which can lead to inappropriate emotional responses, restricted dreams or fantasies, and extremely rigid thinking processes. This leads to greater emotional detachment and difficulty connecting with other people. A 1983 study found that 41 percent of Vietnam veterans with PTSD symptoms also experienced alexithymia.

There is some controversy among researchers over whether it is possible to experience both PTSD and TBI since the post-traumatic amnesia often seen in severe head injuries makes it unlikely that patients develop the flashbacks and other symptoms associated with PTSD. Case histories of head-injured patients with PTSD symptoms have been reported, however, suggesting that traumatic stress can still occur when specific memories of the traumatic event are not available. Even in severe head injury cases, there can still be some "islands" of memory allowing for flashbacks and other traumatic stress symptoms to develop. For mild or moderate head injuries with no real amnesia reported, PTSD symptoms are more common and may be linked to the postconcussive symptoms many head-injured patients report. Any neurological symptoms need to be carefully assessed by qualified professionals, however, to ensure that there are no underlying complications that might be causing the problem.

Conversion Disorder

Patients can be diagnosed as having a conversion disorder when they show neurological problems such as seizures, paralysis, blindness, or numbness without any apparent physical cause. According to the DSM-5, a conversion disorder diagnosis requires:

- One or more symptoms of altered voluntary motor or sensory function.
- Clinical findings showing incompatibility between the symptom and a recognized neurological or medical condition.
- The symptom or deficit is not better explained by another medical or mental disorder.
- The symptom or deficit causes significant distress or impairment in vocational, social, or other important area of functioning.

FACT

Conversion disorder was once known as "hysteria" due to the medical belief that it only occurred in women as a result of problems with the uterus (*hysteria* comes from the Greek word for "uterus"). Identified by physicians for centuries, the diagnosis often masked other mental or physical problems and women patients were frequently subjected to treatments that were traumatic in themselves. Prominent psychotherapists such as Sigmund Freud and Carl Jung largely based their psychodynamic theories on patients with hysteria.

Though the diagnosis of a conversion disorder was used by doctors for any patient presenting unusual symptoms, the DSM-5 warns against making a diagnosis without clear evidence of inconsistent or incompatible symptoms. Cases of conversion disorder such as functional or psychogenic blindness, paralysis, or muteness are often brought on by exposure to some type of traumatic event or extreme stress. They can also be associated with other types of mental disorders and patients with conversion disorders often show more than one kind of symptom. People with conversion disorder often experience anxiety, depression, or panic attacks in combination with their other problems. Approximately 5 percent of all referrals to neurology clinics involve conversion disorder.

While conversion disorder symptoms can be brought on by post-traumatic stress, how those symptoms reveal themselves is usually very different than what is seen in PTSD. Culture can also play an important role in developing conversion disorder symptoms, particularly cultures where certain kinds of conversion disorder are more common. As well, females are more likely to develop conversion disorder than men.

CHAPTER 6

Who PTSD Affects

The preceding chapters showed the different risk factors that can make people more vulnerable to traumatic stress, such as biology, previous experiences, the presence of other medical conditions, the exact nature of the traumatic event, and the resources that are available afterward to help trauma sufferers get on with their lives. While there have been different theories put forward to try to explain how traumatic stress changes people and why some are more vulnerable than others, there are still no easy answers.

Types of Traumatic Events

In exploring how traumatic stress can leave a mark on the ones who experience it, it might be best to focus on the different types of traumatic events that can lead to PTSD. Researchers have identified three types of traumatic stressor events that could potentially result in trauma symptoms. These include:

- Type 1 stressors that are *unexpected, single* events that are beyond the range of normal daily stress and are traumatic in their effects. Most natural and human-made disasters fall into this category including the 2004 Indian Ocean tsunami, Hurricane Katrina, the Japanese earthquake and tsunami in 2011, etc. While some disasters are not necessarily limited to single events (aftershocks following a major earthquake, for example), they are still classified as Type 1. Though Type 1 events are often interpreted as never-ending by people experiencing them, these situations are usually fairly brief, ranging from a few minutes to no more than a few hours.
- Type 2 stressor events occur over long periods of time or involve repeated exposure to trauma. The trauma experienced by soldiers or civilians living in war zones, long-term domestic abuse (battered spouse syndrome), being taken hostage, or being physically or sexually abused over time all involve Type 2 traumatic stress.
- Type 3 traumatic stressor events are harder to classify since symptoms are caused by the combined effect of low-level stressful events that are not necessarily traumatic in themselves, but still produce long-term trauma problems. This is often seen in children who grow up in institutions where they are frequently neglected or exposed to bullying or other stressful behaviors. While the environment is not necessarily considered traumatic, the end result can include symptoms very similar to PTSD including behavioral and emotional problems such as those seen in abused children.

In many cases of PTSD, there can be exposure to more than one type of traumatic stressor event. For instance, while Hurricane Katrina was a Type 1 event, many people who survived the disaster itself faced long-term problems receiving aid or relocating to new communities, which added to the stress they experienced. Victims of rape can often find themselves being re-traumatized by their exposure to the criminal justice system or facing stigma in the communities where they live. In PTSD, the combined effect of multiple stressors can make people even more vulnerable by eroding the inner resources needed for coping with stress.

FACT

Along with the behavioral and emotional problems stemming from neglect, there can be severe serious physical problems as well, depending on the extent to which the child has been neglected. This includes malnutrition leading to stunted growth, brain damage stemming from lack of mental stimulation during critical periods of the child's development, as well as physical impairments due to lack of proper medical care. Studies of neglected children show poor social adjustment, serious depression and hopelessness, and higher-than-average suicide attempts.

Important Factors

While there are different types of traumatic stressor events, most people exposed to these events are not going to develop the same symptoms. In fact, many people that survive horrendous experiences may not develop any symptoms at all. How people are affected by trauma can vary widely depending on personality and temperament factors and the fact that not everybody is going to experience trauma in exactly the same way. For people facing a traumatic event, how that event is experienced can often have as great an impact as the trauma itself.

The presence of other people can also make an important difference in the way a traumatic event is experienced. In cases where trauma is experienced alone (as with sexual or physical assault, for example), not having others to depend on can make victims feel helpless, fearful, and much more vulnerable. People experiencing traumatic events while part of a larger group can also face problems. Having other people around can provide better emotional support, but can also add to stress due to conflicts with other survivors. In cases involving traumatic events affecting entire communities, seeing the wide-scale devastation caused by a natural disaster can be as traumatic as experiencing injury or loss firsthand.

By looking at the different types of traumatic stressors and the influence of social factors, you can see why traumatic events can often affect people in different ways. Overall, there are a number of factors that can play a role in the amount of trauma that people are likely to experience. These factors include:

1. **Degree of life threat**—How close did you come to death or serious injury?
2. **Bereavement or loss**—Was someone close to you killed in the disaster?
3. **Speed of onset and offset**—How quickly did the traumatic event come on and how long before it was over?
4. **Displacement afterward**—Were you and your family forced to evacuate? And for how long?
5. **Exposure to death and chaos**—Was there a wide-scale breakdown of social order or numerous deaths?
6. **The location of the trauma**—Did it occur in a place you had previously thought of as safe (home or school, for instance)?
7. **Complexity of the event**—Was it one stressor or multiple stressors?
8. **Community impact**—Was the entire community to which you belong affected by the event?

As a rule, the greater the number of factors involved, the greater the likelihood of trauma developing. While people can be more vulnerable to trauma due to personality and other factors, how that trauma is first experienced likely plays a role in the type of symptoms that will develop later.

FACT

A study by researchers at the University of Canterbury in New Zealand looked at the survivors of the 2011 Christchurch earthquake and found that people who had pre-existing problems with depression and who scored high in neuroticism (see previous chapter), and low in self-control, were more likely to develop PTSD symptoms. Problems associated with dealing with the aftermath of the earthquake also contributed to developing symptoms.

Famous People Who Developed PTSD

While PTSD was not formally identified as a disorder until 1980, history records numerous cases of people developing unusual symptoms following their exposure to trauma. Here are a few presented for reference:

King Joseph I of Portugal

Following the massive earthquake and tsunami that struck Lisbon, Portugal, on November 1, 1755, the destruction to the city and the deaths of nearly 50,000 people made it one of the worst earthquakes in history. Even after an international relief effort and an enormous rebuilding program that drained Portugal's economy, none of the people who lived through the disaster were ever the same again.

King Joseph I himself developed one highly unusual symptom as a result of his trauma. For the rest of his life, he was extremely claustrophobic and could never trust himself inside a building. The old royal palace had been completely destroyed and Joseph refused to allow it to be rebuilt. Instead, he and his family lived in a series of large tent-like pavilions on the city's edge and even formal government functions were conducted there. After his death in 1777, his daughter Maria had a new palace constructed on the site where the old tents once stood.

Florence Nightingale

In 1854, Florence Nightingale and thirty-eight fellow nurses traveled to Turkey to set up a military hospital near what is now Istanbul to tend to wounded soldiers during the Crimean War. As one of the first female nurses, she became known as the Lady of the Lamp and established many of the principles of modern nursing. Describing the Crimean War as "calamity unparalleled in the history of calamity," she cared for thousands of sick and dying soldiers under appalling conditions and had to fight for every improvement in hospital conditions she could manage.

During the two years she spent in the field, Nightingale experienced many of the horrors of war while reducing the hospital's death rate by two-thirds. Amazed by the hero's welcome she received on returning home, Florence Nightingale helped to reform battlefield medicine and establish better care for soldiers in future wars. For reasons that are still unclear, she became a permanent invalid within two years of returning from the Crimea and was largely bedridden for the next forty years of her life. Despite being an invalid, she published over 200 books, pamphlets, and reports and maintained friendships with some of the most prominent politicians, doctors, and social reformers of her time. Though she was diagnosed with "Crimean fever," which caused her permanent fatigue, some biographers suggest that many of her symptoms were caused by post-traumatic stress relating to her experiences in the Crimea.

Audie Murphy

The most decorated American soldier of World War II, Audie Murphy spent two years with the infantry in southern Europe during which he was wounded five times, earned every medal of valor available from the U.S. military, killed over 200 German soldiers, and was even decorated by the French and Belgian governments. After the war ended, however, Murphy continued to be haunted by his memories of combat. Due to nightmares, he was unable to sleep without his automatic pistol under his pillow. Before his death in 1971, he was asked in an interview how combat soldiers were able to survive a war. "I don't think they ever do," he replied.

Primo Levi

A prominent Italian Jewish scientist and writer, Primo Levi wrote movingly about the year he spent in the Auschwitz concentration camp. Because of his ordeal, he was almost unrecognizable after his return to Italy. Though he recovered physically, married, and raised a family, the emotional impact of his time in the death camps left its mark on him. He was prone to periods of depression despite his success as a writer. He also remained active in Holocaust remembrance organizations though he could never escape the survivor guilt he felt or the memories of his abuse. His death in 1987 due to a fall from his third-floor apartment was ruled a suicide although that verdict remains controversial. In commenting on Levi's death, prominent writer and Holocaust survivor Elie Wiesel said that, "Primo Levi died at Auschwitz forty years earlier."

Spike Milligan

Despite his reputation as one of Britain's best-loved comedians, Spike Milligan spent much of his life dealing with the emotional aftermath of his experiences in World War II. During the war, he had served in numerous campaigns in Italy and was wounded in the Battle of Monte Cassino. Demoted due to an unsympathetic officer refusing to believe he was experiencing post-traumatic symptoms, Milligan eventually went on to become a professional entertainer. He became an international star through his work on *The Goon Show* along with Peter Sellers and Harry Secombe. His old post-traumatic symptoms and the pressures of the show led to manic-depressive illness and an odd breakdown where he was injured trying to kill Sellers. While he continued to be successful with many new ventures in performing, Milligan had at least ten major breakdowns during his life but never lost his puckish sense of humor. Though he wished his tombstone to have the epitaph, "I told you I was ill," the diocese refused to allow it.

Romeo Dallaire

A brigadier-general in the Canadian Forces, Dallaire received a commission as force commander of the United Nations Assistance Mission to Rwanda in 1993. With the outbreak of hostilities in 1994, which led to the deaths of well over 500,000 Tutsis, Dallaire and his undermanned forced attempted to defend key areas and protect as many civilians as possible. While he is personally credited with saving more than 30,000 lives, Dallaire's sense of failure following the genocide caused him to go into a downward spiral due to PTSD. Following an attempted suicide in 2000, Dallaire recovered and remains on medication to control his symptoms and problems with alcoholism. He has been an active supporter of mental health treatment for veterans as well as publicizing the Rwanda genocide to ensure justice for the victims. Appointed to the Canadian Senate in 2005, he has advocated for numerous humanitarian causes including the abolition of child warriors and greater public understanding of PTSD. His book on his Rwanda experiences, *Shake Hands with the Devil*, has been a bestseller since its release in 2003 and has inspired an award-winning documentary.

Senator Dallaire has been appointed the honorary chair of the Post-Traumatic Stress Disorder Association of Canada. As part of his mandate, he is helping promote the association's work in providing greater awareness of PTSD and improving services available to members of Canada's Armed Forces. If you wish more information about the Association and their online resources for people with PTSD, see their webpage at *http://ptsdassociation.com*.

Isn't Everyone a Little Different?

As covered in previous chapters, personality and temperament can make an enormous difference in how people respond to traumatic events. Personality traits can also influence perceptions of new situations and that includes traumatic situations. Ultimately, everyone differs in terms of the kinds of needs they have, which can then influence the sort of subjective response they might have to the trauma. That also depends on their inner resources and the help and support they can draw from afterward. How people adapt and respond can best be explained by five separate (but related) dimensions to adaptive behavior.

Emotional Responding

Traumatic stress is always going to produce powerful emotional responding because it disrupts the normal mental and physical balance of our lives. Though people vary widely in terms of whether they have pre-existing emotional issues that might make them more vulnerable to trauma, the level of distress experienced by a major traumatic event can overwhelm anybody, no matter how well-adjusted they might seem. People can respond to overwhelming emotion through extreme anxiety, paranoia, and depression. They can also respond by shutting down completely leading to the "psychic numbing" often seen in trauma victims. People who successfully cope with traumatic events are often able to handle the overwhelming emotions involved by maintaining an "affect balance" that uses effective coping to keep negative emotions under control.

ESSENTIAL

Psychic numbing in people suffering from trauma is usually characterized by a loss of interest in doing activities that were formerly enjoyed, being detached from other people, and a restricted range of emotion. Therapist Susan Gill argues that psychic numbing stems from being overwhelmed due to feeling extremely stressed. As a result, the numbing results in a zombie-like state that she describes as being in a "dead zone." In many ways, this psychic numbing is a way of coping with memories and emotions that the survivor is unable to handle otherwise.

Cognitive Appraisal

How you handle a traumatic situation is often going to depend on your perception of what is happening. You may not always have the information you need to understand what has just occurred (such as after a natural disaster when survivors often depend on rumors for information on what will be happening next). In cases of extreme traumatic stress, survivors can become hypervigilant or paranoid in always searching their surroundings for potential dangers.

Or else you might deliberately avoid accepting or try distorting what you are hearing as a form of denial. Immediately prior to the Mount St. Helens eruption in 1980, some residents refused to evacuate because they did not believe the volcano would erupt, a decision that would prove fatal to many of them. Denial can often be used as a defense strategy to protect people against possibly wrong information. Extreme trauma cases can also show signs of dissociation, or detachment from reality, which helps control overwhelming psychic stress. They can also experience severe flashbacks in which they re-experience the traumatic situation.

Motivation and Trauma

Everyone has powerful needs that they want to satisfy. These needs drive them toward certain goals, which they feel are important. Whether the needs are for safety, security, friendship, or a range of other things, these needs are usually in balance with emotions and inner resources. Following a major traumatic event, these needs can be changed dramatically and new motivations can develop as well. People whose sense of safety was disrupted by a disaster may find themselves developing a new need for security by becoming paranoid about the world and making elaborate preparations for a future disaster that might never occur. Other people whose sense of community was shattered by a large natural disaster might deliberately cut off personal ties to prevent such a loss from occurring again.

Coping Strategies

People constantly change their methods of coping with life's stresses, usually by trying out new strategies when old ones seem not to be as effective as they would like. According to research by psychologists Richard Lazarus and Susan Folkman and others, coping can be regarded as problem-focused and emotion-focused. These vary depending on the situation and are often linked to underlying personality traits.

Problem-focused coping strategies are usually reserved for situations where you have a reasonable expectation of being able to control the outcome. This usually involves defining the problem that needs to be solved, generating workable solutions, learning new skills as needed to put the solutions into practice, and reappraising the situation to see if the solutions worked. Following a disaster, whether affecting one person or an entire community, problem-based coping typically involves working with treatment professionals and aid agencies to develop plans to reduce the trauma involved and prevent future problems.

Emotion-based coping often arises when you feel that you have no control over what is happening. If the trauma resulting from a disaster you cannot control is so severe that it overwhelms all of your inner resources, you often cope using strategies to regulate your emotions to relieve distress. This can include avoidance of all reminders of the trauma, emotional numbing or distancing, or depersonalization to withdraw from the event completely. Acceptance can be a healthy strategy for emotion-based coping, but not if it means passively allowing the trauma to continue (such as in domestic assault victims). A third type of coping, resilient coping, will be discussed in a later chapter. Ultimately, how you respond to traumatic events is going to change over time and with the nature of the situation.

What is meaning-making coping?
According to the meaning-making model of coping advocated by Viktor Frankl and other therapists, people have an inherent need for the world to make sense. When a traumatic event occurs, questions such as "Why did this happen?" are common among survivors. Meaning-making coping involves coming to terms with trauma by finding an underlying meaning that makes sense in the worldview of the survivor.

Natural Disasters

Imagine that your community has been struck by a severe storm. How severe that storm appears to be often depends on the community and whether this is a rare occurrence or something that happens fairly regularly. In this example, let us say that the storm is causing an unprecedented amount of damage to your home and many other homes in your neighborhood. Though there may not have been any loss of life, you can still feel traumatized at seeing the need to evacuate and the loss of many of your precious possessions. While you are unlikely to develop PTSD as a result of this experience, you can certainly experience post-traumatic stress over what has happened. Still, your community pulls together and provides you with the coping resources you need to recover quickly.

Now, imagine a far-greater disaster striking your community with major loss of life. It need not necessarily be a natural disaster. A school shooting such as the one at Sandy Hook Elementary in Newtown, Connecticut, in 2012 can have devastating emotional consequences for survivors and the community as a whole. While the disaster itself is the greatest source of stress, it can also aggravate problems that existed in the community before the disaster struck. As a result, communities can be very different in terms of how people respond during times of crisis.

During Hurricane Andrew, for instance, some communities had far-greater problems with looting than others. In Florida, many people were afraid to leave their homes despite the damage because of risk to personal safety. It took a major action by the National Guard to blanket the area and reassure people that order had been restored. In Louisiana, on the other hand, there was little looting although inadequate housing meant that more people were left homeless and needed emergency shelter.

Most governments, whether at the federal, state, or municipal level, maintain civil defense plans to be put into effect in the event of a major disaster while relief organizations such as the Red Cross are also on call. While disaster planning primarily focuses on providing food, shelter, and safety for survivors, providing mental health counseling for people dealing with trauma is also becoming more recognized.

PTSD in Wartime

While PTSD was first identified in military veterans, the idea that developing trauma symptoms is a sign of weakness has remained strong in the military culture. The traditional military view was that psychiatric breakdowns for soldiers were usually temporary and that they could be sent back to fighting fairly quickly. That war itself could be traumatic was something few commanders were willing to admit which led to frequent confrontations and accusations of cowardice.

Along with the soldiers themselves are the noncombatants, including doctors and nurses as well as support staff and even civilians, who risk being caught in the crossfire. Although we usually only think of trauma in terms of facing enemy combat, there can also be secondary trauma linked to the general breakdown of society during wartime. As a result, people in war zones face greater risk of all forms of violence, including sexual violence, and may have difficulty receiving medical and legal assistance afterward. This will be covered in greater detail in later chapters.

Refugees and PTSD

According to the 1951 United Nations Convention Relating to the Status of Refugees, a refugee is defined as "any person who: owing to a well-founded fear of being persecuted for reasons of race, religion, nationality, membership of a particular social group, or political opinion, is outside the country of his nationality, and is unable to or, owing to such fear, is unwilling to avail himself of the protection of that country." People can be forced to flee their country for reasons of natural disaster, economic hardship, fear of persecution, or due to war. The United Nations high commissioner for refugees estimates that there are 35.4 million people worldwide who are currently unable to return to their homes. Along with refugees, this figure includes asylum seekers, "internally displaced" people who were driven from their homes but still remain in their country, as well as people who have been declared stateless for political reasons.

Most of the world's refugees are accommodated in refugee camps where many have lived for years, and even decades at times. Despite active efforts by humanitarian aid organizations, life in the camps is often difficult and mental health problems remain common due to limited access to proper treatment. Anyone visiting the camps and talking to the refugees can often hear them describe the various psychological symptoms they are experiencing, including grief over what they have lost and often the brutal deaths of friends or family members. Even those refugees who successfully return home or are able to become citizens of other countries can carry emotional scars that can persist their entire lives, as well as be passed on to their children through intergenerational transmission of trauma.

FACT

Along with the mental health problems faced by refugees in camps around the world, the aid workers who deal with them on a regular basis are also prone to problems as a result of the daily stress they experience. Research studies show that aid workers often report elevated symptoms of anxiety and depression and a large minority also develop PTSD symptoms, depending on their experiences. While older workers are less vulnerable to mental health problems, aid organizations have long recognized the need for stress management training for workers to prevent burnout and other problems.

Personal Trauma

Not all trauma can be linked to wide-scale disasters. Trauma can also occur as a result of experiencing or witnessing violence, including domestic violence, death or serious injury of a loved one, or being involved in a serious accident. Whatever the circumstances, resolving a personal trauma can require time and patience on the part of family members and friends as trauma victims work through their symptoms. While people experiencing a personal trauma need to learn to cope with what they have experienced, the recovery process may be complicated by the lack of an effective support network or the failure to seek needed treatment.

Unfortunately, many friends or family members may not express the necessary sympathy or understanding, especially due to the stigma surrounding mental health issues. Instead of providing support, trauma sufferers can be told to "get over it" and feel isolated as a result. Developing a support network, whether informally from sympathetic loved ones, or formally through support groups, can be critical in the recovery process.

PTSD and Sexual Abuse

Statistics relating to sexual abuse suggest that as many as one girl in three or one boy in five will have been molested at some point prior to attaining adulthood. While definitions may vary concerning what constitutes sexual abuse, many cases of sexual abuse can involve multiple perpetrators and a pattern of abuse that can last for many years. Often the sexual abuse can be accompanied by either systematic physical abuse or verbal threats of harm (usually to intimidate the victim into remaining quiet about the abuse).

For victims of child sexual abuse who remain silent, there are characteristic problems with inability to trust authority figures and intimacy issues due to a sense of betrayal and/or abandonment. Even when child sexual abuse victims do come forward, they are often re-traumatized due to their experience with the criminal justice system, the refusal of many adults to believe their claims of abuse, and frequent anger directed at them over their role in the arrest and conviction of the abuser.

All of these factors can lead to long-term trauma issues that are extremely difficult to treat by mental health professionals and can often last a lifetime. Even family members and friends can often react in unexpected ways that can add to the emotional harm involved and finding the necessary treatment can be a challenge for many survivors.

CHAPTER 7

Special Populations and PTSD

Though the symptoms seen in PTSD can occur following any kind of traumatic event, how those symptoms are expressed can vary widely depending on the circumstances of the trauma and the type of help that victims can receive afterward. Much of the research on PTSD has focused on specific high-risk populations that are seen as being particularly vulnerable to developing post-traumatic symptoms.

PTSD in Veterans

Based on media reports of troubled Vietnam veterans having difficulty becoming readjusted to society following the end of the Vietnam War, the National Vietnam Veterans' Readjustment Study was conducted as part of a congressional mandate in 1983. The study represented the first in-depth look at the psychological problems occurring among returned soldiers and attempted to address whether their actual treatment needs were being met. According to the study results, the majority of Vietnam veterans had successfully returned to civilian life with few symptoms of psychological problems.

But there was a sizable minority who were not so fortunate. Among veterans who had served in the Vietnam theater, 15.2 percent of men and 8.5 percent of women participating in the study met DSM criteria for PTSD at the time that the study was conducted. An additional 11.1 percent of men and 7.8 percent of women showed partial symptoms. Even twenty years after serving in Vietnam, many soldiers reported continuing to experience symptoms. For male veterans, age of entry was the most significant predictor of later PTSD with males going into combat at a younger age being more vulnerable. For females, history of prior victimization (such as child abuse) was a significant predictor.

Along with PTSD, Vietnam veterans reported a range of other problems including alcohol abuse, anxiety, and depression. A substantial minority of veterans also described problems with occupational issues as well as marital and family difficulties. Compared to veterans without PTSD symptoms, veterans reporting issues with post-traumatic stress were also more likely to have significant health problems. In examining postwar variables that played a role in protecting returning veterans from later PTSD issues, social support appeared to be the most important single variable.

While Vietnam veterans continue to be closely studied to gain insight into the long-term consequences of post-traumatic stress, the United States campaigns in Iraq and Afghanistan have produced a new generation of traumatized soldiers. A RAND study released in 2008 determined that over 20 percent of the 300,000 soldiers who had returned from tours of duty reported symptoms of post-traumatic stress. When questioned about what kind of traumatic stress they had experienced, half stated that they had at least one friend who had been seriously wounded or killed. Forty-five percent of the soldiers in the study reported seeing dead or seriously injured noncombatants and 10 percent said they had been injured themselves. Of those soldiers reporting symptoms, however, only slightly more than half actually sought some form of treatment despite programming being available.

"There is a major health crisis facing those men and women who have served our nation in Iraq and Afghanistan," said Terri Tanielian, the project's coleader and a researcher at RAND. "Unless they receive appropriate and effective care for these mental health conditions, there will be long-term consequences for them and for the nation. Unfortunately, we found there are many barriers preventing them from getting the high-quality treatment they need."

As for why many veterans are not getting the help that they need, the veterans in the study reported a variety of reasons including concerns about the side effects of medication and preferring to rely on the emotional support of friends and family. The single most cited reason for not seeking treatment was the fear that the very act of seeking professional help might damage their career in the military or cause their fellow soldiers to lose confidence in them. The stigma surrounding mental illness and psychiatric treatment still remains strong, especially in the military culture. While the rising number of soldiers in treatment is slowly changing those attitudes, greater acceptance will not happen overnight.

ESSENTIAL

The problems relating to PTSD and substance abuse disorders in returning veterans and their later involvement in the legal system have led to the development of diversion programs called Veterans Treatment Courts (VTCs). VTCs represent a unique fusion of mental health and drug diversion programs and are intended to steer court-involved veterans with mental health problems (often PTSD) and/or substance problems to treatment and/or community service rather than incarceration. By helping veterans address symptoms of PTSD, substance abuse, or other psychiatric problems with the goal of improving mental health, reducing substance abuse and resultant recidivism, veterans' groups hope that VTCs can prevent veterans from falling into the trap of arrest, incarceration, release, and recidivism.

The researchers conducting the RAND study estimate that the financial cost of PTSD and major depression in the U.S. military ranges from $4 billion to $6.2 billion during a two-year period alone. That includes the social costs associated with traumatized veterans who manage to commit suicide. Those costs include veterans who develop problems with substance abuse, require expensive psychiatric or medical treatment, and even veterans who develop legal problems.

In a 2010 study released by the Institute of Medicine, criminal justice involvement was identified as being one of the most significant problems faced by veterans returning from tours of duty in Iraq and Afghanistan. Some recent estimates place the number of returned veterans in U.S. prisons as being as high as 200,000, with more than half of those veterans incarcerated for violent offenses. Since veteran status is not always reported at the time of conviction, this number may actually be underestimated. Some U.S. states have even gone so far as to open veterans-only prisons to allow veterans to complete their sentences and avoid prison in future. While many of those veterans undoubtedly suffer from PTSD and related problems, actual research studies remain scarce.

FACT

A study published in the April 2008 issue of *Journal of Traumatic Stress* examined anniversary reactions in mental health disaster relief workers following traumatic exposure at the site of the World Trade Center terrorist attacks. Despite relatively low levels of symptom reporting, workers endorsed an increase in both negative mood symptoms and functional impairment at the one-year anniversary of their traumatic exposure (compared to six months post-exposure). For individuals who met at least some of the criteria for PTSD immediately following exposure, overall self-reported PTSD symptoms tended to increase from six to twelve months afterward. This tendency resulted specifically from an increase in hyperarousal symptoms.

But the problem of veterans with PTSD is hardly limited to the United States military. Virtually every military force in the world that deploys soldiers into combat situations is faced with the problem of traumatized veterans.

Along with the various military conflicts around the world, soldiers who have served as United Nations peacekeepers in troubled regions such as the former Yugoslavia and African countries including Rwanda and Somalia are also being diagnosed with post-traumatic stress problems. Some studies indicate that the nature and degree of trauma experienced by UN peacekeepers varies across different peacekeeping missions depending on the nature and potential danger of the deployment setting.

PTSD in Children

Although children are frequently exposed to potentially traumatic events, collecting statistics on the number of children who develop post-traumatic symptoms remains a challenge for health professionals. Whether the trauma involves being in a life-threatening accident, a natural disaster, or being the victim of physical or sexual abuse, children can and do develop trauma symptoms.

FACT

Studies of abusive parents have found that they were far more likely to have been abused themselves as children. Childhood trauma also appears to be linked to adult psychiatric problems, including anxiety disorders, personality disorders, and depression. Since many children fail to get the help they need as their brains and bodies develop, the consequences of untreated trauma can extend throughout their entire life and even impact how they raise their own children. As a result, the consequences of untreated trauma can last for generations.

Even exposure to the violence seen in mass media can lead to trauma symptoms in children. Following the events of January 18, 1986, when schoolchildren watched the *Challenger* disaster live on television, research showed that many children who had watched the coverage developed symptoms such as nightmares, being easily startled by loud noises, insomnia, and general anxiety over the safety of loved ones. For most of these children, the symptoms did not subside for at least a year. Similar findings have been reported for other high-profile events such as 9/11 and the Oklahoma City bombing.

As news stories become more likely to provide graphic images of death and destruction, the potentially traumatic effect for children can be expected to increase. While most of these stories will probably not lead to long-term emotional problems, the cumulative effect of different kinds of trauma will have an impact on their emotional development. And children do not simply "grow out of it." The trauma that children experience can lead to the development of behavioral and mental health problems later in life. This includes substance abuse, antisocial behavior, and relationship difficulties.

Does Child Abuse Affect Brain Development?

According to research by Dr. Martin Teicher, associate professor at Harvard Medical School and director of the Clinical Biopsychiatry Research Program at McLean Hospital in Belmont, Massachusetts, different types of stress, including child physical and sexual abuse, can have a dramatic impact on brain development. In particular, early childhood traumatic stress produces lasting alterations in patterns of brain development, which, in turn, can lead to different psychiatric disorders. Early stress can program the body's fight-or-flight systems to react more adversely to later stressors.

There is also evidence for different periods during development when different regions of the brain are especially affected by early stress. Therefore, it isn't just the nature of the abuse, but *when the abuse happens* that can affect later development. Early neglect can also be as debilitating as physical or sexual 'abuse. There appear to be different abuse-related syndromes associated with particular ages of abuse and specific regional brain changes. PTSD, major depression, borderline personality disorder, impulse disorders, and aggression may be the result of abuse that only emerges at a much later stage of brain development (or even in adulthood). Even verbal abuse can impact later emotional and social development. In an address given at the 15th Annual Children's Justice Conference, Dr. Teicher argued that early abuse can mold the brain to be more irritable, impulsive, and hypervigilant. He states that "maltreatment is a chisel that shapes a brain to contend with anticipated strife but at the cost of deep, enduring wounds. Early childhood stress isn't something you 'get over.' It is an evil that we must acknowledge and confront if we aim to do anything about the unchecked cycle of violence which often leads victims of abuse to become abusers."

Until relatively recently, child health authorities often dismissed the potentially harmful effect of childhood trauma on later development. Research also tended to focus on trauma in adults while ignoring the harm the children experienced. All of this changed in 1980 with the new DSM-III, which proposed a diagnosis of PTSD that applied exclusively to children. With the increased awareness that children could experience trauma in the same way as adults came new research examining post-traumatic stress in children.

One of the first researchers studying traumatic stress in children was Dr. Lenore Terr who conducted interviews with children following a 1976 kidnapping in Chowchilla, California. In that situation, a school bus with a bus driver and twenty-six children was seized by gunmen who buried the bus, complete with passengers, underground for twenty-seven hours. Although the children were physically unharmed by their ordeal, Dr. Terr's extensive interviews with the kidnapped children presented the first clear indication of what she termed "traumatic symptomatology."

In describing her findings, Dr. Terr reported that the children displayed many of the post-traumatic symptoms commonly seen in adults including nightmares and avoidance behavior. She also found important differences, however, since the children did not report flashbacks or hallucinations and there was also no sign of emotional numbing. Instead, they tended to "relive" the experience through play (including games where they took on roles of kidnapper and victim). They also showed "anniversary" reactions, with a resurgence of symptoms on the anniversary of the kidnapping, dreams of personal death, and pessimism about the future. Over time, their fears appeared to become more general, going from specific fears relating to the kidnapping to more generalized fears about daily events.

During the 1980s and 1990s, new research studies on children following traumatic incidents largely supported Dr. Terr's original findings though the studies often relied on parent and teacher reports rather than on interviewing children directly. This reveals a critical problem in dealing with traumatized children who often have difficulty trusting unfamiliar counselors or researchers. Despite the reluctance of traumatized children and their families to discuss traumatic experiences, new traumatic events provided opportunities for more rigid research studies to understand how children and adolescents coped with grief and loss.

Further Research

Following a school shooting in the mid-1980s in which a sniper killed one child and wounded thirteen others, research comparing trauma reactions in children who were present during the attack with others who had been absent that day showed important differences in trauma symptoms. Not only did children closer to the shooting show higher signs of trauma, the symptoms were found to persist well over a year after the shooting. The majority of the children who had been in the playground when the shooting occurred became emotionally distressed over any reminders of what had happened. They also reported having intrusive thoughts of the shooting with strong fear of a similar shooting happening in future. Their reported distress was linked to the feeling that their recovery was taking far longer than they had expected.

Natural disasters provided another opportunity to study how trauma affected children. After Hurricane Hugo in 1989, a research study of 5,687 young Americans aged nine to nineteen was carried out to determine how widespread PTSD symptoms were in younger disaster survivors. What the researchers found was that 5.4 percent of the children met DSM criteria for PTSD (6.9 percent of girls vs. 3.8 percent of boys). Children aged nine to twelve were more likely to be diagnosed with PTSD than older children.

As the diagnostic criteria were widened in the DSM-IV, more children were found to meet the requirements for a PTSD diagnosis, and it can apply to children as young as preschoolers all the way through adolescence. A meta-analysis of DSM-IV criteria in children suggest that they may be more vulnerable to post-traumatic stress than adults, with 39 percent of children exposed to trauma being diagnosed with PTSD versus 24 percent of adults with similar exposure.

The symptoms often reported by traumatized children include:

- Inability to concentrate
- Bad dreams of the event
- Intrusive memories of the event
- Talking excessively about the event
- Trauma-specific fears
- Loss of interest in previously enjoyed events
- Avoidance of reminders

- Reliving the traumatic event

While most of the symptoms are similar to those seen in traumatized adults, children experiencing PTSD are also more likely to report additional symptoms including low self-esteem, separation anxiety, depression, and generalized anxiety. A small percentage of traumatized children also report panic attacks, self-destructive behavior (including self-cutting), eating problems, and sleepwalking.

Other signs to watch for in children dealing with trauma include antisocial behavior (stealing, fighting, defiance to authority) and regression (which can include bedwetting or thumb sucking in smaller children). These signs are especially common in preschoolers who have been exposed to a traumatic event but can be seen in older children as well.

QUESTION

Can PTSD in children be linked to ADHD?
The relationship between trauma in children and Attention-Deficit Hyperactivity Disorder (ADHD) is often hard to establish, especially in children who have been exposed to long-term trauma such as physical or sexual abuse. Many of the symptoms seen in ADHD such as concentration problems, hyperactive behavior, and opposition to authority can also be seen in children diagnosed with PTSD. Although the trauma symptoms usually only arise after a child has been exposed to a traumatic event, this can be hard to determine without better awareness of a child's background and long-term history.

In traumatized children, how well they recover often depends on the nature of the trauma. For children exposed to one-time traumatic events that do not involve abuse, symptoms usually peak for about a year after the trauma before subsiding. In a large minority of children, however, traumatic symptoms can persist for much longer. For children who are exposed to multiple traumatic stressors or who live in traumatic environments where abuse can continue for years, trauma symptoms can persist well into adulthood.

For children who witness the violent death of a parent, especially due to homicide, the intense stress that they experience can often disrupt their normal development. If the perpetrator of the homicide is the other parent, then there is typically double grief since the child is essentially losing both of their parents, one to homicide and the other to the criminal justice system. Being called into court to testify against a parent's murderer, whether a family member or a stranger, can add to the sense of trauma and delay the normal recovery.

Risk Factors in Children

There are also risk factors that can increase the likelihood of children developing PTSD. Much like in traumatized adults, females are more likely than males to develop symptoms. Also, children with pre-existing learning problems, exposure to violence at home (whether being abused directly or witnessing violence), or who experienced other stressful events at home are more likely to be diagnosed. That can include financial stress since children from low-income homes are more vulnerable to PTSD than children from more affluent homes. Families that have been left in poverty by a natural disaster are less likely to provide traumatized children with the resources they need to cope effectively. Parental conflict with parents frequently fighting in front of their children can also weaken a child's ability to cope with stress.

As well, having a strong social support network in place including supportive parents, family members, and friends can have a powerful protective effect that can reduce the number of PTSD symptoms children experience after a traumatic event. Some researchers have suggested that having a good parenting style including being warm and caring can help protect children, while having a rigid and authoritarian parenting style can reduce children's self-esteem and make them more vulnerable.

Although research about the changes that trauma produces in the neurobiology of survivors has mainly focused on adults, some studies have identified similar changes in traumatized children. As one example, children raised in Romanian orphanages where they experienced extreme neglect often showed lower cortisol levels than children raised in normal settings. Lower cortisol levels have also been found in six- and seven-year-old girls who were abused. Mistreated children also show greater differences in other hormones such as norepinephrine and dopamine. Researchers have also found reduced brain volume in severely abused children, depending on how young they were when they were first exposed and how long the abuse continued. Not only are severely traumatized children affected emotionally, but their cognitive development can be affected as well.

Much like with adults, there can be enormous cultural differences in how children respond to traumatic stress or in the resources they would have to cope. As one example, sexual abuse of children is far less likely to be reported in many cultures and caregivers are also less likely to believe stories of abuse. Suicide is far more likely to occur in Asian cultures as a result of unresolved trauma though there can be significant overlap among different cultural groups. Urinary symptoms such as bedwetting appear more likely to be found in children of European background and least likely in children of Asian background. Anger, sexual acting out, and depression also vary widely depending on the cultural background of the child exposed to trauma. In many countries with a diverse ethnic population, there can be wide differences among traumatized children depending on the cultural background of their parents.

Overall, the health and well-being of children around the world can be affected by trauma arising from natural disasters, serious accidents, fires, war, life-threatening illnesses, domestic and sexual violence, bullying in schools, or other calamities. Though the traumatic events may differ, the resulting post-traumatic symptoms often occur due to children's attempting to adjust to experiences that challenge their entire view of the world. Their limited experience of the world up to that point leaves them more vulnerable to trauma than adults and makes treating PTSD in children especially difficult.

PTSD in Victims of Violence

Violence can produce far more victims than most people realize. Along with people who are directly victimized, whether the violence is reported to authorities or not, there are also the secondary victims who can also develop trauma symptoms. In the United States alone, millions of people over the age of eighteen have lost family members either to criminal homicide or to automobile accidents related to alcohol (which is another form of violence). People experiencing trauma can include relatives, close friends, and even people who witnessed what occurred.

People traumatized by acts of violence, whether or not they were directly affected, can often find themselves re-traumatized by sensational news stories, rumors, and the general community reaction that follows. Often they can hear thoughtless remarks from friends trying to be kind, from clergy who often say the wrong thing, or even from mental health professionals who lack the proper training in grief counseling.

There can be a wide range of emotions associated with trauma stemming from violence that is usually more severe and long-lasting than the trauma associated with a natural disaster or an accident. This is typically due to the traumatic violence being of "human design," which can make the sense of danger from re-victimization far stronger than with other traumatic situations. People who witness a violent death are especially prone to flashbacks and intrusive thoughts as well as the sense of reliving what was experienced.

When dealing with trauma due to violence, survivors not only need to cope with grief and loss, but also with the often impersonal nature of the criminal justice system, which will rarely provide a proper sense of closure. Not only are police required to follow set procedures in their investigation which makes them seem unsympathetic and hostile at times, but also, survivors called to give testimony can face hostile questioning from defense attorneys, which can distort the facts of the case. While victims' rights legislation has cut back on many of the traumatic experiences that victims used to face in courts, recent surveys suggest that only around half of all individuals dealing with the criminal justice system report any kind of satisfaction with the outcome.

For victims of sexual violence, the outcome can be even more serious, whether the victim is male or female. Victim surveys suggest that the actual incidence of sexual assault in adults is largely underreported and, of the crimes that are reported, only a small percentage will ever lead to a conviction. Research has shown that adult sexual victimization often leads to a variety of psychological problems, including PTSD and substance abuse. Men or women suffering from post-traumatic symptoms resulting from sexual assault are urged to seek help from local groups or one of the organizations listed in Appendix C.

QUESTION

What is betrayal trauma?
First proposed by Jennifer Freyd of the University of Oregon, betrayal trauma refers to a violation of trust that occurs when a person or institution that someone depends on for survival betrays that trust and inflicts physical or emotional harm as a result. Examples include a caregiver or representative of a government agency sexually abusing a child or physically dependent adult. Freyd suggests that betrayal trauma can escalate the trauma resulting from the abuse itself.

PTSD and Traumatic Brain Injury

Diagnosing a traumatic brain injury (TBI) is always difficult since there are often no signs of physical injury and symptoms can even develop when there has been no head injury at all. While the old "shell shock" diagnosis was based on the belief that symptoms were due to soldiers being exposed to the shock of explosions that led to brain damage, it is possible for soldiers to develop TBI that way. The force of an impact, whether due to an explosion or the sudden deceleration after an automobile accident, can shake the brain within the skull producing a brain concussion and potentially long-lasting symptoms.

Though most people experiencing a mild TBI will be back to normal within a few months, pre-existing medical issues including a history of previous head injuries, psychiatric symptoms, or even geriatric problems can lead to complications that can delay recovery. As was noted previously, there can be a significant overlap between TBI and PTSD symptoms and many people exposed to trauma can experience both. People with mild TBI symptoms often recover on their own although this usually depends on the amount of support they have, including family and friends, who can help them overcome problems caused by symptoms such as depression, greater impulsivity, memory difficulties, and reduced concentration.

For people with more severe TBI symptoms, however, the outcome can be much worse. In the United States alone, TBI is a leading cause of death or disability with TBI-related deaths accounting for a third of all injury deaths. Long-term TBI-related disability is a major drain on health-care resources with approximately 3–5 million people in the United States (approximately 1–2 percent of the population) living with long-term disability due to TBI. Along with frequent inability to continue working in jobs they held before their injuries, people with TBI are also prone to social difficulties including greater isolation, increased likelihood to develop substance abuse issues, and legal difficulties. Though the actual incidence of TBI in prison inmates is hard to estimate, some reports suggest that 25–87 percent of prison inmates have a history of TBI, which may have contributed to their offense.

People with TBI-related disability are also far more likely to be victims of violence, emotional abuse, or neglect than people in the general population. Children with disabilities are also far more likely to be physically or sexually abused than nondisabled children. While the proportion of women with disabilities being abused is roughly comparable to what nondisabled women face, they are more likely to report being abused by more than one perpetrator and over longer periods of time.

FACT

A study by researchers at the University of California, San Francisco, suggests that military veterans with a history of traumatic brain injury, PTSD, and depression are at increased risk for developing Alzheimer's disease and other types of dementia later in life. Based on their findings and what is now known about dementia risk factors, the authors suggest that there may be 423,000 new cases of Alzheimer's disease among veterans by 2020. The costs associated with these new cases may range from $5.8 to $7.8 billion.

The abuse that disabled people receive often comes from family members or personal care workers and is most likely to occur while in institutional settings such as prisons and long-term care facilities. Even for disabled people living on their own, their limited income often means having to live in marginal conditions and even being reduced to homelessness. As a result, they are far more vulnerable to being robbed or assaulted. Even after being victimized, they are more reluctant to ask for help from police and care workers because of mistrust of authority figures and dealing with agencies that are not equipped to handle the special needs of people with disabilities.

Cognitive problems resulting from TBI can also lead to showing poor judgment in many social situations, as well as the inability to recognize or handle potential threats effectively. They can also engage in drinking or drug use or other unsafe behaviors that can increase the likelihood of negative consequences. With reduced cognitive ability comes reduced ability to cope with traumatic situations when they do occur. As a result, the potential for post-traumatic stress problems remains high.

CHAPTER 8

The Role of PTSD in Building Relationships

No man is an island, Entire of itself, Every man is a piece of the continent, A part of the main.

—John Donne

Every human being is part of a community, whether consisting of family members, friends, extended acquaintances, people at work, colleagues, or members of a parish or church. No matter how isolated people with PTSD may regard themselves as being, there will be people who care about them. While PTSD can often lead to major interpersonal problems that can damage their relationships with the people around them, there has been surprisingly little research into the powerful role that family and friends can play in either helping or delaying a trauma patient's recovery.

Impact of Trauma

This chapter will provide an extended look at the impact that trauma can have on personal relationships and cover some of the research that has been done to date. Though every relationship is different, maintaining that relationship while dealing with the often-devastating symptoms associated with trauma requires tremendous patience, both on the part of trauma patients and the ones who are trying to understand them. Perhaps above all else, it means not giving up hope and recognizing how different PTSD symptoms can affect the patients' behavior and emotions.

The interpersonal problems that trauma survivors often have tend to fall into two broad categories: emotional detachment and aggression. Family members and friends dealing with survivors need to be aware of these issues and make allowances when possible as they occur.

Emotional Detachment

Emotional detachment stems from the emotional numbing seen in many trauma sufferers and typically involves a general sense of anger over their perceived vulnerability. This can stem from:

- Feelings of grief and the fear of re-experiencing their overwhelming loss
- Survivor guilt ("Why did I survive when others didn't?")
- Feelings of shame, poor self-esteem, and self-loathing
- Feeling overwhelmed by the trauma symptoms they are experiencing

The most common coping strategy used in trauma survivors is to avoid all reminders and potential triggers for traumatic flashbacks. Survivors may also find themselves preoccupied with their own memories and emotional issues, which can distract them from paying much attention to the personal lives of the people around them. When family members or friends experience their own problems or setbacks, the lack of apparent sympathy they receive from trauma survivors can lead to hurt feelings and damaged relationships.

Trauma survivors may also deliberately drive people away out of a fear of loss or a sense of a foreshortened future, which may make them uncomfortable with long-term relationships. The *ambiguous loss* (see sidebar) can often take a powerful psychological toll on family members.

Dealing with ambiguous loss often leads to depression, anxiety, and guilt for family members. It also places an additional burden on spouses who have to take on more responsibility as a result.

QUESTION

What is ambiguous loss?
Ambiguous loss refers to the uncertainty that can surround family members who are absent in some ways, but not in others. Spouses and family members of military personnel deployed overseas in dangerous places often experience a form of this due to the uncertainty over whether their loved one will return safely.

For families of PTSD survivors, dealing with someone who is psychologically absent, whether due to emotional numbing or the survivor preferring to be alone, can be especially hard. When a family member who was once a vital part of everyday life is no longer there to take part in important decisions and special occasions, that loss is felt, even when he or she is physically present. Since there is no way of telling whether things will ever return to normal, spouses and family members can often feel "frozen" in terms of their relationship with PTSD survivors.

Aggression

Many trauma survivors have enormous difficulty controlling their emotions. That can include irritability over even minor problems and people around them can find themselves walking on eggshells as a result. While trauma survivors are often afraid of losing their temper for fear of their own self-control, the possibility of their lashing out verbally or physically in extreme cases needs to be recognized. Domestic and emotional abuse in PTSD survivors is well-documented, and they may try to isolate themselves out of fear of harming the people around them.

Any of the symptoms associated with severe PTSD can lead to problems with violence including flashbacks, hyperarousal leading to chronic irritability, low frustration tolerance, hypervigilance, and avoidance symptoms. Feelings of guilt and self-loathing can even be projected onto others leading to confrontations.

There are cases of PTSD survivors, especially veterans, committing acts of violence while experiencing flashbacks and the PTSD diagnosis has been used as a legal defense in a number of court cases. This violence can be aimed at family members or total strangers depending on where or when the flashback occurs. Family members need to recognize that loved ones with PTSD symptoms are going to experience anger issues and may even be prone to violence, especially if they are experiencing symptoms such as flashbacks. Helping people with PTSD overcome these problems is going to require both patience and caution.

ALERT

A recent study by researchers at the University of North Carolina at Chapel Hill looked at more than a thousand veterans who served tours of duty in Iraq and Afghanistan and found that 13 percent reported violence against a family member and 9 percent against a stranger during the time period when they participated in the study. Anger symptoms and flashbacks were the two biggest predictors of violence occurring, with male veterans being more likely to commit stranger violence while female veterans were more likely to commit family violence.

According to Robert Rosenheck and Jane Thomson in their 1986 review of research of families of traumatized veterans, dealing with the emotional emptiness resulting from severe PTSD symptoms can be one of the most serious problems faced by family members. This detachment can have different degrees of severity ranging from "spacing out," leaving home for days at a time, sitting in front of a television set for hours at a time, or self-isolation in a private room that acts as a "bunker" where the PTSD survivor avoids the world.

Family members and friends often cope with this detachment in different ways, depending on their own inner resources and the extent that they are able to cope with the difficult circumstances of their daily lives. How long they are able to cope depends on the treatment they and the PTSD survivor receive. For this reason, family-centered treatment of PTSD remains an important part of the recovery process for most people with trauma.

When Parents Have the Disorder

The risk of PTSD survivors indirectly passing on their trauma symptoms to their children is an ever-present concern, especially in victims with severe trauma. Though there is no clear model to explain how parents can pass these symptoms on to their children, research studies have shown that people who have had extremely traumatic experiences can inadvertently influence their children to develop problems with emotional detachment, depression, and hypervigilance similar to what the traumatized parent is experiencing. Some children of trauma survivors can report these symptoms well into adulthood.

Much of the research looking at intergenerational transmission of trauma has focused on the children of Holocaust survivors. The existence of a "second-generation syndrome" remains controversial with many researchers pointing out that most second and third-generation offspring of survivors never develop psychological problems. There is also controversy over whether problems being passed on to children are due to "impaired parenting" or the trauma they experience from hearing about what their parents endured.

FACT

A team of researchers at Oklahoma State University examined the role of parenting style in maternal trauma passed on to children. The researchers found that mothers with a history of interpersonal trauma were more likely to be authoritarian in raising their children. This includes a tendency toward verbal hostility, physical coercion, and low nurturing style. Children exposed to verbal hostility were also more likely to develop emotional and behavioral problems later in their childhood.

Attachment and Trauma

Another concern, especially in children in the early stages of development, deals with the emotional attachment that all children need to form with their parents as they grow and develop. According to the attachment theory first proposed by psychiatrist John Bowlby in the years following World War II, infants need to develop a warm and loving relationship with at least one primary caregiver to develop normally. Though Bowlby mainly focused on infants deprived of maternal affection due to neglect, he noted that children bonded to a primary caregiver out of a need for security. Children deprived of a parent upon which they had previously depended undergo separation anxiety and eventually become alienated from that parent due to the lack of an emotional bond. As part of his theory, Bowlby proposed a sensitivity period between six months to early toddler stage when children especially need to develop emotional attachments. Although researchers have extended this sensitivity period, children deprived of emotional attachment to a parent for an extended period of time are at risk for developing problems as they grow older.

While having at least one parent capable of providing children with the love and attachment that is needed for normal development can help prevent most upbringing problems, children often have difficulty understanding why one parent is so emotionally distant. As well, witnessing other symptoms such as traumatic flashbacks, lashing out emotionally, and the loss of intimacy between both parents can also have impact on the normal development of children.

How Do Children See Trauma in Parents?

While research into how PTSD affects parenting styles has largely focused on emotional numbing, the symptoms parents show can affect their relationship with their children in different ways. Along with emotional detachment and avoidance behavior, which can lead to reduced attachment and alienation, parents showing hypervigilance symptoms are also more likely to trigger verbal and physical conflicts due to problems managing their own emotions. Also, due to exaggerated fears for the safety of their children, parents with trauma issues may become overly protective and prevent their children from engaging in activities they see as potentially harmful. Such overprotectiveness can lead to resentment on the part of children forced to forego experiences they regard as enjoyable. Parents with PTSD may also experience significant doubt as to their own ability to be a good parent. This fear, combined with their other symptoms, can influence how they interact with their children.

For many parents dealing with trauma symptoms, the symptoms may change rapidly over time and often without warning. This can lead to considerable confusion as children try to adjust to a parent who can be moody and withdrawn or overly protective depending on how he or she is feeling at the time. It is often left up to the other parent to act as peacemaker and to explain to their children why their mother or father is so unpredictable or distant.

FACT

A recent study conducted by Norwegian researchers looked at the post-traumatic symptoms developed by parents and children exposed to the 2004 Indian Ocean tsunami. Results showed that parents having strong post-traumatic symptoms, especially hyperarousal and intrusive memories, were more likely to influence their children to develop strong trauma symptoms as well. The researchers concluded that how children cope with disasters is strongly influenced by whether their parents are showing emotional distress as well.

Children who become alienated from their parents are often vulnerable to psychological problems of their own, including acting-out behavior (temper tantrums, school truancy, and other antisocial actions), emotional instability, and increased rebellion. Problem behavior in children can make the home situation far worse for people recovering from PTSD, leading to greater family disruption and an increased risk of domestic violence or substance abuse.

Therapists working with PTSD patients often involve family members, including spouses and children, to help their patients learn to handle the pressures of dealing with trauma and being an effective spouse and parent as well.

Social Relationships

Attempting to maintain a social relationship with someone who has become emotionally detached and prone to mood swings and anger episodes is difficult, and many people report being emotionally drained as a result. Having a relationship with someone experiencing PTSD often means taking on the role of "ambassador" between that person and the rest of the world. Explaining to others why he or she is so moody, argumentative, and distant can be frustrating, especially if you have difficulty understanding what the loved one has gone through. There is also the very real sensation of being "stuck in two time zones" when dealing with someone who is unable to move on from a traumatic event that is being constantly re-experienced. Things they have experienced years or decades previously can seem more important than day-to-day activities with spouses, children, or friends. Many people find themselves reluctant to compete with such memories and often feel insecure and unimportant by comparison.

At the same time, you can also lose patience with people who seem rooted in the past and who are unable to "just get over it." People with PTSD are often confronted with this attitude and feel that their unique experiences are being ignored or dismissed by others who are unable to understand what they have endured. All of which can contribute to undermining the relationships that they have with the important people in their lives.

Friends of people with PTSD should recognize the various symptoms that can emerge and how they are likely to affect social behavior. This includes watching for things such as sudden irritability, apparent loss of interest in activities and topics they used to enjoy together, a tendency to obsess on topics relating to the trauma (or a complete refusal to discuss the trauma at all). Emotional withdrawal should also be expected since many trauma victims find themselves afraid of being abandoned or allowing others to "get close" to them. People with trauma can also become overprotective with friends the way they might be with close relatives.

Along with understanding how PTSD symptoms are going to affect social relationships, people attempting to preserve their friendship should encourage open and honest communication as well as defuse any talk of giving up on problems. Encourage problem-solving and keep watch for maladaptive coping strategies such as substance abuse. Above all else, stay committed to the relationship. People with PTSD need the social support they get from their friends and family. Even if they often refuse to admit it.

QUESTION

How should you react when a loved one tells you about his or her trauma?

As part of their research into the importance of listening skills when trauma victims share their experiences, Jennifer Freyd and her colleagues at the University of Oregon developed a set of skills-training materials covering the verbal and nonverbal ways of responding to disclosures. These include the need for attentive body language, verbal encouragement, and responding supportively and without judgment. More information can be found online at *http://dynamic.uore gon.edu/jjf/disclosure/SkillsExperimental.pdf*.

Professional Relationships

While many people with PTSD are able to hold down jobs and function professionally, that often depends on how severe their symptoms are and whether they have the mental and emotional capacity to do what their employers demand. It is hardly surprising that unemployment is a common problem faced by trauma survivors, many of whom find themselves unable to cope with the stress being placed on them.

Trauma that occurs in the line of duty, whether for people in the military or emergency workers such as police, firefighters, or paramedics, can often lead to long-term inability to return to work due to constant reminders of that trauma. Following the events of September 11, 2001, the public became more acutely aware of the stresses, dangers, and risk of fatality emergency workers face whether during mass emergencies or in the course of their daily working lives. And the trauma is not necessarily limited to the frontline workers. Support staff, including counselors, are also vulnerable to secondary trauma dealing with the often-graphic experiences being related to them by their friends and colleagues.

The potential for traumatic stress can also occur in other occupational settings where workers face possible death or injury, including construction sites, public transportation services, factories, prisons, or public utilities, among others. Even people working in supposedly "safe" workplace settings can develop post-traumatic symptoms following natural or human-made disasters such as workplace shootings or accidents.

Though trauma is usually expected following major traumatic events, it is also often seen as the result of smaller and less sensational events, including suicide or domestic violence resulting in death or serious injury. Survivor guilt following the death of a fellow emergency worker or a victim who might have been saved can be especially overwhelming. In many cases, such deaths are followed by inquests where the judgment and actions of surviving emergency workers are called into question. This can add additional stress.

FACT

A research study conducted by Cheryl Regehr and her colleagues at the University of Toronto found that over 80 percent of paramedics and firefighters are regularly exposed to death of patients, including children, while nearly 70 percent reported having been physically assaulted. More than half of all paramedics and firefighters studied also reported to have been in situations where their lives were at risk. Studies of volunteer firefighters, police officers, and other emergency workers show similar findings.

For the family and friends of emergency workers, their role as a personal support network can be critical in helping to protect against post-traumatic stress, both immediately after being exposed to trauma and in the months that follow. They also need to be aware that they are at risk for secondary trauma affecting them as well. While family members of police, military personnel, and firefighters must cope with the daily stress brought on by shift work and irregular hours, not to mention long-term deployments in the case of military families, there is also the constant fear for the loved one's safety. During critical events, these fears become even stronger.

When emergency workers are dealing with traumatic stress symptoms, their emotional detachment and increased irritability can lead to tension and strained relationships. There can also be a greater sense of isolation due to the feeling that people outside the closed community of fellow emergency workers are unable to understand what they are facing. As a result, many police officers and firefighters along with their families develop informal "cultures" to provide themselves with emotional support when dealing with outside criticism.

Recognizing that trauma can often develop for military personnel and emergency workers, most emergency service organizations have formed trauma teams to deliver emergency debriefings after traumatic events to prevent later emotional problems. Trauma team workers are typically recruited from within the organization and provided with special training that is regularly upgraded to ensure that their skills remain current.

While trauma teams help prevent long-term problems, many people exposed to traumatic events at work find themselves unable to return to their jobs due to potential reminders of the event and the overwhelming fear of a similar event occurring. Whether they are able to overcome the symptoms and return to work or the job loss becomes permanent often depends on their individual circumstances and effective treatment.

Romantic Relationships

Considering the loss of intimacy often seen in people dealing with PTSD, the psychological impact on their spouses can be just as devastating as what they experience themselves. Along with emotional detachment and moodiness, spouses also have to deal with all the other adverse symptoms associated with PTSD. It is hardly surprising that research studies looking at spouses of traumatized veterans often experience problems with tension, loneliness, stress, and somatic problems depending on the severity of their spouses' symptoms. Along with an increased risk of intimate partner violence, research has shown that veterans diagnosed with PTSD are also more likely to have their marriages end in divorce.

According to a recent Department of Veterans Affairs survey, 42 percent of veterans receiving treatment three years after coming home from deployment report difficulties getting along with their partners while 35 percent report separation or divorce. Overall, the stronger the PTSD symptoms are, the greater the level of dissatisfaction in a relationship. Similar findings have been reported for sexual abuse survivors, adult children of alcoholics, and other people whose lives were affected by PTSD. For the purposes of treatment, however, encouraging PTSD patients and their spouses to maintain a strong relationship, including developing effective communication skills and positive emotional bonding, can be an important part of making a good recovery.

For many people dealing with trauma, problems with intimacy often come from a fear of being abandoned by their partners and, at the same time, a fear of losing control over their own lives. Dealing with trauma can mean feeling afraid of those inner feelings of anger and anxiety and how people might react at seeing those feelings come out. Spouses need to be alert for those symptoms in their partners and not feel hurt or angry if they lash out verbally. There can also be a certain amount of limits testing in traumatized people as they try to see how far they can go in letting out their inner anger before a partner decides to walk away.

Why Are You in This Relationship?

For anyone in a long-term relationship with someone showing the various devastating symptoms associated with chronic PTSD, the question often arises of whether to remain in the relationship or to end it. Ultimately, that is a decision that everyone affected by PTSD, whether directly or indirectly, needs to make for themselves. Being able to cope with the challenges associated with preserving a relationship that has been affected by trauma often involves tremendous internal resources as well as support from family and friends and treatment professionals.

Although the social support from an intimate relationship often provides PTSD patients with the stability and emotional balance they need to get their lives back on track, keeping that relationship going while a partner is coping with trauma is going to be a challenge. If you are the one trying to keep that relationship going, you need to be honest with yourself about whether you have the inner resources to face what that might mean.

Unfortunately, there are no guarantees that things will necessarily get better although many families emerge from the crisis stronger than ever. Some of the coping strategies that many families use to help a family member deal with post-traumatic stress will be covered in a later chapter. For now, just recognize that hope is the key. So long as you can maintain that hope, the relationship will survive.

CHAPTER 9

PTSD Paired with Other Disorders

Trauma is surprisingly common, and traumatic events can occur at any time. Trauma does not even need to be experienced directly to lead to PTSD. Witnessing or hearing about the circumstances surrounding the violent death or injury of a loved one can be enough to cause post-traumatic stress symptoms that can linger long afterward. While not everyone exposed to traumatic stress will develop PTSD, they are certainly vulnerable to a range of different health problems, including psychiatric disorders and medical conditions.

Trauma and Your Health

In her classic book, *The Body Remembers*, Babette Rothschild wrote, "Trauma is a psychophysical experience, even when the traumatic event causes no bodily harm. That the traumatic event exacts a toll on the body as well as on the mind is a well-documented and agreed-on conclusion of the psychiatric community as attested to in the DSM-IV." She goes on to write, "Trauma continues to intrude with visual, auditory and/or other somatic reality on the lives of its victims." The effects of trauma can have a major impact on the mental and physical health of survivors.

Though researchers have identified the impact that PTSD has on health in military veterans and other high-risk populations, they are also finding that untreated PTSD can have a major impact on health-care costs as well. Trauma interacts with how people use health care in three different ways:

- **Direct health-care needs.** Experiencing a traumatic event can also involve additional medical problems that need to be treated, such as soldiers being wounded in battle and rape victims needing medical services for their injuries.
- **Health risk behaviors.** Trauma survivors can develop high-risk behaviors as a result of trauma exposure. That can include drug and alcohol abuse, cigarette smoking, obesity, neglecting one's diet, or other factors that can increase the risk of developing long-term health problems. Many of these risk factors develop as a way of coping with traumatic stress but can also damage the body.
- **Somatization.** Trauma exposure often leads to medically unexplained physical symptoms. The symptoms can mimic neurological disorders despite the lack of any real evidence to back them up. Trauma victims may even fake symptoms as a way of gaining sympathy from medical doctors and in extreme cases, this is known as Munchausen syndrome. Even patients with legitimate medical issues can find themselves experiencing far more distress than the symptoms actually cause. One example of this is when trauma sufferers with chronic pain problems resort to illegal sources for pain relievers that doctors are otherwise reluctant to prescribe.

Depending on the nature of the trauma and their personal background, survivors may not necessarily ask for help. Victims of childhood neglect or abuse may be too mistrusting of medical caregivers to seek treatment, even when it is needed. Unfortunately, while "overusers" who make repeated requests for medical help are well-documented in the clinical literature on traumatic stress, "underusers" who prefer not to rely on medical doctors for even serious problems are not as widely researched. As a result, ignoring serious medical problems can lead to people needing far more expensive treatments when they are finally forced to get help.

FACT

A research study published in 2000 by the *Australian and New Zealand Journal of Psychiatry* examined 641 Australian Vietnam veterans and found that a diagnosis of PTSD was associated with medical costs that were 60 percent higher than average. Those higher costs were associated with overall higher treatment costs for physical conditions as well as mental health treatment. Mental health factors such as depression and anxiety were significant predictors of health-care costs along with age and number of medical diagnoses. For mental health factors such as depression and anxiety, overall health-care costs increased substantially with each symptom reported as well as each medical diagnosis.

PTSD and Substance Abuse

According to the National Vietnam Veterans Readjustment Study (NVVRS), 75 percent of Vietnam veterans who met diagnostic criteria for PTSD also met the criteria for a lifetime alcohol abuse problem and 15 percent met criteria for drug abuse. Substance abuse, whether involving drugs or alcohol or both, is also a common problem in veterans attending inpatient psychiatric programs. The true extent to which substance abuse occurs in people with trauma symptoms may be hard to measure given that many people with drug or alcohol problems often deny abusing substances, at least in the early stages. Researchers have also linked substance abuse to various other emotional problems including depression and anxiety disorders. Along with treating PTSD symptoms, counselors are also often called upon to treat drug and alcohol abuse problems as well.

For people dealing with post-traumatic stress, relying on drugs or alcohol to suppress or avoid painful memories or other symptoms often seems like the only way to manage crippling thoughts and emotions or simply to sleep at night. For many Vietnam veterans, drug and alcohol use often began while they were still deployed to help detach themselves from their daily exposure to death and dying. For other veterans, the chemical use was the only way to get to sleep at night and the pattern of abuse would continue even after they returned home. Veterans who also had physical injuries frequently developed a dependence on pain medication that aggravated their other substance abuse problems.

Even veterans who returned home without any substance abuse problems or post-traumatic symptoms were often at risk for delayed onset of post-traumatic symptoms triggered by reminders of their wartime experiences. In many cases, self-medication with alcohol or narcotics seemed to be the only way to relieve what they were experiencing.

ESSENTIAL

If you are dealing with PTSD symptoms and feel that you have become dependent on drugs or alcohol just to keep those symptoms under control, seek immediate help either by contacting one of the organizations listed in Appendix C or by contacting your family doctor and asking for a referral to a program in your area. While those programs nearest to you may not help you deal with the combined symptoms of PTSD and substance abuse, a local counselor can make referrals to treatment professionals who might work with you to confront your problems and to get your substance abuse issues under control.

While alcohol can be legally purchased in most places, getting access to drugs often meant either purchasing street drugs or getting prescriptions from medical doctors who were unaware of the potential dangers of over-prescribing psychiatric medications for symptom relief. To get around the problem of dealing with suspicious doctors, many veterans seeking high dosages of a preferred medication engaged in "doctor-shopping" to receive prescriptions from different doctors. Many states have introduced patient registries to prevent drug-seeking patients from seeing multiple doctors but the problems associated with substance abuse still remain.

Family members and friends need to stay vigilant to ensure that people with PTSD are not becoming dependent on medication, whether they have been prescribed by medical doctors or not.

Mood Disorders

Along with substance abuse, mood disorders such as depression are extremely common in people with PTSD. According to the National Vietnam Veterans Readjustment Study, 28 percent of veterans with PTSD were also diagnosed with major depression. Other studies suggest that almost half of all veterans diagnosed with PTSD will develop strong depression along with their post-traumatic symptoms with similar findings being seen in other PTSD patients. As you have seen in previous chapters, people with long-term depression are also much more vulnerable to developing PTSD after being exposed to a traumatic event.

The most common depression diagnosis seen in PTSD patients is major depressive disorder, depending on the type of symptoms being reported. Major depressive episodes usually last two weeks or longer and often come on unexpectedly or following an upsetting event. The symptoms required for a DSM-5 diagnosis of major depressive disorder are:

1. Depressed mood, either daily or nearly every day.
2. Loss of interest or pleasure.
3. Significant weight loss (not related to deliberate dieting) or weight gain of more than five percent of body weight in a month.
4. Too much or too little sleep.
5. Psychomotor agitation (observed by others, not just self-reported).
6. Fatigue.
7. Feeling worthless or excessive feelings of guilt.
8. Diminished ability to think or concentrate.
9. Recurring thoughts of death, including suicidal thoughts.

As you can see, there is some overlap with symptoms seen in PTSD, and a diagnosis of major depression should only be made by a qualified professional. Even though the symptoms of major depression can be understandable after a traumatic loss, they can be severe enough to disrupt normal life and keep people from returning to their normal lives. Although major depressive disorder is the most common mood disorder, there are other diagnoses depending on the type of symptoms being shown and how long the symptoms might persist. Fortunately, people with depression often respond well to medication and psychotherapy similar to what works with PTSD patients.

For some people though, the depression can be so severe that it can mask the PTSD symptoms that may have caused the depression in the first place. This is often seen in survivors of child sexual abuse who never reported what had happened to them and only sought help years later for apparently unrelated problems such as depression. Treating the depression often involves having the patient open up about unresolved trauma, a process that can make recovery especially difficult.

While most people with PTSD will not develop major depression, prolonged post-traumatic symptoms will often lead to low self-esteem or pessimism about the future that can lead to increased risk of depression. It is especially important for people dealing with PTSD symptoms to be open with friends and family about what they are experiencing rather than concealing their depression due to concerns about "bothering" loved ones or being thought "crazy." Keeping depression hidden usually means a critical delay in getting the help that you need.

Anger

Not surprisingly, many PTSD survivors also report significant problems with anger and hostility along with their other symptoms. Anger symptoms can be expressed in different ways including passive anger (anger directed inward) and aggressive anger (anger directed outward). Aggressive outbursts can range from verbal abuse to physical violence directed against people or inanimate objects. Although anger symptoms are most commonly associated with combat veterans, research studies looking at different groups of PTSD survivors have found that anger is a common response to many traumatic events, especially events that can be linked to a specific cause. Along with general symptoms of anger, some PTSD survivors may also develop problems with poor impulse control, especially in social situations where they may experience stress.

Anxiety Disorders

Besides PTSD, there can be other anxiety disorders that can arise as well, depending on the symptoms than can develop as a result of trauma. Although the anxiety experienced by people with PTSD is usually limited to places and situations that act as reminders of the traumatic event, some trauma survivors develop excessive anxiety or worry about a wide range of activities in their daily lives. This can lead to a diagnosis of generalized anxiety disorder if the anxiety persists for longer than six months and prevents them from leading a normal life. Symptoms of generalized anxiety disorder can include: muscle tension, general restlessness, fatigue, insomnia, irritability, and concentration problems. While generalized anxiety disorder linked to PTSD usually begins with exposure to trauma, people with pre-existing anxiety problems are also more vulnerable to post-traumatic stress.

In addition to generalized anxiety disorder, there are more specific anxiety disorders that can develop in addition to PTSD. Many of the symptoms for these different disorders overlap. It is possible to have more than one diagnosis depending on the symptoms involved. Along with panic disorder, which was covered in a previous chapter, people experiencing trauma can develop specific phobias related to the traumatic event. As an example, people who survive traumatic automobile accidents can find themselves unable to drive again due to crippling fear of being in another accident.

Phobic reactions to trauma can extend to *agoraphobia*, e.g., intense fear or anxiety of using public transportation, being out in open spaces such as parking lots or shopping malls, or being inside public buildings. In extreme cases, people with agoraphobia may be afraid to leave their homes and prefer to remain shut in, often for years. The anxiety resulting from trauma can also affect how people cope with social situations, including social anxiety disorder (also known as social phobia) and even selective mutism in which children or adults find themselves unable to speak in social situations.

For people coping with trauma, separation anxiety disorder can often be reported though this is more common with children than adults. Due to the need for emotional reassurance of a trusted family member or even an inanimate object, people suffering separation anxiety experience extreme fear whenever they are separated from home or the person or object that makes them feel safe. They are often reluctant to be alone or in an unfamiliar place without their attachment figure. Children suffering separation anxiety may be unable to stay by themselves and prefer to "shadow" a parent around the house rather than go into another room. They may also be reluctant to sleep alone and need the reassurance of their parents' bed.

Both adults and children experiencing separation anxiety may experience nightmares of death and destruction when separated from their attachment figures. Adults and older children can also experience heart palpitations, dizziness, and fainting whenever they are experiencing separation. As a result, they may restrict any independent activities away from home and become more dependent on parents or other attachment figures.

Whatever form the anxiety disorder takes, people with anxiety disorder symptoms experience fear or anxiety that prevents them from getting on with their lives. Whether this anxiety begins with exposure to trauma or is part of a long-time problem with anxiety that made them more vulnerable to trauma, many PTSD patients have anxiety episodes triggered by the apparently minor difficulties they may face. While medication and psychotherapy can help people learn to cope with the anxiety, treatment still needs to be tailored to the specific symptoms being reported.

PTSD and Infection Resistance

Can being stressed lower the body's ability to fight infection? According to research into the growing field of psychoneuroimmunology, the answer appears to be yes. Though medical doctors noticed that psychiatric patients are more vulnerable to infectious diseases as far back as the nineteenth century, it was not until the twentieth century and research into how the immune system worked that a formal connection between stress and immunity could be demonstrated.

According to Hans Selye and his general adaptation syndrome model as well as McEwen's concept of allostatic load, the body's ability to fight disease becomes strained in the final stage of coping with stress when the body's inner resources become exhausted. Based on this research, many of the physiological markers linked to acute stress, including enlargement of the adrenal gland, smaller spleen and thymus gland, and changes in brain chemistry, are accompanied by reduced activity of the immune system and production of fewer antibodies.

Research examining stressful events in humans and animals has shown a consistent link between stress and different measures of immune functioning including antibody response as well as production of antigens and T cells. Children exposed to neglect in early childhood are also more vulnerable to infectious diseases and other medical problems associated with a reduced immune system.

QUESTION

What is psychoneuroimmunology?
The term "psychoneuroimmunology" was first coined during the 1970s by researchers at the University of Rochester, who discovered that laboratory animals could learn to suppress their immune response. This suggested that resistance to disease was at least partially controlled by the nervous system. The immune system and the brain apparently communicate through a network of nerves leading to key components of the immune system, including the thymus gland and the spleen. Based on later research, the brain and the immune system are part of a single system with stress boosting the production of antibodies to help resist infection during crises. Both the sympathetic nervous system and the hypothalamic-pituitary-adrenal (HPA) axis appear to be major pathways allowing for interdependence between emotions and immune resistance.

Other emotional problems including depression have been positively linked to reduced immune functioning. People with depression are more vulnerable to chronic heart disease, premature aging, impaired wound healing, chronic pain syndromes, and Alzheimer's disease.

Though research looking specifically at the link between traumatic stress and immunity is more limited, studies of PTSD patients have shown greater vulnerability to a range of different medical conditions that can be linked to reduced immune functioning. This includes increased inflammation, which plays a strong role in cardiovascular disease.

In recent years, research has linked traumatic stress to increased production of cytokines, which can also be linked to problems with inflammation. Cytokines are a diverse group of chemical substances including proteins that are secreted by cells in the immune system and act as chemical messengers. Along with playing a role in how the immune system works, they can also boost immune responses including inflammation, leading to increased autoimmune problems such as rheumatoid arthritis and cardiovascular disease.

Research studies examining high-risk PTSD populations including rape victims and survivors of domestic abuse have shown a higher rate of inflammation and related health problems.

Cardiovascular Disease

People suffering from PTSD show an increased risk for many serious illnesses and premature death than people without post-traumatic symptoms. As one example, the National Comorbidity Survey showed that women who had been mistreated as children were nine times more likely to develop cardiovascular disease (CVD) than women without a history of abuse. According to the Canadian Community Health Survey, people with PTSD show a significantly higher rate of developing illnesses such as CVD, cancer, respiratory diseases, and chronic pain.

FACT

Cardiovascular problems are a special concern with depression, even more so than for PTSD. In a large study of U.S. veterans, people diagnosed with depression have an increased risk of dying of heart disease over a five-year period. No similar link was found for veterans diagnosed with PTSD alone, but people with both depression and PTSD symptoms also appear to be at increased risk of heart disease.

A 2007 study of people in the Netherlands affected by a human-made disaster found a strong increase in medical complaints relating to CVD, muscle, and skin problems even when previous health problems were taken into account. People with PTSD are also more likely to request medical services and make more visits to hospital emergency departments than people without trauma. Not surprisingly, most PTSD patients demanding medical services also scored high on symptom screens for depression.

Chronic Pain

Researchers and treatment professionals have recognized a strong link between chronic pain and PTSD over the past two decades. Not only can the same traumatic event cause people to develop lingering pain problems along with post-traumatic symptoms, people suffering from chronic pain are also more vulnerable to developing post-traumatic symptoms after being exposed to a traumatic event.

Though pain is usually temporary, it is considered to be *chronic pain* if it endures longer than three months and is severe enough to disrupt the lives of the people experiencing it. While most pain problems have a clear origin and can be treated along with the condition causing them, other pain disorders such as fibromyalgia are harder to treat since the underlying cause remains obscure. Chronic pain is the most common complaint among people requesting medical services and the leading cause of disability in most countries around the world. Illegal opium-based painkillers easily outsell almost all other street drugs, and medical doctors are warned to watch out for legally prescribed pain medications being diverted to illegal sales. The cost involved in dealing with chronic pain, whether in terms of time lost from work or the money spent on pain medications is astronomical. In the United States alone, the economic costs of lost productivity due to pain have been estimated at $61.2 billion a year.

FACT

Chronic pain is a particularly large problem in military veterans with more than 50 percent of the returning veterans in some studies reporting regular pain issues. Of the Iraq and Afghanistan veterans seen at one Veterans Affairs Polytrauma Network site, more than 80 percent met criteria for chronic pain.

Considering that people with chronic pain also experience related psychiatric problems, it is hardly surprising that a number of studies have found high rates of PTSD among chronic pain patients. For example, a St. Louis University study of automobile accident victims with chronic pain showed that nearly 30 percent were also diagnosed with PTSD. In studies of veterans dealing with chronic pain, those veterans reporting PTSD as well have ranged from 50 to 66 percent. Even in PTSD patients with no identifiable injury, chronic pain due to fibromyalgia is also commonly reported, with some studies finding as many as 57 percent of fibromyalgia cases also reporting post-traumatic symptoms.

Though female veterans are less likely than male veterans to report both PTSD and chronic pain, there is still a considerable overlap as women with PTSD are more likely to report pain problems than women without trauma issues. Veterans with PTSD are also more likely to report specific types of chronic pain, including headache problems, than non-PTSD veterans. Chronic pain is also more strongly associated with PTSD than with other anxiety disorders.

For people with PTSD and chronic pain problems, the long-term outcome is often worse than what might be expected for either disorder separately. Symptoms of PTSD often aggravate pain and vice versa due to greater emotional distress and pessimism about eventual recovery. Chronic pain can also interact with specific PTSD symptoms such as flashbacks, hyperarousal, and avoidance behavior.

According to the mutual maintenance model proposed by Timothy Sharp and Allison Harvey, chronic pain and PTSD can maintain one another due to the cognitive, emotional, and behavioral problems seen in both disorders. In other words, specific factors seen in chronic pain can make PTSD worse while PTSD symptoms can make recovery from chronic pain more difficult. This mutual maintenance can occur due to coping through avoidance, which can reinforce both disorders and also make patients less likely to participate in treatment.

Treatment

Treatment for people experiencing PTSD and chronic pain symptoms needs to take both disorders into account since treatment is less likely to be successful if they are treated separately. In fact, patients experiencing both disorders may be less motivated to attend any treatment that does not address both trauma and pain issues. In veterans particularly, pain may act as a reminder of the traumatic event that caused both problems, and veterans may want to discuss how and why their pain problems began. For a veteran saying, "Every time my shoulder acts up, I think about what happened that day," treatment providers and family members often need to be aware of the psychological issues involved with both chronic pain and trauma.

Unfortunately, there are still relatively few joint chronic pain/PTSD programs available except through the Veterans Administration or other agencies and getting to the needed program may often involve traveling long distances. The only alternative is to seek treatment for the different disorders separately, which can raise new problems due to the lack of communication between different treatment providers. Friends and family members have to stay vigilant to warn treatment providers of any changes that might occur, especially with new symptoms as they develop.

ESSENTIAL

People experiencing both PTSD and chronic pain need to be especially careful about using opioid-based pain relievers such as morphine, methadone, oxycodone, Fentanyl, or codeine, which are more likely to lead to problems with chemical dependence and adverse reactions. Research shows that veterans with chronic pain and PTSD who were treated with opioids showed increased high-risk behaviors such as using higher doses for long periods of time, using more than one type of pain medication at the same time, and adverse side effects. Opioid use should be carefully monitored by your doctor.

Medical doctors prescribing medication for both pain and trauma symptoms also need to keep careful watch to ensure medications are not being misused or overprescribed. Many jurisdictions now require patient registers to keep track of pain medication being prescribed to prevent "doctor-shopping" that might allow pain patients to receive prescriptions from more than one doctor. On the other hand, veterans or other people with legitimate pain and trauma symptoms may be reluctant to take needed medication due to a fear of becoming dependent and can find themselves being over-whelmed by their symptoms. Since people with both PTSD and pain can often develop substance abuse problems, relying on medication to deal with troubling symptoms should only be considered in consultation with trained professionals.

CHAPTER 10

Can PTSD Be Prevented?

There has always been controversy over what to do immediately after a major traumatic event occurs. Depending on the scope of the event, whether it involves an entire community or a single individual, treatment is usually focused on dealing with symptoms of acute traumatic stress as they occur. Since it can often take months before a formal diagnosis of PTSD can be made, emergency workers dealing with people showing emotional or physical distress can be called on to offer whatever help and support they can provide. The type of help being given often depends on what is needed most at the time, however, based on the principle of triage (see following sidebar).

Immediate Help

Triage is the process of determining the priority of the help a patient needs, depending on the severity of his or her condition.

In emergency situations involving mass casualties, every patient is evaluated based on how immediate their need is. Each patient is then tagged in terms of priority, which helps personnel keep track of them through the triage process. People with life-threatening injuries are treated first while people with less serious injuries may be treated later on. Depending on the severity of the disaster and the number of emergency workers available, patients with relatively minor injuries may even be recruited to assist with more serious cases.

FACT

The term "triage" comes from the French word *trier* meaning to "sift" or "sort."

Along with medical emergencies, triage can also be applied in dealing with immediate needs of survivors. As one example, immediately following a disaster that has left people homeless, the first priority is to provide them with food and shelter, with other needs regarded as being of secondary importance. People reporting psychological issues due to traumatic grief or separation anxiety many need verbal reassurance, but whether or not psychological treatment can be provided often depends on the number of mental health workers available and how acute the symptoms may be.

ESSENTIAL

According to mental health research about disasters, 11–38 percent of people in distress who arrive at emergency shelters and family assistance centers after a disaster have stress-related and adjustment disorders. Problems with bereavement or family separation, major depression, and acute anxiety are also commonly seen. Also, up to 40 percent of people in distress have pre-existing problems that are contributing to their mental health issues following a disaster.

The psychological treatment provided for survivors immediately following a traumatic event has changed over time based on research into which approaches were most likely to prevent later post-traumatic problems. Since triage policies usually mean that only people showing severe symptoms of trauma are most likely to be treated first, counseling can often be delayed for weeks and even months due to waiting lists and lack of available counselors.

It is also important to identify all the people who might be potentially affected by a traumatic event, many of whom can be overlooked because the emotional impact is not as easy to determine. These can include:

- People directly involved, whether physically injured or not
- Family members of people directly involved
- Those experiencing the loss of a loved one
- Rescue personnel and helpers
- Eyewitnesses and bystanders

The likelihood of developing trauma is determined by how strongly people identify with the victim and the traumatic event itself. The reactions are always more intense if the victim is a child or if what happened seemingly strikes at random, leaving people to wonder, "*What if it had been me?*" Many traumatic events also produce "hidden" victims who were not present but who experience trauma because they missed out on being a victim due to an unforeseen circumstance, e.g., someone who misses a plane that later crashes.

There are always more psychological victims of a traumatic event than there are people in medical need. On average, there can be as many as twenty or thirty psychological victims for every medical victim (dead or injured). Since psychological victims can be scattered around the world, it is often left to them to seek out help rather than relying on disaster relief organizations working where the traumatic event physically occurred.

Not everyone developing post-traumatic symptoms are going to show signs of distress right away. Some people may refuse any treatment being offered them only to develop post-traumatic symptoms months or years later. According to psychiatrist Johan Cullberg, how people process a crisis experience has four basic stages. The extent to which someone later develops PTSD often depends on how well they are able to work through these stages.

Shock

Psychological shock occurs when we see or experience something our minds cannot accept or endure. A traumatic event that hits without warning can make the entire world seem unpredictable and dangerous. When we go into shock, our minds are essentially declaring a time-out until we are able to come to terms with what happened. How long people remain in shock often depends on the help they receive immediately after the trauma occurs. This is where front-line workers and helpers are especially important since they are often the first people the shocked victim deals with. They are also extremely vulnerable to any negative comments made by bystanders or well-meaning helpers who accidently say the wrong thing while trying to comfort them.

Above all else, psychological shock is a survival technique. Trauma victims can often recall what happened to them in complete detail even years afterward, including the sounds and smells they experienced. There is also complete emotional numbing as people are still trying to process what happened. This can include the inability to feel pain as people in shock can move and behave almost normally without realizing they have been injured.

People who are in shock can also react by either panicking or becoming hysterical, or else by freezing and becoming completely unresponsive to what is happening around them. In traumatic situations where there seems to be only a slight chance of surviving, people are more likely to react with panic while people who see the situation as completely hopeless often freeze instead. Containing panic is especially important in mass evacuations since even a small percentage of victims panicking can endanger other survivors and their rescuers.

Reaction

People use shock as a way of protecting themselves from the mental chaos and feelings of hopelessness that can set in if they think about their situation too much. Once the immediate shock fades, reaction can set in, at which point that mental chaos often comes to the surface. The transition from shock to reaction is usually gradual and typically only occurs when the survivor feels relatively safe. The reaction stage is often marked by emotional turmoil, including crying episodes, sadness mixed with feelings of relief that it could have been worse, despair at the prospect of rebuilding, guilt, and self-accusations. Anger and blame are commonly seen as well with accusations and even aggression, whether verbal or physical.

There can also be embarrassment at the thought of dealing with friends and strangers offering sympathy. People interacting with them can also be afraid of saying the wrong thing. Families that have experienced a traumatic loss find well-meaning friends pointedly not mentioning their loss unless they bring it up first. Others can be unwilling to talk about the trauma at all out of fear of the emotions it would raise.

People in the reaction stage often experience physical symptoms including trembling, vomiting, nausea, a feeling of heaviness in the chest, muscle pain, and fatigue, all common stress reactions. Insomnia is also frequently experienced and some people may report being afraid to close their eyes. Though the emotions experienced in the reaction stage serve an important purpose by helping us get them out of our system, many people can insist on medication to help them sleep or to numb what they are feeling. This in turn leads to the possibility of becoming physically dependent on medications or even self-medicating with whatever other chemical aids are available.

Working Through and Processing

After the reaction stage comes the working-through-and-processing stage. Once people go through the previous two stages, they often find themselves unwilling to discuss what they have experienced any further. Trauma victims recognize that they need to come to terms with what happened, but this process is largely internal. Though the shock and reaction stages can end fairly quickly, the working-through stage can take much longer. Dealing with grief after a traumatic loss can require years or even decades of handling each day as it comes.

This is also the stage where people are moving on with their lives. While they may be preoccupied with thoughts about what happened in the first few months, this gradually changes as the daily business of living pushes those thoughts into the background. As they become aware that feelings of traumatic loss are occurring less frequently, it also becomes possible to recognize that they are making progress in their recovery.

That does not mean that strong emotions will entirely disappear. There will always be reminders that will trigger flashbacks, memories, and feelings of guilt, but they will occur less frequently as the person works through his or her trauma.

Reorientation

The final stage, reorientation, involves making the changes needed to move on with life. This usually means taking concrete actions such as selling the belongings of loved ones who have died, moving to a new neighborhood to escape tragic reminders, starting a new career or going back to school, or whatever is needed to reinvent oneself. The end result of reorientation is to incorporate the traumatic experience into life and recognize that it is a part of who the person is. People who have survived a major traumatic event and who have learned to reorient their lives around it often form communities of like-minded survivors or else join organizations to preserve the memory of what they experienced as a legacy for the future.

While helping people who have experienced severe trauma can often be a lifelong process requiring intensive treatment, mental health professionals working with disaster victims and people in high-risk professions have developed specialized counseling procedures to be applied immediately after the trauma in an attempt to prevent later problems. Although triage usually focuses on providing food, shelter, and medical care, counselors providing debriefing and short-term treatment after a disaster have become more widely accepted as well.

Ideally, trauma counseling begins within the first forty-eight hours following a traumatic event, although it can also be applied days or even weeks after the event depending on the symptoms being displayed or whether counselors are available. During this early period, many survivors are experiencing psychological shock or are entering the reaction stage of their crisis experience.

Critical Incident Stress Debriefing

Originally developed for emergency service workers who experienced acute stress on the job, critical incident stress debriefing (CISM) later became widely used by emergency responders as part of the disaster response process. The interventions that are part of the CISM model developed by psychologist Jeffrey Mitchell include:

Defusing

Carried out on the day of the incident, often before the people affected have a chance to sleep, defusing can involve either individual or group sessions in which people exposed to trauma are educated about the possible symptoms that could develop and to stress that such symptoms are normal. Counselors doing defusing also monitor for individuals who are at risk for later problems or who are showing symptoms such as shock, anger, depression, or anxiety. Defusing sessions are usually informal and are intended to address *immediate* needs.

Debriefing

Debriefing sessions are meant as a follow-up for people who have already been through defusing, but can also be used for people who were not directly affected by the traumatic event. Done within seventy-two hours of the event, debriefings can be conducted individually or in groups, but are more structured than defusing sessions. Along with giving people a chance to talk about their experiences, debriefings also provide an opportunity for brainstorming about coping strategies and to inform people about resources available in their community.

A typical debriefing session has seven phases:

1. Introduction phase and establishment of session guidelines
2. Fact phase during which people recount the event from individual viewpoints
3. Thought phase with people describing how they personally experienced the event
4. Reaction phase in which people discuss their emotional reaction to the event

5. Symptom phase and the discussion of symptoms and changes following the event
6. Teaching phase in which people are instructed about stress reduction techniques and ways of using personal support to deal with trauma
7. Re-entry phase where people are given the chance for feedback and the termination of the debriefing

Follow-Through

In all cases following a debriefing, people are contacted within a week to ensure that the debriefing was effective and to learn if new problems have developed. People who were previously identified as being at risk can also be contacted and referred to treatment professionals if the trauma symptoms persist.

While participation in the debriefing process is strictly voluntary, many organizations can make attendance compulsory, which can be regarded with resentment by people preferring to rely on their own coping strategies. Although CISM was initially developed for people suffering from occupational stress, using debriefing with trauma patients remains controversial.

Research studies looking at whether CISM actually benefits trauma cases have found little evidence to support its continuing use except in helping emergency workers dealing with occupational stress. Not only has CISM not been shown to prevent later PTSD following trauma, some researchers have suggested that forcing people to attend debriefings may actually make symptoms worse. Psychiatrist Arieh Shalev has suggested that forcing people to participate in debriefing sessions too soon after the initial trauma may lead to increased arousal and re-traumatize individuals who are still coming to terms with what they experienced.

Though some professionals still advocate CISM for use in trauma cases, most mental health professionals have shifted to a new approach that seems to have more promise.

Psychological First Aid

Developed jointly by the National Center for PTSD and the National Child Traumatic Stress Network, *psychological first aid* (PFA) was specifically designed to help people immediately following a natural or human-made disaster. PFA can be administered by first responders to an emergency scene, school crisis response teams, medical professionals, disaster relief workers, and Citizens Corps workers. Intended for use in diverse settings, PFA can be conducted in emergency shelters, field hospitals, medical triage areas, crisis hotlines, and community centers. It is also intended for use with people of all ages, including young children, and includes special handouts providing important information for youths, adults, and families to use while they are recovering.

FACT

The *Psychological First Aid: Field Operations Guide* is available free of charge online at *www.ptsd.va.gov.* Along with a comprehensive overview of PFA principles and procedures, the online guide also includes handouts for survivors and worksheets. Online training in PFA is available at *http://learn.nctsn.org,* while hard copies of the guide can be purchased for $10 each at *www.castlepress.net/nctsn.*

Almost hidden among the first responders dealing with the aftermath of the Boston Marathon bombings on April 15, 2013, were the mental health professionals providing *psychological first aid* to the survivors. Although an estimated 50–60 percent of all people directly or indirectly affected by a traumatic event will recover without the need for mental health services, professionals dealing with post-traumatic stress in survivors have long recognized that a large minority of survivors require psychological support to recover.

Since earlier critical incident stress management approaches have often been found to do more harm than good, the newer system of PFA is now the preferred method of dealing with trauma cases. Developed jointly by the U.S. Department of Veterans Affairs and the National Child Traumatic Stress Network, PFA is intended to help people during the immediate aftermath of traumatic events such as terrorism or natural disaster.

Among the mental health professionals called in to help survivors of the 2013 Boston bombings was Kermit Crawford PhD of the Boston School of Medicine. A licensed clinical psychologist who specializes in disaster behavioral health response, Crawford is well experienced in dealing with trauma survivors in previous disasters such as Hurricane Sandy and recognizes that the PFA counseling provided to date is only the first stage in the recovery process. In describing his initial work with Boston Marathon survivors and their families, he stated that the early goals of PFA were to establish safety and emotional stability, reduce stress, provide comfort, and provide access to whatever information they may need. "They need to be in the place where they're certain that they are protected, that their fears and anxieties about what happened are somehow managed, that their emotions are somewhat stable," he added.

While providing victims with the answers they needed about the causes of the bombing as well as new information as it became available, victims also needed to be reassured that the immediate danger is past and that they are safe for the time being. Helping trauma sufferers recognize the symptoms linked to post-traumatic stress will follows as well as training them to handle flashbacks and other delayed reactions to what they have gone through.

QUESTION

How should psychological first aid be done with children?
When dealing with children, especially young children, responders should sit or crouch at the child's eye level. They should help school-age children express their feelings verbally and use age-appropriate words such as "scared," "mad," or "worried." By listening carefully and checking in with the children to make sure they are understood, responders can determine whether children are showing signs of regression in how they speak or behave. Responders also need to talk to children "adult to adult" while still matching their vocabulary to the children's age level. For very young children, concepts such as death may be too abstract for them to understand. Once the children are reunited with their parents or caregivers, responders need to ensure that the caregivers are able to continue providing the children with the needed support.

The basic objectives of PFA are to establish a human connection in a non-intrusive and compassionate manner, to reassure survivors who might be in shock or experiencing emotional distress, to provide physical or emotional comfort, and to gather information about their immediate needs that can guide responders in providing the most effective care. PFA responders also work to connect survivors with social support networks, including reuniting them with family members, friends, neighbors, or community groups. Through the training they receive, PFA responders encourage survivors to cope with what they are experiencing and to connect with available mental health resources in the area as soon as possible depending on what is needed.

What Not to Do after a Disaster

Along with specific guidelines for providing PFA to children and adolescents, older adults, and people with disabilities, PFA responders are also trained in what *not* to do in an emergency. This includes:

- Do not make assumptions about what survivors are experiencing or what they have endured.
- Do not assume that everyone exposed to a disaster is going to be traumatized. Many survivors are going to be able to weather what happened without needing more than minimal help.
- Do not try labeling what survivors are experiencing as "symptoms" or attempt to diagnose them on the spot. They don't need to be told about "pathology" or "disorder." Even if you suspect traumatic stress, share these suspicions with the appropriate mental health professional, not the survivor.
- Do not talk down to survivors or focus on their helplessness. Focus instead on what the survivor has accomplished or contributed to others while waiting for help.
- Do not assume that all survivors are going to want to talk to responders. Simply being there and offering support may be enough.
- No "debriefing." If they want to talk about what they experienced, they will do it on their own without prompting.
- Don't speculate or provide wrong information or rumor. If you don't know the answer to a question, say so and then do your best to get the right information to the survivor.

The Psychological First Aid Process

There are eight core actions that lie at the heart of the PFA process, although workers are encouraged to adapt the core actions as needed given the special needs of survivors and available resources.

1. **Contact and engagement**—The responders introduce themselves to survivors in a nonintrusive and helpful manner. Responders should also respect the wishes of survivors who are not interested in talking but reassure them that help is available if they need it. For those survivors who do wish to talk, responders need to reassure them about confidentiality and gather the information needed for providing further help.

2. **Provide safety and comfort**—This includes attending to children and adults who are anxious and separated from family members to attempt to reunify them as quickly as possible. Responders also need to provide whatever source of physical comfort the survivor requires as well as information about where they can get the services they might need. This stage can also include emotional comfort, especially for survivors dealing with a traumatic loss.

3. **Stabilization (if needed)**—Though not every survivor is going to need emotional support, PFA responders will be alert for signs that a survivor is in shock or is having a strong emotional reaction to what he or she has gone through. Survivors may also be experiencing flashbacks or showing other signs of acute distress. Stabilizing survivors may simply involve providing calm comfort or else giving them time to calm themselves. For many survivors, simply reuniting them with friends or family may be all that is needed, especially with children separated from their parents.

4. **Information gathering**—People providing PFA need to gather all information about a survivor's immediate needs in a reassuring manner to get the proper help. The PFA manual provided by the Center for PTSD includes worksheets for providers to gather as much information as possible and to relay it to aid agencies as quickly as possible. The information-gathering stage usually begins with: "You've been through a lot of difficult things. May I ask some questions about what you've been through?" Questions can focus on any traumatic loss that survivors experienced or whether they had post-disaster concerns relating to safety. Survivors are also questioned about medical needs, risk of self-harm, and how to

contact family members. Learning about previous history of trauma can also be important.

5. **Practical assistance**—Once the survivor's needs are identified, responders should offer practical assistance to address those needs. Once again, triage is important in responding to the most immediate needs first. That can include medical needs, providing food and shelter, and family reunification (especially with children or adolescents). For those needs that cannot be immediately addressed (such as a home or business that has been destroyed), PFA responders can help survivors develop an action plan to put into effect.

6. **Connection with social supports**—Traumatized survivors will need as much emotional and physical support as possible. After a disaster or loss, providing survivors with a hug, a willingness to listen, understanding, and acceptance can be essential, whether it comes from a family member or a PFA provider. Reassuring people that they have self-worth and are not to blame for what happened to them is an important part of the PFA process. Survivors may also benefit by forming support groups with fellow survivors who have gone through similar experiences. This can be especially important for survivors who are cut off from their regular emotional support or who cannot be immediately reunited with their families. PFA providers and other volunteers can help children and adult survivors by providing games, arranging sing-song sessions, or other group activities. It is also important to respect the wishes of survivors who refuse support for whatever reason so long as they are not in immediate distress.

7. **Information on coping**—Many survivors need to be educated about many of the common symptoms that often arise after a traumatic event. They also need information on the most effective ways of dealing with traumatic stress as well as basic information about the events that are unfolding around them. This information needs to be practical and accurate with no speculation about what is happening. Information on stress reactions should avoid "blanket" reassurances providing fixed timetables about when stress symptoms will disappear since this might create unrealistic expectations about when people can recover and even make survivors feel "abnormal" if their symptoms take longer to subside.

Information on coping can include telling survivors about the different kinds of PTSD symptoms and how those symptoms can appear to other people. It is also important to warn survivors about the role of trauma reminders, including anniversary dates and potential flashback triggers. The PFA manual available online also includes useful handouts that can be given to survivors covering helpful tips for parents to use with children of different ages (ranging from preschoolers to adolescents) as well as the maladaptive coping strategies to avoid. Survivors can also be trained in basic relaxation techniques that can help with stress.

FACT

A Simple Relaxation Technique
For people who are feeling stressed, it can help to sit in a quiet place and close your eyes. Inhale slowly while counting to five (one-thousand-and-one, one-thousand-and-two, etc.). Breathe through your nose and fill your lungs all the way to your belly. Silently and gently tell yourself that your body is filling with calm. Exhale slowly through your mouth and feel yourself deflating like a balloon. Silently and gently tell yourself that your body is releasing tension. Repeat this breathing exercise five times slowly and make sure you are not distracted while you are relaxing. If there is background noise, try playing soft music.

8. **Link with collaborative services**—This includes referring survivors to mental health professionals or relief agencies that can provide the help that PFA providers may not feel qualified to give. Survivors with acute or chronic medical problems or who have pre-existing mental health problems should be referred as soon as possible. Many survivors may belong to another culture and might prefer to speak to someone from another faith or who speaks their language.

Whatever the referral, PFA providers should be certain that they have the survivor's permission to provide information about what the survivor needs. Some survivors may feel uncomfortable dealing with government agencies due to past experiences or legal issues and might prefer to rely on family or friends for help instead. Always share with the survivor what you will be telling other agencies about them. For children under the age of consent, always get permission from a parent or guardian before making referrals.

When passing survivors on to other helpers, a personal introduction can be important so that the survivor does not feel that he or she is simply being "handed off" and that they learn the names of these other helpers. Other helpers should know as much as possible about the survivors to prevent them from having to repeat their story again and again. While it may not be possible for them to contact the PFA provider who first helped them, they should have names and addresses of people who can provide them with additional help as needed.

Does Psychological First Aid Prevent PTSD?

While PFA shows enormous promise in helping survivors in the very early stages after a traumatic event, there are still very few studies so far showing that it can prevent later psychological problems. Early intervention may not be enough to keep post-traumatic symptoms from developing since a traumatic event can affect different people in different ways depending on their previous history of problems, how severe the trauma was, and whether survivors have access to the right resources. Not all trauma survivors are going to receive help when they need it and many may even refuse help when it is offered. Though PFA has become the intervention of choice in recent years, the kind of treatment that a survivor receives can often depend on what becomes available.

Forming Social Support Networks

By most estimates, it usually takes up to seventy-two hours for government and nongovernment aid agencies to mobilize a relief effort when dealing with a major disaster. Even for smaller emergencies affecting a handful of people, emergency crews or medical staff may not have time to provide survivors with emotional or physical support. In many cases, it is often left up to survivors and their families to organize their own support systems while waiting for help to come along.

After Hurricane Katrina battered Louisiana, many local communities organized their own informal relief efforts while waiting for FEMA and the other big aid agencies to begin operations. While many of these informal relief programs were eventually taken over by the Red Cross and FEMA, the emotional support provided by volunteers to people in their own communities helped survivors cope more effectively than they otherwise could have if they had waited for the formal agencies instead.

For family members and friends of people who have experienced severe trauma, lack of formal training in emergency mental health care can lead to mistakes that could make recovery more difficult for survivors. On the other hand, the emotional and physical support that loved ones can provide may well be one of the most important factors in helping people with trauma cope.

Often, a strong desire to help and a willingness to do whatever is needed can make a difference in helping traumatized people. In later chapters, you will see some of the recommended steps to follow in helping people deal with the various symptoms that are commonly seen in trauma patients.

Using Online Resources

While there are numerous online resources that can be helpful in dealing with trauma patients, there are important cautions as well. A simple online search can turn up suggestions for people and organizations to contact for help, and Appendix C contains some ideas for a starting point for help.

Some online PTSD support resources you might want to consider include HealthyPlace PTSD forums (*www.healthyplace.com*), My PTSD forum (*www.myptsd.com*), and DailyStrength (*www.dailystrength.org/c/Post-Traumatic-Stress-Disorder/support-group*).

Some important caveats need to be followed through:

- First of all, you need to be careful about the different sites that can provide helpful hints for trauma care. Not all these sites can be considered trustworthy and some of the treatments they offer can be harmful. Do your research before entrusting your life and mental health to someone you don't know. If any of the treatments being suggested make you suspicious, check with the local professional governing body for that professional.

- People with serious trauma symptoms should seek help from *qualified* treatment professionals. These are people with experience in dealing with trauma issues and who are fully licensed by professional organizations in the area where you live. The treatment program they offer should also be widely accepted and backed up by strong evidence that it is effective. Some of the best treatments for PTSD will be covered in a later chapter.

- While self-help groups for survivors can provide valuable support, be certain you know what you are signing up for and that the group meets your needs. Attend a couple of meetings first and don't commit yourself to joining without proper research. Once again, don't do anything that makes you feel uncomfortable or that you might see as being harmful. You are the best judge of what is right for you.

CHAPTER 11

If Someone You Love Has PTSD

Not everyone with PTSD is going to want help. They may not even be aware of what is happening to them. In many cases, the people around them will be the first to realize how much their loved one has changed in the time since the traumatic experience happened. Whether or not they have been formally diagnosed with traumatic stress, what they have gone through is going to have an impact on their lives, and on the lives of the people around them. Family members and friends need to stay alert for potential signs that problems are developing. That includes familiarizing themselves with the symptoms most commonly seen in PTSD and trying to help if needed.

Being Supportive

If you are a friend and relative of someone with PTSD, they are going to need you to be as supportive and nonjudgmental as possible. That means:

- Offering emotional support, understanding, patience, and encouragement.
- Learning about PTSD so you can understand what your friend or loved one is experiencing.
- Talk to your friend or relative. And listen *carefully*.
- Be aware of what your friend or relative is feeling. That includes being alert to situations that might trigger PTSD symptoms.
- Don't take offense if your friend or relative appears emotionally withdrawn or hostile at times. There will always be some variability.
- Remind your friend or relative that improvement is possible with time and treatment.
- Invite him or her out for positive distractions such as walking or other fun activities.
- Help him or her to find comforting places and activities that could be used as part of a coping strategy.

Although most people dealing with the emotional aftermath of trauma are able to handle the symptoms and move on with their lives, there will still be some rocky moments when friends and family are especially important. Friends and relatives also need to keep an eye out for maladaptive coping strategies such as substance abuse or other high-risk activities.

ESSENTIAL

Please bear in mind that you should not try to diagnose PTSD yourself, no matter how many of the diagnostic criteria you think you see. If there are signs of psychological problems in a friend or relative, you should encourage them to seek out a qualified professional for a proper diagnosis to be made and to arrange treatment.

When to Intervene

So what happens if you become concerned that your friend or relative is failing to improve or developing symptoms you find worrying? If the person with PTSD has not already been diagnosed or received previous treatment, you may need to be the one who needs to find a qualified professional and, if necessary, make the appointment yourself. Since your loved one may be reluctant to go on their own, it can help to go with them to meet the professional and convey your own concerns. For many professionals dealing with patients reluctant to share their concerns about what they are experiencing, having another person present who can provide additional details can be invaluable. It is also helpful to be there while your loved one and the counselor discuss different treatment options and make sure that he or she does not develop any unrealistic expectations about how quickly the symptoms will go away.

But your involvement won't end there. Keep an eye on your loved one to make sure he or she continues to attend treatment (many people with PTSD drop out early since progress doesn't seem to be moving fast enough). If the treatment doesn't seem to be helping after eight sessions or so, you can encourage your loved one to change counselors if someone else seems more suitable. This is a major step however and PTSD patients often need to be reminded that change does not happen overnight. If they are getting pessimistic however, you need to encourage them to continue attending treatment and keep them from becoming discouraged. Improvement is going to happen gradually.

Even when they are in treatment, people with PTSD are still going to need friends and family to provide emotional support. You also need to be ready to intervene if they are showing signs that their symptoms are becoming worse or that they are developing a substance abuse problem. While controlled drinking in a social setting is likely nothing to worry about, signs that they are becoming dependent on drugs or alcohol to manage stress (self-medication) should be shared with the treatment professional. If they are showing problems with insomnia, try to encourage them to practice sleep hygiene. Understanding techniques such as grounding (see following sidebar) can be helpful with people experiencing flashbacks or other intrusive memories.

In dealing with agitated survivors who need to be stabilized as quickly as possible, a technique known as *grounding* may be helpful. Grounding basically involves turning your attention away from internal thoughts and becoming focused on the world around you. Survivors can be trained to ground themselves by reconnecting to the real world using different psychological techniques.

Secondary Gain

Another problem that you need to be aware of is called *secondary gain*. The longer one spends being a patient, whether in a hospital or lying in a bed with their family caring for them, the harder it becomes to get out of that sickbed and to take charge of one's own life. Putting your life back together can be scary and the temptation to delay that a long as possible by embracing the sick role becomes stronger with time. As a friend or family member of someone with PTSD who keeps putting off his or her recovery, encouraging that person to get well and stop making excuses can be hard. Don't allow that person to make excuses, especially if their therapist agrees that secondary gain has become a problem. You are doing your loved ones no favors by continuing to take care of them when they should start taking care of themselves.

Above all else, never ignore or dismiss statements they make relating to threats of suicide or violence against others. While they may view it as a breach of trust, threats should be passed on to mental health professionals whether they want you to say anything or not. Whether or not the threat is really serious, it is best to err on the side of life. That also includes self-harming behaviors that do not appear to be due to wanting to commit suicide. Traumatized adolescents may engage in "cutting" behaviors (such as slashing their wrists or inflicting other injuries on themselves) that are more likely to be an extreme way of relieving tension than an actual suicide attempt. Though it can also be seen in traumatized adults, it is much more rare. Self-harming behavior needs to be reported to their doctor or therapist, even if the ones cutting themselves insist that they were not trying to kill themselves.

What is sleep hygiene?
For people dealing with PTSD, insomnia is going to be a major problem. While doctors may prescribe medication to help people get to sleep at night, this is not a long-term solution due to the risk of becoming dependent on medication. A better alternative is to learn to sleep on your own through *sleep hygiene*, or developing good sleep habits. This can include maintaining a regular sleep schedule (fixed times for going to bed and waking up in the morning); avoiding naps during the day; avoiding food or beverages that contain caffeine (that includes coffee and soft drinks); increasing regular exercise but not doing anything strenuous within two hours of bedtime; reducing light and noise in the bedroom; and relaxing during bedtime by playing soft music or otherwise "winding down" at the end of the day.

Expressing Your Concerns

Be as supportive as you can and try to educate yourself about the symptoms of PTSD and what you may encounter in dealing with someone experiencing those symptoms. Although you should try not to lecture people about potentially harmful coping strategies, you also need to let them know that you are worried about them.

Most of the organizations listed in Appendix C will provide information to family members or friends concerned about loved ones. That can include online discussion forums, hotlines, and links to local treatment professionals in your area who might be able to intervene. While people with PTSD need to be willing to attend treatment, family members can often find support groups providing help for caregivers.

Don't be afraid to show that you care and that they are scaring you with some of the symptoms they are displaying. It is also important to recognize the different symptoms of PTSD and to help your friend or family member work through them as much as possible. While he or she may refuse to admit that there is a problem or that they prefer not to confide in you, accept that without hurt feelings or anger at being shut out. Being part of the treatment process means respecting their wishes so long as they are not actively harming themselves. Never doubt that you matter to them.

Dealing with Denial and Confusion

For people dealing with trauma, especially in the early stages, there will be a gross sense of denial and a general disbelief that something so terrible is happening to them. This denial can lead to a rejection of reality and a feeling that they are in a dream from which they will awaken at any moment. Many people experiencing trauma are going to be in an extended state of shock and will need time and support to help them work through that shock.

In extreme cases, there may also be dissociation in which they become detached from reality. There can be different degrees of dissociation depending on the severity of the trauma and the inner resources needed to cope with that trauma. This can lead to loss of memory, especially of the traumatic event (psychogenic amnesia) and even a loss of identity.

Though mild dissociation is not particularly harmful (you do it whenever you find yourself daydreaming), seeing a loved one rejecting reality because they are unable to handle what they experienced can be frightening, to say the least. Encouraging loved ones to face the reality of what has happened to them can be difficult and should be done as gently as possible to avoid confrontations that may make the problem worse.

Part of the treatment process is going to involve memory work or learning to come to terms with traumatic memories, especially the ones that have been repressed through dissociation. Recovery is not going to happen without learning to embrace those painful memories. While this is something that all people with PTSD need to learn on their own, friends and family members can help this process along by helping them to process what they experienced and integrate it into their normal lives.

What Should You Say?

It is important to make those people in your life dealing with PTSD symptoms feel loved and needed as much as you can. Unfortunately, that can be difficult at times and some spouses and family members describe their experience dealing with traumatized family members as if they were walking on eggshells out of fear of saying or doing something that might upset them somehow. Although you may often need to follow your own instincts about what to say or do, it might help to remember the following guidelines:

- Be willing to listen. Even if you have heard the story of his or her traumatic experience many times before, it is always going to feel as if it just happened to the person with trauma.
- Be positive and upbeat. Try to defuse any pessimistic statements the person with PTSD is making. Even if you are not optimistic yourself, try to focus on the positive achievements made so far.
- Accept that the person with PTSD may not want the help that you are offering. And don't be offended if that help is refused.
- Don't be put off if he or she becomes angry or irritable. Mood shifts and angry outbursts are to be expected, especially in the early stages. That is not to say that you should tolerate verbal or physical abuse. Establish boundaries and make sure he or she knows they've been crossed.
- Be supportive but don't make statements such as "I know how you feel." Unless you've been through the same experience before, you likely don't.
- Don't talk down to them or lecture them on what they should or shouldn't be doing at this stage in their recovery. Everyone recovers at their own pace.
- Encourage them to stay in treatment, even if they are not recovering as fast as they would like.
- Be patient. Showing that you are there for them can be the most important help you can provide.

Always remember that people with PTSD need your love and support. They don't necessarily need your advice (unless they are doing something particularly destructive) and they definitely don't need you to judge them. If what they are telling you about what they have experienced sounds frightening, say so. Let them know that they are perfectly justified to react in the way that they are reacting but try to avoid pinning the "victim" label on them. It is always best to think of them as people who survived a terrible experience rather than victims.

What Should You Do?

One of the keys to helping a loved one recover from trauma is to provide them with a strong social support network. That includes family, friends, treatment professionals, support workers, clergy if you belong to a church, or other people that your loved one with PTSD can draw on for emotional support when needed. Social support networks can come from virtually anyone with whom you have regular contact. That can include coworkers (this is especially important for people dealing with workplace-related PTSD), social clubs, fellow hobbyists, and even volunteer organizations to which you might happen to belong.

Social support can come in many forms. These can include:

- Making them feel as if they are needed. Are they useful? Productive? Is their contribution valued? Make certain that they know it.
- Emotional support. This can include hugging, a willingness to listen, complete acceptance, and hearing them talk about their experiences or what they have lost.
- Feeling connected. This can include shared activities, providing them with a sense that they are part of an extended community.
- Reassuring their worth. Many people with PTSD have a sense that they have no value. Recognize that they can often feel this way and try to provide them with a sense that they are important to you.
- Providing them with advice and guidance. If they are feeling lost, try to provide them with guidance. Don't force advice on them if they are truly not willing to accept it, but be willing to provide the information they might need to move ahead with their lives.
- Providing them with assistance, financial or otherwise. As you have seen in a previous chapter, many people with PTSD find themselves unable to work or have extremely limited financial resources. Be

willing to help as much as you can. The help need not be financial though, it can include helping them care for themselves or driving them to appointments as needed.

Basic nutrition can be an important part of the recovery process for many trauma survivors. Sensible eating with a balanced diet and avoidance of junk food and unnecessary calories will help encourage healthier attitudes. Also remember the need to avoid becoming dehydrated by drinking plenty of water during the day. That also means avoiding alcohol and caffeinated beverages as much as possible.

- Treatment programs often assign "homework" assignments (see next chapter) for patients to learn new skills that can help them cope more successfully. Encourage them to do their assignments and, if possible, help them so that you can develop a better understanding of what is happening in treatment.
- Encouraging them to do regular exercise programs and exercising along with them. Make it a shared activity but make sure first that the exercise program is approved by their treating physician. Keep an eye on them to make certain that they are not overdoing the exercise. The hyperventilation that comes from overexertion can also trigger a panic attack so they need to pace themselves.
- Encouraging them to form action plans for the future and to solve the problems facing them. Combat the feeling of helplessness that many people with PTSD often have. If they are unable to work, encourage them to look into retraining programs that can get them back on their feet. You can also encourage them to try writing as a way of coping with their symptoms. If they need treatment for a problem, encourage them to attend counseling or join a support group.

Whether the family member with PTSD is an adult or a child, "normalizing" the relationship you have with them can help with the recovery process. No matter how much the traumatic event may have disrupted their lives, establishing a normal daily routine can help them restore some of the predictability in their lives. That includes a regular schedule of waking up, having a shower, getting dressed, meals at set hours, recreational time, and bedtime. Don't forget to schedule regular shared activities and even reading time.

FACT

Many people with PTSD fear that they will become a burden to friends and family or that their requesting help might lead to rejection. Recognizing why people might refuse the help they really need can help you to decide how best to convince them to accept your assistance.

Developing Healing Rituals

Healing "rituals" can also be important. Veterans coming to terms with their trauma can get comfort from attending war memorials or revisiting the sites of battles. People dealing with the traumatic loss of a family member can benefit from taking a wreath to the site where the loss occurred. The ritual can be either spontaneous (as part of a vigil organized by friends and family) or part of a larger ceremony (such as on Veterans Day), but the opportunity it provides for friends and family members to offer love and support can be of enormous help in the healing process.

Creating a ritual need not be complicated. Families and friends of victims of the Oklahoma City bombing and 9/11 terrorist attacks continue to meet annually at the sites where the tragedies occurred. Designing your own personal ritual can make it even more meaningful. Suggested steps in planning the ritual include:

1. **Specifying the trauma that occurred**—What happened and how has it changed your life?
2. **Identifying all the ones who have been affected**—This includes family and friends along with the person experiencing PTSD.
3. **Developing symbols of life before, during, and after the trauma**—Photos of lost family members or showing life before the loss occurred along with a chance to show how your life has changed.

While a pilgrimage to the place where the loss occurred may not always be practical or safe, gathering at a place that has related meaning can be important. This can be a cemetery near the grave of a loved one or a public spot with special meaning. Religious symbols of hope and comfort can be used as well.

What If Your Child Has PTSD?

Parents of children who have had a traumatic experience, whether it is a life-threatening event or sexual abuse, need to watch for potential signs of post-traumatic stress. Appendix A presents some of the symptoms to watch for in potentially traumatized children. These can include:

- **Bedwetting**—especially in children who have already been toilet trained. This can be a sign of psychological regression.
- **Psychological regression**—traumatized children often begin relying on coping strategies they had previously outgrown such as thumb sucking or imaginary playmates.
- **Nightmares or nocturnal terrors**—children dealing with trauma may be terrified of being alone at night and may insist on sleeping with a nightlight or sleeping with a parent even though they had previously been able to sleep alone.
- **Avoidance behavior**—children are often more sensitive to things that remind them of the traumatic events than adults are and may go to extreme lengths to avoid any reminders.
- **Extreme "startle" response**—traumatized children may overreact to any stimulus that can potentially make them feel they are in danger.
- **Re-enactment of the trauma while playing**—while children with PTSD may not experience flashbacks as adults do, they may re-enact what they experienced while playing. For children who have been sexually abused, this can include inappropriate sexual behaviors while playing.
- **Behavioral problems**—This includes being more restless, aggressive, and general inattentiveness in school and at home.

Not all children exposed to a traumatic event are going to develop symptoms immediately. Though PTSD symptoms may never develop in many children, others may develop new symptoms months or even years after their traumatic experience. Parents and caregivers need to monitor at-risk children and take note of any adverse symptoms as they occur. That includes providing a warm, stable environment where they can recover from their experience. In cases of PTSD developing later, there may be no clear triggers though early signs that problems are occurring may be overlooked. Whenever these symptoms develop, children should be referred to a mental health professional for treatment. Long-term consequences for children with untreated PTSD can include later psychiatric problems, substance abuse, or antisocial behavior.

The process of healing after a traumatic experience can take a lifetime in some cases, but life can still be good in spite of that. Just bear in mind that your previous experience can make you stronger going forward, but it can also make you a little more vulnerable as well. This is especially true for people encountering stressful situations that act as reminders of their previous trauma. Recognizing the potential for new trauma and using the tools learned from previous traumatic experiences can help prevent further symptoms.

CHAPTER 12

Treatment for PTSD

While not everybody experiencing post-traumatic symptoms will need treatment, it is important to understand how post-traumatic stress works and how symptoms may arise that can affect you and the people around you. Even if you have no interest in treatment, basic information on post-traumatic stress and stress management can keep the symptoms from overwhelming you when they do occur. Just being aware of how triggers can invoke unpleasant memories and that anniversary dates can have a powerful effect on people dealing with trauma will give you the tools you need to move on with your life.

Treatment Basics

For people with strong social support networks and whose symptoms seem more or less under control, basic information may be all that is needed. For other people whose PTSD symptoms are more overwhelming, there are additional options available. But many people who need help often find themselves reluctant to ask for treatment. There can be different reasons for this and these barriers to treatment need to be overcome before therapy can begin. When you have never dealt with a mental health professional before or you are afraid of what might happen as a result, seeking treatment can be a scary experience.

ESSENTIAL

Even if you believe that the PTSD symptoms you are experiencing are manageable at the present time, there is no harm in looking into the different treatment options that you have open to you. Compile a list of names and contact numbers of treatment professionals or organizations in your area. It is better to have that information available in case you need it later than to be left scrambling at a time when you might be in crisis.

Why Are People Reluctant to Ask for Treatment?

Many people who might benefit from treatment often refuse to consider it because of the stigma attached to mental health care. While PTSD is more widely accepted that it once was, the fear that being in treatment would make them look "crazy" can often stop people with PTSD symptoms from asking for the help that they need. This is a common problem in the military and with people working in emergency services that are afraid that asking for help might damage their careers somehow. Also, people experiencing trauma from physical or sexual assault might be afraid of being forced to go public with their experience or else face an unsympathetic court system. Feeling pessimistic about the future or being convinced that "nothing can help" can also act as a barrier to seeking help. Some people may also be convinced that they can get well on their own or that talking to friends and family members will be enough. Though this may be true for people experiencing relatively mild symptoms, the ones with more extreme symptoms preventing them from functioning the way they should need professional attention.

FACT

There are enormous cultural differences in how people look at mental illness. People in a variety of cultures have a strong stigma against admitting that they need professional help. As a result, mental health professionals are far more common in North American and western European countries than they are in Asian, African, and South American countries. Immigrant communities are also less accepting of mental illness, which makes seeking treatment for PTSD especially difficult for members of those communities.

When Is Treatment Necessary?

According to the DSM-5, a formal diagnosis of PTSD requires that the symptoms cause a significant disruption in a person's life (whether at work, at school, socially, etc.). The symptoms also need to persist for longer than a month and cannot be related to another medical condition or being under the influence of drugs or alcohol. If you are experiencing flashbacks, emotional distress, or other problems that are clearly linked to exposure to a traumatic event, you should begin by seeing your family doctor to look into other medical explanations and to look into short-term medical aids that may help keep the symptoms under control for the time being. Just recognize that these are *short-term* solutions, especially if you are prescribed tranquilizers or sleep medication. Do *not* try self-medication, whether with alcohol or drugs! If you do decide to seek treatment, remember to keep your family informed since they will be part of the treatment process as well.

Treatment is *especially* important:

- If you need drugs or alcohol to keep the symptoms under control
- If friends or family members report that your symptoms are disturbing them (you may be the last to realize this)
- If you are prone to angry outbursts or strong thoughts about violence

- If you are having persistent thoughts about suicide, including making plans
- If your symptoms are preventing you from working, attending school, or getting on with your life

Before beginning treatment, it is also important to make your life as stable as possible. People recovering from a major disaster may be too preoccupied with rebuilding their lives or handling the various upheavals involved to handle treatment as well. That includes making sure of the social support network they will be depending on during treatment. Since that treatment can take months or even years to get the symptoms under control, it is essential that there be as few disruptions as possible during that time.

Another way of making your life as stable as possible is to take care of your own health through good nutrition and regular exercise. While you should never begin a new exercise program without medical approval, a regular routine of *modest* exercise can help manage stress, manage muscle tone, and improve cardiovascular fitness. Whether the exercise is daily or semi-daily, it should include aerobic fitness training and stretching as well as calisthenics or other strength-training exercises.

ESSENTIAL

People suffering from panic attacks often find themselves feeling as if they are not getting enough air in their lungs. Treatment often involves teaching breathing exercises, including making certain that all air is expelled from the lungs before new air is taken in. Also, panic sufferers are encouraged to learn belly breathing by inhaling through the nose and pushing out the stomach rather than the chest. During the breathing exercise, breathe more slowly than usual. Since this type of breathing is different from the chest breathing most people do, there is often some resistance, though learning to breathe through the abdomen can help curb hyperventilating.

Once again, do not begin a new exercise program without medical consultation and preferably under the supervision of someone trained in good exercise techniques. If you are prone to panic attacks, be extremely careful about overexertion since hyperventilation can often trigger attacks. You should also learn about controlled breathing to deal with hyperventilation when it happens and to get your breathing back to normal. Learn to pace yourself and discover how useful exercise can be as a way of coping with stress. Also, allow five to ten minutes before and after your exercise routine for warming up and cooling down. For people with sleep problems, make certain that you don't do any exercise after dinner or within three hours of bedtime.

Where to Go for Help

Getting help may be easier than you think. Appendix C contains just some of the addresses for available resources you can contact. Military personnel dealing with trauma and related mental health problems can request help from the Veterans Administration or similar organizations in other countries. If you are an emergency service worker experiencing symptoms resulting from a work-related traumatic event, your own department may have an in-house counselor who can provide treatment or refer you to a treatment program in the community. Following a wide-scale disaster, you may receive psychological first aid that, among other things, will provide you with information about available treatment programs. For victims of sexual or domestic violence, most communities maintain a hotline for accessing trauma services and getting additional support as needed.

ESSENTIAL

When you and your friends and family are searching for treatment professionals, make it into a team exercise with all of you working toward a common goal. Along with learning about treatment options, it can also build up the sense of social support that can be important in reducing the feeling of isolation that many PTSD survivors experience.

Most medical doctors providing first-line medical services (including your family doctor or walk-in clinic) can provide you with a referral to a local therapist or support organization. Also, if you belong to a church or other religious organization, your local priest or pastor may be able to make a referral as well. If you are experiencing immediate symptoms, including persistent suicidal thoughts, the emergency department at your nearest hospital or a suicide hotline is likely your best option. Do not take chances with your life.

Always remember that the right help is out there, but you should do your research ahead of time to make certain you know where to go when that help is needed. Your friends and family members can help with this by doing their own research and finding possible treatment options for you.

Finding Information

Virtually all information on local resources for PTSD can be found online, although you may find yourself overwhelmed by all the different options available to you. It is always best to go through a national mental health organization such as Mental Health America in the United States or the Canadian Mental Health Association. For other countries, you can try contacting the International Society for Traumatic Stress Studies for information on local organizations or treatment professionals. The American Psychological Association and *Psychology Today* both provide professional directories that list therapists by specialization and location. Bear in mind that there are different kinds of therapists offering treatment services and you should be aware of the different services they can offer.

QUESTION

How can I find a therapist online?
The American Psychological Association provides an online psychologist locator at *http://locator.apa.org*. When you enter your zip code or city and state, the locator provides names and contact numbers of psychologists in your area. The Anxiety Association of America also provides a Find a Therapist website at *www.adaa.org*.

Treatment professionals providing mental health services can include:

• **Clinical psychologists**—Licensed psychologists are registered with the local governing body and are trained to provide assessment and treatment. There are different specialties depending on whether they are dealing with children or adults and most psychologists dealing with trauma patients have additional training in trauma psychology. Often confused with psychiatrists, psychologists cannot prescribe medication in most areas.

- **Psychiatrists**—Psychiatrists are medical doctors who specialize in the diagnosis and treatment of mental disorders. Again, there are different specialties depending on additional training and whether they are dealing with children or adults. Psychiatrists can prescribe medication and some also provide psychotherapy.
- **Clinical social workers**—Certified social workers typically have a master's degree or doctoral degree in social work. They are involved in linking service users with community agencies or programs, providing mental health counseling, and promoting general well-being.
- **Master's level clinicians**—Usually working under the supervision of a psychologist, master's level clinicians have postgraduate training in psychotherapy and can provide mental health services, including counseling and assessment.
- **Pastoral counselors**—Priests, rabbis, pastors, or other religious workers with additional training in counseling can provide treatment integrating psychotherapy with religious practice. Pastoral counselors can help people with spiritual needs learn to cope with life crises.

While telephone directories are going out of fashion, they can still provide a useful reference for finding resources in the community. In the yellow pages, look under "psychologists," "social workers," "psychotherapy," or "mental health." The pages for government services can also direct you to government offices such as the Veterans Administration. Look under "health services" or "mental health." You can also try contacting the psychology department at the local college or university. Your local hospital may have a psychology or social work department as well.

There is also the financial cost of treatment to consider. If you have health insurance coverage (whether through work or your own policy), contact the health insurance company to find out which mental health providers are covered by your policy. You should also look into what out-of-pocket expenses you will need to pay in addition to the treatment sessions. Don't be afraid to discuss these details with your therapist at your first meeting. He or she should be able to tell you what kind of insurance the therapist accepts.

Also, your insurance company should have a list of approved therapists or provide a referral to professional organizations that can help you decide on which therapist to choose.

You will also find a wide range of self-help books dealing with PTSD that can include information on how to find local resources as needed (the reading list in Appendix D would be a good start). They can also provide advice on how to deal with short-term problems such as stress management and handling intrusive memories. While the advice can be useful, these books should not take the place of a caring professional who can give you the guidance you need. Reading about PTSD can show you how to ask the right questions when choosing a therapist and also give you some ideas about what kind of treatment you might need.

Sifting Through Information

When finding a mental health professional, it is important to be as informed as possible in choosing the therapist or program that is best for you. While this is not always feasible for people in distress (which is why you should do your research early instead of waiting until the symptoms overwhelm you), a certain amount of caution is also needed since many forms of treatment can be completely inappropriate for people with PTSD. Being a good mental health consumer means not being afraid to ask tough questions about the proposed treatment program that you are considering.

This can include:

1. **What are the credentials of the counselor or therapist?**—Is he or she registered with a local governing body? Who can you complain to if the therapist ends up doing more harm than good?
2. **Does the proposed treatment have a good track record for success?**—Some forms of treatment are more reputable than others (see the next chapter). Be *very* suspicious of anyone promising quick relief or miraculous cures.
3. **What do other therapists think of this type of treatment?**—Do not be afraid to get a second (or third) opinion.
4. **How will progress be measured in treatment?**—Most therapists will prepare progress notes after a fixed number of sessions, which can include

psychometric testing to see how much benefit patients have received from the treatment.

Unless you're in immediate distress, you have time to weigh the information that you are given as well as to do your own research on the Internet or by checking with other professionals.

Is It Working?

From the very beginning, you and your therapist should establish what you hope to accomplish from the treatment. While you want the symptoms you are experiencing to go away (or at least to get under control), you also have an idea in mind of where you want to be in ten years or so. That means developing short-term and long-term goals as well as an action plan to make those goals happen. As you have seen in the previous section, your therapist will evaluate treatment progress over time and you will also get your own sense of whether or not the treatment you are receiving is helping or not.

While improvement is going to be gradual, you should still be using the techniques you are learning in treatment to control some of the most distressing symptoms and be making some progress toward the short-term goals in your life. Your family and friends may have better insight than you do as to whether you are really improving. While it is important not to have unrealistic expectations, both you and your therapist should have some sense that things are getting better for you.

You may also decide to attend more than one treatment program at the same time. If your therapist is seeing you for PTSD problems, you may also want to attend a support group with fellow survivors or, if you have an additional problem such as substance abuse, you may want to attend a support group for that. Just make sure you budget your time properly and that you don't exhaust yourself by trying too many different things at once. Your therapist can advise you whether extra treatment groups are a good idea (he or she might even recommend it). You may also be seeing your family doctor and/or a psychiatrist as well. If so, make sure that they can contact one another in case of emergencies or if you develop suicidal symptoms.

Still, problems can develop. You and your therapist may have different ideas about the direction your therapy takes. Or, there can be a personality clash (it happens). Your therapist may even do something you decide is unethical or that makes you uncomfortable. How you respond to that is your decision, but the choice to go to another therapist is something you and your therapist should arrive at together. Don't just arbitrarily stop treatment unless you feel there is no other choice. Otherwise, your therapist is likely best suited to tell you about the different treatment options you have available.

The ultimate goal of treatment for PTSD is to help people move on with their lives and to overcome symptoms that are preventing them from functioning, whether it be vocational functioning, social functioning, or simply being able to handle daily stresses without falling apart. While symptoms may never disappear completely, successful treatment should make them more manageable. Some people who develop work-related trauma may find themselves unable to return to their previous job, but they should be capable of finding another job in which they can support themselves and pursue their future goals. This may not be a realistic hope in extreme cases although some degree of coming to terms with what they have experienced should still be possible.

Above all, don't give up on treatment just because of one bad experience with a therapist or because you didn't get the benefit that you hoped you would. In the following chapter, you will see the different treatment options that are available to you. You may need to experiment a little to find the treatment program or combination of different programs that work best. Every case can be a little different.

Group Support

Group therapy for trauma survivors is one of the oldest and most common treatment options, although a local group program may not be available for every person in need. Groups are usually intended for people who survived specific types of trauma, e.g., groups for veterans with PTSD, groups for sexual abuse survivors, etc. Since chronic PTSD often involves losing the ability to trust other people, especially with victims of violence, group sessions where survivors can interact with other people who have had similar experiences can be a valuable part of the recovery process. It is also more cost-effective than other forms of treatment since one therapist can meet with many patients at once.

The group therapy option can also be useful for survivors who are not ready for individual psychotherapy due to problems they are facing. Many Veterans Administration clinics treating wounded veterans as inpatients also offer group counseling to allow survivors who are still in the early stages of trauma a chance to talk with fellow veterans who have undergone the same experiences. Though early groups relied on a self-help model with veterans running groups with little or no professional guidance, there has been little research showing how effective they were. In recent years, therapists developed different group treatment options to help survivors handle their symptoms and learn to address life problems. Groups can be either open-length with people joining or leaving at any time and with no fixed termination date, or can run for a fixed number of sessions (usually ten to fifteen). Different types of group therapy include:

Supportive Group Therapy

Supportive group therapy for PTSD is usually problem-oriented to allow group members to act as a social support network to work through problems. Supportive groups (also known as support groups) usually avoid having members provide details of their traumatic experiences but focus instead on how those experiences have affected their lives. They also rarely involve homework assignments, although group members can be given written handouts with information on treatment options or community resources they can use as needed. A group leader encourages members to participate as they see fit but avoids confronting people in the group who may not feel ready to contribute. Groups can also provide crisis intervention for members going through life changes such as divorce, job loss, or other problems. Supportive group therapy can be used in combination with individual psychotherapy or as a stand-alone treatment program.

For supportive groups with a fixed number of sessions, there is usually a beginning phase where the rules of the group are laid down and group members come to know one another; a middle phase as the group becomes more integrated; and an ending phase in which treatment gains are reviewed and new treatment options are explored. There can also be monthly follow-up sessions in which people who graduate from the group can check back to review their progress over time.

Psychodynamic Group Therapy

Usually consisting of five to seven group members along with two group leaders, psychodynamic group therapy involves having each member tell their own story of what happened to them with the other members helping to explore different details. Using a psychodynamic approach based on the psychology of Sigmund Freud and his followers, the painful emotions being felt as the stories are told are tied back to how people feel about themselves and others. The therapy also allows people in the group to identify irrational beliefs that reinforce PTSD symptoms. Group leaders encourage frank discussions among group members to work through disagreements. Typically running to twenty-four sessions, the earlier stages of the therapy include presentation of psychoeducational material and laying down the ground rules for later sessions. The structure of the group becomes more relaxed as group members become more comfortable with the other group members. The group leader's role is then reduced and the group members are largely in charge of setting the agenda for later group sessions. The final group sessions focus on termination of treatment and preparing group members for follow-up as needed.

Cognitive-Behavioral Group Therapy

Based on the same principles as individual cognitive-behavioral therapy (CBT), group CBT focuses on helping people reduce PTSD symptoms and develop good coping strategies. Using prolonged exposure and cognitive restructuring, group members work through their individual traumas by telling their stories to the other group members in a supportive setting while hearing the stories that other members tell. There is also a focus on relapse prevention training to help people with PTSD learn to cope with new high-risk situations as they arise. Along with the group sessions, people in therapy also receive homework assignments to work through on their own or with the help of family members.

Though group CBT can vary depending on the type of patient being treated and the issues that need to be addressed in treatment, many groups can run from twenty to thirty sessions. During the first eight sessions (the introductory phase), the group leader educates group members about PTSD and coping and has them describe their lives before the actual trauma occurred. They are also trained in coping strategies such as stress management, sleep hygiene, and positive and negative ways of coping. The middle phase focuses on members retelling their traumatic experiences and how to handle the symptoms as they arise. The support they receive from other group members is a key element in helping them to reveal details of their experiences they might not have shared with anyone else.

ESSENTIAL

One example of a homework assignment involves keeping a regular diary. Being able to put what you experienced into words, whether by talking about it or writing, can be an excellent way of dealing with traumatic memories. Many therapists recommend that patients write about their traumatic experience, using as many details as possible. If you have more than one traumatic event, write about the one that upsets you the most. Putting your feelings into words can be anxiety-provoking at first and you may need all of your skills at coping, but it should become easier with time.

In the final phase, group members are trained to deal with relapses as they occur and learn to make the trauma part of their overall life stories. That includes learning to recognize high-risk situations likely to trigger PTSD symptoms and how to defuse anxiety as it occurs. They are also provided information on community resources and follow-up treatment as needed.

Which Group Therapy Is Best?

Research has not shown one group therapy treatment to be better than the others for people coping with PTSD. They can even be used one after the other or in addition to individual psychotherapy, depending on the individual needs of the patient. Overall, group therapy works best for PTSD patients who:

- Are able to trust other group members and the group leader
- Have previous group experience (including twelve-step programs such as A.A.)
- Have had individual counseling to help prepare for talking about trauma in a group setting

- Do not have serious issues such as being suicidal or violent
- Have had traumatic experiences similar to the other group members
- Are willing to respect the confidentiality of the group

ESSENTIAL

For PTSD survivors who do not feel ready to talk about their trauma, individual psychotherapy is the best option at this time. Once they are ready, however, joining a treatment group can be a valuable experience that helps survivors learn to interact with other survivors and develop coping strategies that can protect them from future stress.

Treating PTSD in Children

Research into how effective different treatment methods are for dealing with adolescent trauma is still fairly limited compared to similar research in treating traumatized adults. Still, cognitive-behavioral therapies (CBT) are the leading choice for most therapists, particularly since the available research tends to be far stronger than research looking at psychoanalytic or purely medication-based treatment. While CBT was first developed for trauma in adults and later adapted to adolescents, the special needs that adolescent trauma patients have has inspired the development of treatment methods focusing on children and adolescents alone. These treatment approaches include:

1. **Multimodality trauma treatment (MMTT)**—First developed in 1998, MMTT is based on the idea that trauma at a young age can disrupt normal physical and emotional development and uses age-appropriate CBT strategies to help children or adolescents cope with trauma. Usually conducted in school settings, MMTT programs have a fourteen-session format that can include psychoeducation, narrative writing (writing about the traumatic experience), exposure and relaxation techniques, and cognitive restructuring. Empirical studies of MMTT have shown marked reduction in trauma symptoms with similar results for symptoms of depression, anger, and anxiety. The chief advantage of MMTT is that it was specifically developed for traumatized adolescents

although the nature of the program focuses on adolescents who have experienced only one traumatic event. The value of MMTT for treating adolescents experiencing multiple traumas is not as well-researched.

2. **Trauma-focused cognitive behavioral therapy (TF-CBT)**—First developed in 2006 by Judith Cohen and her colleagues, TF-CBT was specifically developed for children between the ages of three and eighteen. Treatment programs using TF-CBT usually range from eight to twenty sessions involving the child alone or the child and a parent/caregiver. The main goal of TF-CBT is to help children and adolescents learn coping skills that will help them deal with traumatic memories. A component-based model, TF-CBT is organized using the acronym "PRACTICE." In treatment, children receive *p*sychoeducation, are taught *r*elaxation skills, as well as *a*ffective expression and modulation, and *c*ognitive coping skills. Children are also encouraged to use *t*rauma narration and to cognitively process the trauma, use *i*n vivo exposure to master trauma reminders, have *c*onjoint parent-child sessions, and *e*nhance safety. First developed for use with victims of sexual abuse, TF-CBT has been found to be effective with other forms of trauma as well and has been widely used in treatment settings around the world.

3. **Stanford cue-centered therapy (SCCT)**—Developed by researchers at the Stanford School of Medicine's Early Life Stress Research Program, SCCT is a short-term treatment approach focusing on individual therapy for children and adolescents dealing with trauma. Designed to treat problems with a child's cognitive, affective, behavioral, and physical functioning, SCCT uses cognitive-behavioral techniques, relaxation training, narrative use, and parental coaching. The goal of SCCT is to reduce the child's negative thoughts and cognitions as well as sensitivity to traumatic memory. Typically fifteen to eighteen sessions long, SCCT encourages children to build coping skills including relaxation and self-empowerment. By helping children learn *how* trauma affects them, they are able to control how they respond to traumatic reminders. Despite its promise, SCCT requires extensive one-to-one therapy sessions that can be extremely time-consuming. Research testing SCCT's value tends to be limited to case studies.

4. **Seeking Safety**—First developed for use with substance abuse as well as trauma in adults and adolescents, Seeking Safety has five basic

principles: personal safety as a priority; integrated treatment of trauma and substance abuse; focusing on the client's needs; attention to the therapy process; and focusing on cognitions, behaviors, interpersonal interactions, and case management. Seeking Safety was specifically adapted for treating adolescents and, like the other treatment models, uses psychoeducation, training in specific coping skills, and cognitive restructuring. Parental involvement is only needed in one Seeking Safety session and training programs are available online.

5. **Trauma Affect Regulation: A Guide for Education and Therapy (TARGET)—** First developed and tested on young offenders, TARGET can be used individually or in group sessions. The goal of TARGET is to teach clients to understand how trauma changes the brain's normal stress response and how to manage and control emotional responding to trauma. The TARGET model uses the FREEDOM acronym (*f*ocus, *r*ecognize triggers, *e*motion self-check, *e*valuate thoughts, *d*efine goals, *o*ptions, and *m*ake a contribution). Most similar to TF-CBT, one of the advantages of TARGET is that parents are not involved in the treatment. At this time, most empirical research on TARGET's value is with young offenders.

Although there are other approaches that can be used to treat trauma in children and adolescents including art therapy and EMDR (eye-movement desensitization and reprocessing), it is CBT-type approaches that seem to work best for dealing with post-traumatic symptoms. For the CBT methods that have been developed specifically for younger clients, there are some common features including psychoeducation to teach children about traumatic stress and the effects it can have on them, relaxation techniques, a trauma narrative to encourage children to describe their experience in detail, and some sort of cognitive restructuring to correct maladaptive thoughts about the traumatic experience.

For all of the recognized approaches for treating traumatized children, it is vital that children be encouraged to face their traumatic experience gradually and only in a way that they can handle emotionally. Since all children do not develop emotionally at the same pace, it is important to tailor the treatment to the child's level of emotional and cognitive development. Otherwise, the therapist could end up doing more harm than good by re-traumatizing their child patients.

CHAPTER 13

Therapy Options for PTSD

Treatment for PTSD can involve either psychotherapy, medication, or a combination of the two, depending on how severe the PTSD symptoms are and whether there are additional mental health problems such as substance abuse that also need to be treated. When meeting with a counselor for the first time, it is essential to be honest about whether you are experiencing other symptoms that do not appear related to the PTSD, including suicidal or violent thoughts. You may also be asked to complete questionnaires and psychological tests similar to the PTSD Checklist in Appendix B. This testing may also be repeated at different stages in your treatment to check your progress and after the therapy is completed to see how successful it was.

Psychotherapy

There are many different types of psychotherapy or "talk" therapy, although they usually fall into one of three categories: individual therapy involving one-to-one sessions with the therapist, group therapy with a number of patients meeting with a group leader directing how the members of the group interact, and couple/family therapy where couples or even entire families have therapy sessions with a counselor to address the problems they are having. There can also be different therapy programs depending on the age of the patient receiving help, with programs for young children, adolescents, and adults. Therapy can focus on specific symptoms that patients are having or address particular problems including substance abuse, job-related concerns, or stress management.

ESSENTIAL

For someone who has never attended therapy before or whose only impression of what happens in therapy is what they see in movies or television, beginning therapy can seem extremely awkward. Just remember that attending therapy is the first step toward getting things back under control and dealing with the symptoms that are interfering with your life. While there are no guarantees about therapy, cooperating with the therapist will become easier after the first few sessions.

The first two or three therapy sessions will usually focus on gathering information so that the therapist can learn about how your life has been affected by the symptoms as well as what kind of social support network you have in place. The therapist may also ask to meet with family members who can provide additional information and may involve them in the therapy process. In some types of therapy, a spouse or even the entire family can take part in the treatment process. The early stages of therapy also allow you to learn more about what PTSD is and how it can affect your life. Though you may have already done some reading on the subject, the therapist can help answer any questions you might have and show you how to begin applying specific coping strategies to get your symptoms under control.

That can also include assigning homework that you can complete on your own or with the help of family members. These assignments will give you a chance to practice the coping skills you are learning during your therapy sessions. While these exercises will seem awkward at first, the skills will become easier with practice. Don't be afraid to involve friends and family either, as they will want to help and may find the skills useful themselves. As you have seen in the previous chapter, real change will not happen overnight but you should note some improvement as you get your most distressing symptoms under control.

Acute Post-Traumatic Interventions

Though psychological first aid (PFA) and debriefing have already been covered in a previous chapter, there are other kinds of treatment that can be used within the first few weeks of traumatic experiences to prevent later problems from developing. These can include:

Crisis Intervention

While originally designed to be used following stressful life events that can drain a person's ability to cope, crisis intervention has also been found to be beneficial in dealing with traumatic events, including serious motor vehicle accidents, loss of a family member, or having a serious injury. Crisis counselors are usually called in for people who are felt to be at risk of developing symptoms of PTSD and need help as quickly as possible. Much like with PFA, crisis intervention involves teaching people in crisis about the different symptoms that can develop and the different ways of coping. Since these people may still be in shock, crisis counselors help them work through their feelings and process what they have experienced. Formal crisis intervention usually involves three stages: assessment of need (including triage to identify who needs immediate help), providing stress management training and short-term psychological treatment to address immediate psychological symptoms, and then directing them to counseling as needed to prevent later PTSD symptoms. Although crisis intervention can be useful for relieving short-term stress, researchers have questioned whether it can prevent later PTSD, especially since many people may not develop symptoms until long after the traumatic event occurred.

FACT

Crisis intervention typically focuses on the most immediate problems and helps stabilize people in distress so they are prepared for more long-term treatment. This includes dealing with issues such as suicidal thoughts or attempts, panic attacks, emotional distress, drug or alcohol detox, and all the other issues that need to be under control before regular treatment can begin.

Short-Term Trauma Counseling

Following a traumatic event such as a sexual assault, trauma counseling can be provided to help survivors cope with what they experienced and to prevent later PTSD. Short-term trauma counseling is usually intended to comfort survivors during the acute period (one to two weeks after the traumatic event) and focuses on their reaction to the trauma to help them confront what they experienced and to work through their feelings. As opposed to debriefing, short-term counseling works best in the early weeks after a traumatic event and can include techniques such as relaxation training, cognitive restructuring, and exposure therapy (see section in this chapter). Counselors use cognitive-behavioral principles to help change poor coping behaviors and depressive thoughts by teaching survivors how to solve problems, form action plans for the future, handle stress, and work out ways to prevent relapses.

Grief Counseling

Following a traumatic loss such as the unexpected death of a family member or even a major life change (e.g., divorce), grief counselors are available to help survivors cope with the emotional aftermath. Grief counseling focuses on the process of resolving grief issues, usually on a short-term basis, to help people who have been so overwhelmed by grief that normal coping is no longer enough. There is also a distinction between grief counseling that is provided to people dealing with normal grief, and grief therapy that is needed when survivors are experiencing psychological or physical problems related to traumatic grief. While some controversy has arisen over whether grief counseling is needed in many cases, grief therapy can be essential for people dealing with grief as well as traumatic stress or other psychiatric symptoms.

Research on trauma counseling for children and adults has shown it to be extremely effective depending on the symptoms being shown and whether the survivors are getting help from other disaster relief agencies. Short-term treatment has been found to be especially helpful for female sexual assault survivors and people recovering from natural disasters to prevent survivors from developing later PTSD symptoms.

FACT

Again, it can take months before a survivor can be formally diagnosed with PTSD. People in distress immediately after a traumatic event may only need short-term counseling to help them make the needed adjustments so they can move on with their lives. Others may not show any symptoms only to develop PTSD much later.

Drug Therapy

Medication for treating symptoms linked to post-traumatic stress can be prescribed at any time though the type of symptoms being treated can vary depending on whether they are occurring in the weeks following the traumatic event (acute phase), or more than a month afterward (post-acute phase).

Acute Phase (Within a Month of Trauma)

During the acute phase, people are more likely to need medication for anxiety, sleep, and agitation. Medications given during the acute phase are only meant for short-term use and need to be reviewed regularly to see how well they are working. Although medication should also be provided along with counseling to help people with trauma issues learn to cope on their own, this may not always be an option if counselors are unavailable. Due to the possibility of drug interaction, it is extremely important that doctors prescribing medication be informed of other prescription or nonprescription medications that are also being taken.

Anxiety medications that can be prescribed during the acute phase can include:

- **Benzodiazepines such as lorazepam or clonazepam**
  These can be useful for anxiety and panic attacks though it is possible to become physically dependent on them if they are taken for more than three weeks. There are also non-benzodiazepines that can be prescribed and psychiatrists may change prescriptions over time to avoid dependency issues. For cases of mild anxiety, acetaminophen with diphenhydramine can be acquired over-the-counter.

- **Sleep medication**
  Research into sleep medication for use in patients with acute stress disorder or PTSD is still limited but there are some commonly prescribed medications for insomnia. These medications are for *short-term use only* and should not be prescribed for longer periods without being reviewed by a physician. Some common insomnia medications can include trazodone, zolpidem, and eszoplicone. Side effects with these medications include extreme sleepiness and dizziness.

- **Medication for agitation**
  People can become extremely agitated immediately after trauma though doctors need to be careful to ensure that the agitation is not occurring because of other medical problems such as head trauma, substance abuse, or serious medical conditions. Medications that can be prescribed include haloperidol, lorazepam (high-dose), or diphenhydramine (high-dose). Low-dose antipsychotic medications can also be prescribed.

Post-acute Phase (Greater Than One Month after Trauma)

In the weeks or months following a traumatic event, the symptoms become more settled and medical doctors can get a better sense of the long-term problems survivors may be experiencing. Along with making formal diagnoses such as PTSD and major depressive disorder, psychiatrists can prescribe medications to control symptoms for longer periods ranging from months to two years or more. Medications can include:

- Antidepressant medications specifically approved for treating PTSD symptoms. These include selective serotonin reuptake inhibitors (SSRIs) such as sertraline and paroxetine. Other antidepressants that can be used with PTSD include citalopram (Celexa), fluoxetine (Prozac), and venlafaxine. They can also be used for related conditions including sleep symptoms.
- Antianxiety medications, including benzodiazepines such as lorazepam and clonazepam, are useful although they have a high risk of chemical dependence. Longer acting benzodiazepines such as propranolol, prazosin, and noradrenergic agents like clonidine and guanfacine can also be used.
- Other medications that can be helpful for treating PTSD can include mood stabilizers such as lithium and carbamazepine. "Typical" and "atypical" antipsychotic medications including haloperidol, risperidone, and olanzapine can be useful in treating agitation and related symptoms. They are also more likely to result in severe side effects including movement problems. Opiates (e.g., morphine) and related pain medications have also been found to reduce post-traumatic stress symptoms in children and adults who also have pain problems.

People on medication for PTSD symptoms often need more than one type of medication since symptoms can change over time and their systems can adjust to the medication. Also, doctors need to monitor how the medication is affecting their bodies and will often need blood tests and regular checkups to watch for side effects. PTSD patients with additional problems such as substance abuse, chronic pain, or traumatic brain injury can require multiple medications to control their symptoms.

There are also experimental programs looking at newer treatment options that have not been formally approved for use with PTSD patients. Some treatments have been sponsored by the Veterans Administration and military researchers.

Can Anesthesia Treat PTSD?

A specialized anesthetic procedure used for treating chronic pain disorders and symptoms associated with breast cancer may also be useful in treating PTSD. A stellate ganglion block (SGB) involves injecting a local anesthetic into the stellate ganglion just below the subclavian artery on or above the neck of the first rib. Though the effects of the local anesthetic usually wear off after a few hours, SGB has already been found to be beneficial for a range of pain-related and vascular medical conditions including complex regional pain syndrome and frostbite. Anesthesiologist Eugene Lipov has also reported positive results in treating hot flashes in women as well as PTSD. Through his research on patients being seen at his Advanced Pain Centers clinic in Hoffman Estates, Illinois, Dr. Lipov reported anxiety relief as early as thirty minutes following an injection into the stellate ganglion leading to the right hemisphere of the brain.

One potential explanation for the effectiveness of SGB for trauma is that anesthetizing the right-sided stellate ganglion blocks right hemisphere structures of the brain that produce autonomic responses to emotional stimuli. This includes the right amygdala that has been linked to unconscious emotional memories. In a recent *Psychiatric Annals* report coauthored by Dr. Lipov, SGB is shown to be a promising approach for PTSD despite the risk of potential complications including seizures or infection. Reported improvement in psychiatric patients receiving SGB has been described in medical journals as far back as 1947 for disorders such as depression and schizophrenia.

Despite these findings, SGB use in psychiatry remains controversial. The results of a clinical trial conducted at San Diego's Naval Medical Center were published in 2013 in the *American Journal of Psychiatry*. According to lead author Anita Hickey and her colleagues, preliminary findings for nine military patients with chronic PTSD showed significant improvement in five of the nine patients receiving SGB. Two other patients reported only mild improvement. The benefit from SGB appeared to fade within one or two months after the procedure. In commenting on SGB treatment for trauma, Naval Medical Center commander, Rear Admiral Forrest Faison said that the results appear promising though further research is ongoing.

While many people with PTSD report good results with medication, some prescribing psychiatrists have warned that medications such as quetiapine and other antipsychotic drugs are being overprescribed. Many of these medications are prescribed "off-label" with little real evidence that they can help people with PTSD. People being prescribed unfamiliar medications should do their own research, including looking into possible side effects, before beginning treatment. It is also important not to have unrealistic expectations since some medications can take weeks before taking full effect.

It is also essential that patients educate themselves about the different possible side effects of the medication being prescribed for them as well as possible toxic effects resulting from taking more than the recommended dosage. People on medication also need to be educated about the potential interaction effects with other medications as well as other psychoactive substances such as alcohol, caffeine, and recreational drug use.

Cognitive-Behavioral Therapy

Of the different schools of psychotherapy most commonly offered for people with PTSD, the most evidence-based is cognitive-behavioral therapy (CBT). This is a general label covering a range of different techniques and theories combining cognitive and behavioral scientific principles. CBT is designed to be problem-focused to address specific problems that are contributing to patient distress. Patients are also trained in different coping techniques depending on their specific symptoms, including exposure therapy, stress inoculation, cognitive processing therapy, and cognitive restructuring.

QUESTION

What is evidence-based therapy?
Since the 1990s, "evidence-based practice" has become increasingly important in many different areas of health care including medicine, nursing, and psychology. In evidence-based psychotherapy, all practical decisions relating to providing care to patients are based on well-designed research studies that provide hard evidence that the treatment is effective. Since some forms of psychotherapy are more evidence-based than others (such as cognitive-behavioral therapy), patients are encouraged to do their own research and weigh the available evidence before choosing a therapist.

Stress Inoculation

Stress inoculation therapy (SIT) involves teaching patients to become more resistant to stress by "inoculating" them with better coping strategies to deal with stress effectively. Most SIT programs are extremely flexible but typically involve three phases:

1. The *conceptualization* phase in which the patient and the therapist develop a formal relationship where they agree to work together to help the patient learn to cope with stress. Patients are encouraged to recognize stressful situations as problems that need to be solved and to identify what can be changed.
2. The *skills acquisition and rehearsal* phase involves learning different coping strategies such as relaxation, self-soothing and acceptance, problem-solving, and emotional regulation. Along with the training they receive in the treatment sessions, patients are also given homework assignments they can complete on their own or with the help of friends or family to rehearse the new skills.
3. The *application and follow-through* phase allows patients to practice their new skills in real-life settings, whether at home or in public. By using the skills in situations with different degrees of stress, patients develop confidence in the new skills. They are also taught relapse prevention techniques such as identifying high-risk stress situations, warning signs of stress, and how to handle setbacks. This phase also includes "booster" sessions at a later date to allow patients to refresh their skills and measure their progress.

Though stress is often unavoidable, SIT teaches patients to change their lifestyles to control the amount of excess stress they experience and handle what cannot be avoided. SIT can be administered either individually or in group therapy sessions and typically involves eight to fifteen sessions over a three- to twelve-month period including booster sessions. Research has shown that SIT can help people deal with stress in a wide variety of situations. It is often used in combination with other CBT techniques.

Exposure Therapy

Exposure therapy is a specific CBT technique frequently used to treat PTSD symptoms and phobias. To help patients come to terms with the fear and distress resulting from traumatic memories, they can be systematically confronted with reminders under safe conditions to desensitize them. The exposure therapist first identifies the emotions, thoughts, and physical arousal that patients associate with the reminder and then creates a hierarchy of different levels of exposure. This allows a patient to gradually become more desensitized to the reminder. This exposure can be either imaginary, such as asking patients with a fear of snakes to visualize being in the same room as a snake, or real life, such as taking a patient back to the scene where the trauma occurred.

Systematic desensitization (SD) was one of the first exposure techniques used with PTSD patients. Developed by psychiatrist Joseph Wolpe, SD involves having patients use muscle relaxation to reduce anxiety after which they are asked to imagine a mild anxiety-provoking situation. With repeated trials, the anxiety-provoking situation loses its ability to provoke anxiety. The SD sessions are continued with increasingly stronger anxiety-provoking situations to systematically reduce anxiety. Although early research has suggested that SD can be effective, it has been replaced in recent years by prolonged exposure (PE) therapy.

Developed by psychologist Edna Foa, prolonged exposure therapy involves helping patients develop confidence in their ability to cope with anxiety-provoking situations through direct confrontation with what frightens them. This exposure can be either imaginal ("talking through" anxiety while imagining being in a frightening situation) or in-vivo (confronting anxiety in actual situations). Some clinicians have also reported positive results using virtual-reality simulations of traumatic situations to help patients work through their fears. Prolonged exposure therapy depends heavily on homework assignments to help people become desensitized to traumatic memories and reduce avoidance behavior. To help with homework and keep track of assignments, the VA has also developed a mobile phone application for veterans.

Cognitive Processing Therapy

Cognitive processing therapy (CPT) is a form of CBT specifically developed for use with PTSD, and clinicians report excellent results with trauma patients including combat veterans. Offered both individually and in group formats, CPT typically runs for twelve sessions following a format containing four phases:

1. **Learning about PTSD symptoms**—People in the program are educated about their specific PTSD symptoms and work with the therapist to develop a treatment plan and the different skills to be learned in later phases. It is also during this phase that the therapist and patient come to know one another to develop a good rapport.

2. **Becoming aware of thoughts and feelings**—This can include imaginal exposure to come to terms with traumatic memories as well as processing how different thoughts and feelings are affecting the patient's life. People in treatment are asked to "step back" and consider how their trauma is affecting them and the people around them. Some versions of CPT involve patients writing down their memories of what happened or else talking about it with the therapist to work through the experience.

3. **Learning skills**—Once patients become aware of negative thoughts and feelings, they are taught coping skills to identify and question negative thoughts. Many of these thoughts leave people with PTSD "stuck" because they obsess on them and are unable to move on with their lives ("If only I had . . ."). Patients learn to "become their own therapist" by challenging negative behaviors and learning new coping strategies.

4. **Understanding how beliefs change**—Many people surviving a traumatic experience find their beliefs about themselves and the world have changed as a result. That includes beliefs about personal safety, self-control, self-esteem, other people, and intimate relationships with others. By exploring these beliefs in therapy, patients learn to develop a more realistic view and correct negative beliefs that are delaying their recovery. The cognitive skills learned in the previous phase are put into practice to develop alternative beliefs that are more balanced.

Can PTSD treatment be given online?
A new online treatment program has been developed by the National Center for PTSD to help veterans with PTSD and alcohol abuse problems get the help they need. Titled VetChange, the program is designed to be fully computer-automated and to help veterans learn to cope with different high-risk situations in which they might encounter PTSD triggers and be tempted to have a drink. A recently published study looking at the effectiveness of VetChange indicates that participating in the program helps reduce PTSD symptoms and alcohol use over a three-month period. While dropout rates were high, the program remains popular and can be used as a stand-alone treatment program as well as part of face-to-face treatment.

Cognitive Restructuring

Cognitive restructuring (CR) focuses on helping patients identify and challenge negative thoughts about themselves, other people, and the world that might be damaging their ability to cope with stress. Certain "automatic" thoughts can sabotage efforts to get better by convincing people that nothing they do will be effective. These include "magical thinking" such as patients believing that a traumatic experience is a punishment for some misdeed on their parts, or persistent beliefs about their own inability to rebuild their lives. Patients are encouraged to write down the situations that trigger their negative thoughts, to identify the moods they associate with those situations, to identify the negative thoughts produced, and to challenge the thoughts using skills learned in treatment. CR is especially useful in treating anxiety and depression, which are reinforced by negative thoughts and poor self-esteem. While it is not a stand-alone therapy for PTSD, it can be an important component of broader therapy programs.

Does EMDR Help?

Eye movement desensitization and reprocessing (EMDR) was developed by psychologist Francine Shapiro during the 1980s as a way of helping people work through traumatic memories using eye movements. According to Shapiro, traumatic events "upset the excitatory/inhibitory balance in the brain," which could be manipulated using rapid eye movements, and she reported positive results with trauma patients. EMDR can be considered a form of imaginal exposure since it involves guided imagery in which patients relive traumatic memories guided by verbal instructions by the therapist. Patients are then trained to relieve their anxiety using rapid eye movements.

EMDR uses an eight-phase program developed by Shapiro during which the patients are trained in eye movement and relaxation to handle the anxiety triggered by traumatic memories. They develop positive thoughts to replace the negative thoughts linked to the memory and are also trained to "scan" their bodies for tension or physical discomfort. During the EMDR process, patients are also encouraged to keep a journal as a record of their progress. In the final phase, the therapist evaluates progress to determine the effectiveness of the treatment and to explore other trauma symptoms. Though EMDR resembles CPT, there are important differences including no direct challenging of beliefs, no homework assignments, and no direct exposure to trauma reminders.

Despite the popularity of EMDR, with more than 60,000 clinicians becoming trained in its use and an official endorsement from the American Psychiatric Association, there is still some controversy over whether eye movements are an effective way of relieving trauma symptoms. While controlled studies have found significant improvement in trauma patients compared to trauma patients not receiving treatment, direct comparison with other treatments including standard exposure therapy have yielded mixed results over whether EMDR is better than the other treatments.

Counseling/Psychotherapy

Though CBT programs such as cognitive processing therapy and prolonged exposure are the most commonly used for treating people with PTSD, many patients may drop out of treatment or refuse the treatment programs completely because they feel they are "not ready" for formal treatment. Since some survivors may still be actively avoiding any reminder of their trauma, they would not want to attend treatment programs requiring them to work through their experiences. Considering how severe their PTSD symptoms are, many survivors may require full-time help, whether from family members or caregivers, or through the use of service dogs.

QUESTION

Can service dogs help people with PTSD?
Though service dogs are more usually associated with people with vision and mobility problems, training dogs to help people suffering from psychiatric problems, including PTSD, has become more common in recent years. According to the Americans with Disability Act (ADA) and similar laws in other countries, a service dog must be "individually trained to do work or perform tasks of benefit to a disabled individual in order to be legally elevated from pet status to service animal status." That includes tasks such as guarding their owners while they are sleeping, acting as protectors to relieve their hypervigilance symptoms, and helping them to cope with isolation.

For veterans dealing with PTSD, one alternative to the standard cognitive treatment programs is to attend adjunct therapy, either individually or as part of a group that can help them work through their emotional issues and become more comfortable talking about what happened to them. This therapy can even continue while they are attending the other CBT programs. Two forms of adjunct therapy that the VA provides for veterans resistant to other forms of treatment are:

Mindfulness Therapy

One type of mindfulness therapy, known as mindfulness-based cognitive therapy (MBCT), focuses on developing greater *mindfulness* (see sidebar later in this chapter) while learning more about emotional problems such as trauma and depression. The goal of MBCT is to recognize automatic thought processes that can trigger negative emotions such as depression and anxiety. By learning not to react to unpleasant experiences but instead embracing them without judgment, MBCT allows people to stop automatic thought processes from happening and to learn to be more accepting instead.

MBCT can be given as a group program that usually lasts eight weeks. Along with two-hour weekly sessions and a daylong class after the fifth week, people in the group also receive homework assignments to practice the skills they learn in their daily lives. By learning how some negative thoughts and emotions can leave them "stuck" and unable to concentrate on the present, MBCT patients can develop mind management skills and eliminate potentially destructive automatic thought processes. Mindfulness therapy in PTSD can allow survivors to let go of traumatic memories and emotional states like guilt or anger. Different forms of mindfulness therapy include:

- **Acceptance and Commitment Therapy (ACT)**—Described as "the third wave of behavioral and cognitive therapy" by psychologist Stephen Hayes, the goal of Acceptance and Commitment Therapy is to increase psychological flexibility and make patients more committed to identifying and moving toward specific goals in their lives. Using mindfulness exercises to make patients more willing to experience thoughts, memories, and emotions, ACT encourages patients to cope with avoidance by learning how to examine painful memories under safe conditions and reduce emotions such as fear and anger. By working through the painful memories and emotions, patients learn to *Accept* their reactions and be present, *Choose* a valued direction, and *Take* action.

  ACT is structured around core principles such as cognitive diffusion of troubling thoughts and emotions, accepting thoughts rather than struggling with them, discovering what is really important, having contact with the present moment, and taking committed action. Since its development in the 1980s by Stephen Hayes and his colleagues, thousands of therapists around the world have been trained in ACT and it continues to be used for a wide variety of psychological problems, including PTSD.

- **Dialectical behavior therapy (DBT)**—First developed by psychologist Marsha Linehan drawing on her own history of suicide attempts and depression, dialectical behavior therapy (DBT) combines cognitive-behavioral techniques and mindfulness exercises for emotional regulation and reality testing. Originally intended as a treatment for symptoms of borderline personality disorder and related problems, DBT has been adapted for use with patients suffering from

PTSD, traumatic brain injury, and substance abuse, and survivors of sexual abuse. DBT involves individual and/or group skills training in distress tolerance, interpersonal effectiveness, emotional regulation, and mindfulness. In PTSD patients, DBT is often used before more intensive treatments such as exposure therapy so that patients can develop the distress tolerance and emotion regulation needed for later treatment. DBT can also be used as a stand-alone treatment or in conjunction with other therapy programs.

- **Mindfulness-based stress reduction (MBSR)**—For PTSD patients dealing with stress and anxiety issues, Mindfulness-Based Stress Reduction (MBSR) can be useful. First developed by psychiatrist Jon Kabat-Zinn as part of his work as a founding member of the Cambridge Zen Center, MBSR focuses on mindfulness meditation to help patients manage stress. Combining hatha yoga and Buddhist Zen techniques, patients being trained in MBSR are encouraged to "scan" their bodies for signs of stress and to develop a decentered view of the self that avoids judgment of thoughts, emotions, and physical sensations. Research into MBSR has found it to be useful in treating anxiety disorders, depression, and substance abuse, all of which are common problems in PTSD patients. Unlike other mindfulness programs, MBSR training materials recommend that PTSD patients need to attend other treatment programs in conjunction with MBSR since untreated PTSD patients may find their symptoms worsening otherwise.

Since research on the effectiveness of mindfulness therapy in treating post-traumatic stress is still limited, its value as a stand-alone treatment has not been proven though it can still be used in addition to other treatment programs. Many VA clinics offering PTSD counseling to returning veterans offer mindfulness training either individually or in groups. For PTSD patients who have problems regulating emotions, extended mindfulness exercises are not recommended and therapists are usually advised to limit the exercises to no more than five to ten minutes at a time until the PTSD symptoms are stabilized.

What is mindfulness?
Based on the concept of mindfulness in Buddhist meditation, mindfulness is usually regarded as having two components: (1) focusing on the present moment through developing greater awareness, and (2) nonjudgmental acceptance of the flow of emotions, experiences, and sensations being experienced. Awareness is developed through meditation exercises focusing on the "here and now," while acceptance means developing greater open-mindedness in accepting new experiences. Another concept linked to mindfulness is Shoshin, or "beginner's mind," meaning to have enthusiasm and a lack of preconceptions when considering something new. Buddhist philosophy holds that mindfulness should be maintained through a calm awareness of feelings, mind, body, and desire.

Anger Management Therapy

For many trauma survivors, anger can be the most significant problem they experience, especially when dealing with hyperarousal. Though anger is often treated along with other PTSD symptoms as part of the therapy process in most cases, some survivors may find their anger symptoms continuing even when other issues improve. To help survivors deal with anger, many VA hospitals have developed anger management programs focusing on controlling aggressive behavior and teaching more appropriate ways of interacting with others. Typical anger program modules include:

- Learning about the difference between anger and aggression and how anger can be expressed appropriately
- Learning how hyperarousal can lead to anger and aggression
- Learning to take charge of your own actions
- How to correct mistaken impressions of the behavior and attitudes of others
- How to communicate needs and feelings appropriately
- How to negotiate conflicts and solve problems

Research has found that anger management programming can be an effective way of curbing anger and helping survivors develop self-confidence in how they interact with others. Anger management treatment can be given in groups or to individual patients. Couples counseling focusing on anger control is also available in some places. Anger management programs are also often recommended for PTSD survivors who have been convicted of violent offenses as a condition of supervised release or to avoid incarceration. Many anger management programs are available in the community though survivors and their families need to do their own research to see if the program suits their needs.

CHAPTER 14

The Family and PTSD

As you have already learned in previous chapters, family members can play an important role in helping PTSD survivors learn to deal with their symptoms and overcome the sense of isolation that keeps them from rejoining their community. For that reason, couples and family therapy is often used to help keep troubled families together and encourage greater cooperation in learning to cope with post-traumatic stress.

PTSD Symptoms in the Family

Depending on the type of trauma and the symptoms that survivors are experiencing, family members can often find themselves helping loved ones work through issues such as grief, feelings of guilt or shame, the fear of some new devastating catastrophe, or the general loss of morale and pessimism that often comes with severe post-traumatic stress. Many survivors try to isolate themselves from family members as much as they can, whether through a fear of intimacy or because they are too emotionally numb to be able to function as a member of a family.

Another common feature that can frighten family members is the aggression shown by many PTSD survivors. Trauma survivors are often afraid of losing control of their temper and research shows that they have an increased risk of domestic violence and emotional abuse. As a result, many people with PTSD may isolate themselves from their families out of fear of hurting loved ones. Symptoms such as flashbacks (especially flashbacks of violent experiences) and hypervigilance can lead to chronic irritability, persistent feelings of danger, and a tendency to overreact to the unexpected.

Reacting to this irritability can often lead to hurt feelings, anger at what the trauma survivor may say or do during one of these outbursts, or guilt at unintentionally triggering the anger. Not surprisingly, family members dealing with this kind of aggression can develop emotional problems of their own, including depression, anxiety, and even secondary trauma on the part of spouses and children.

ESSENTIAL

The Support and Family Education (SAFE) Center at the Oklahoma City Veterans Affairs Medical Center provides a comprehensive online list of resources for families dealing with PTSD. The list includes recommended books, websites, phone numbers, and information on different mental disorders that can affect how families are functioning. The list can be found at: *www.ouhsc.edu/safeprogram/ResourceList.pdf*.

Family members can learn to deal with PTSD symptoms as they occur by educating themselves about post-traumatic stress and possible symptoms. By developing a working relationship with the treatment professionals who are dealing with their family member, they can also be better prepared to handle what may happen. It is also essential that they remain patient since people with PTSD need time to work through their symptoms.

Characteristics of the Family System

Handling the emotional isolation resulting from PTSD can be the most serious problem that families face. Whether the trauma survivor refuses to pay attention to their spouses or children, spends hours in front of a television set, or "spaces out" during conversations, family members can often find themselves walking on eggshells out of fear of triggering new symptoms. Along with a sense of feeling rejected and unloved, family members often develop a sense of resentment or feel abandoned.

Family members can also develop a sense of competing with the memories of the past that people with PTSD are unable to set aside. Flashbacks and other trauma symptoms that lead survivors to re-experience what happened to them makes their memories seem more real than the actual world around them. Family members need to understand that this is not a deliberate rejection of them even though they may feel that they are less important than the memories their loved one keeps reliving.

Aside from the isolation resulting from PTSD, families also feel the gap from losing a valuable family member. Whether the person with PTSD was a husband, father, mother, son, etc., the various family activities they used to play a role in become that much harder for families to enjoy. With emotionally numb family members acting as if they were on the outside looking in, landmark family events such as birthdays, graduations, etc., are more subdued as a result.

This also leads to the lopsided relationships that many spouses of people with PTSD describe since they are often required to compensate for their spouse's lack of active involvement with family members. The added resentment of spouses finding themselves running the show by acting as caregivers for both their traumatized spouses as well as their children can strain many relationships to the breaking point. This is especially true for spouses who have to take over as chief financial supporter for the family replacing the former breadwinner who is no longer able to work due to PTSD.

Despite the emotional numbness and isolation, people with PTSD often develop mixed emotions relating to their families. Along with a fear of harming others by giving in to the anger inside of them, trauma survivors can often have an intense fear of being abandoned. Though they love their family members intensely, they have difficulty expressing that love in a way that they can understand. Some trauma survivors even go so far as to insist that their family is the only thing keeping them alive. This can lead to an understandable sense of confusion over how the trauma survivor regards them and adds to their sense of insecurity.

All of this contributes to the strong feelings of guilt that can overwhelm people with PTSD and their families. Not only do trauma survivors feel guilty over the impact their symptoms are having on the people around them, the family members feel guilty for doing anything that might potentially make people with PTSD even worse.

ESSENTIAL

Without treatment or education about PTSD and why people suffering from post-traumatic stress cannot simply "get over it," families will not be able to survive the relationship problems that develop. At that point, family or couples therapy may be the only option to prevent marriages or families from falling apart.

Creating Social Support Networks

Family members of trauma survivors can often feel completely isolated. It is that feeling of isolation that can make the emotional burden involved in caring for someone with PTSD even harder to deal with. Building a social support network to provide emotional and physical support can be as important for family members as it is for trauma survivors.

For many survivors, social support networks already exist in the form of family members and friends who care about the survivor and are ready to assist them. Along with these natural support networks, survivors can also have formal support networks made up of mental health workers, fellow survivors meeting in support groups, or community volunteer organizations ready to provide assistance.

The type of support that a network of concerned family members, friends, and treatment professionals can provide usually takes different forms. Perceived support (knowing that these people are ready and willing to offer help as needed) and received support (the aid that has already been given) are two of the most common. Functional support refers to the specific type of help that a person can provide (such as a counselor providing therapy). Structural support comes from the feeling of connectedness that a survivor may have by being part of a larger community.

But what about survivors who don't have a support network in place or who feel isolated because they don't wish to rely on friends or family members (as with many victims of sexual assault)? Depending on the type of trauma experienced, survivors can form new support networks by getting help from community groups or national organizations formed to help people in their situation. Appendix C gives some examples of different resources available for survivors of physical and sexual violence, veterans, and other people who have been affected by trauma.

QUESTION

What is the Caring Letters Project?
Recognizing how isolated many veterans dealing with emotional problems can feel, the National Center for Telehealth and Technology (T2) and the Defense Centers of Excellence (DCoE) for Psychological Health and Traumatic Brain Injury have launched a new pilot project. Called the Caring Letters Project (CLP), the new project involves sending brief letters to discharged inpatients considered to be at high risk for suicide following hospitalization. Though still in the early stages, the Caring Letters Project appears to be an effective way of helping potentially suicidal military personnel.

For those survivors without a support network in place, seeking help is more crucial than ever since dealing with trauma symptoms alone will only make them worse.

Defusing Stress

Every family deals with stress. With traumatic stress, however, it is essential to be aware of the different symptoms that might occur and to learn how to defuse them as they arise. This is especially true for persistent PTSD symptoms that can be as emotionally draining for family members as they are for survivors.

Along with providing emotional support and making sure that loved ones in need get the proper treatment, friends and family members can help defuse the symptoms of traumatic stress by following some basic common-sense strategies. These can include:

- Encourage survivors to stay in treatment. If there is no real progress after a reasonable amount of time (about six to eight weeks), talk to the therapist yourself or else participate in the treatment directly to learn how to help with treatment.
- Learn as much about PTSD as you can. Along with doing your own reading on the subject, help the survivor with his or her homework assignments to learn more about the coping skills being taught.
- Be willing to listen to what the survivor is saying. Be alert about feelings and emotions as well as what triggers PTSD symptoms.
- Suggest different distractions. Anything from a walk through the park to seeing a movie can help survivors take their minds off their troubles for a while. Make certain the movie doesn't contain any inappropriate material that might act as a trigger, however.
- Be optimistic about recovery and try to share that optimism. This is especially important during times when survivors seem particularly anxious or depressed.
- Never ignore comments suggesting that the survivor is feeling suicidal. Report these comments to the survivor's doctor. Make certain that your friend or relative is aware that you will be doing this, however.

Along with providing emotional support to PTSD survivors, it is also important to recognize that friends or family members acting as caregivers can become stressed as well. For many spouses or other family members, caring for a loved one with serious PTSD can be a full-time job. If you have a friend or relative in this position, offer to take over caregiving duties for an afternoon so he or she can have a break for a while. These rest breaks can be critical in preventing the kind of health problems often seen in long-term caregivers.

FACT

A recent research project suggests that caregivers with a history of depression or other emotional issues are especially vulnerable to developing stress-related problems due to caring for others. The same study also shows that caregivers need to be prepared for the challenges of providing long-term care and that caretaker stress can lead to greater problems with chronic illnesses such as heart disease or cancer.

Learning to Cope in the Present

Recognizing that their loved ones have undergone a traumatic experience that led to them becoming "different" is a hard lesson for many families to learn. As you have seen in previous chapters, many trauma survivors can become stuck in the past and unable to move on from a traumatic experience. Part of the recovery process for survivors involves learning how to ground themselves in the present, especially when triggers lead to flashbacks causing them to relive a past trauma. Along with grounding exercises learned in treatment programs, encourage survivors to engage in everyday tasks such as chores around the house, participating in family activities, attending community events, or physical exercise. All of these activities help ground them in the here and now and can be especially important in showing survivors that life can still go on.

Family members participating in treatment should learn about different grounding techniques and coach survivors who appear to be experiencing distress to help them cope. Above all else, they need to be patient since learning to live with PTSD can take years, even with treatment.

Family and Couples Therapy

Since trauma patients often feel alone and disconnected from the people they care about, part of the treatment process involves helping them repair the important relationships in their lives. The damage resulting from symptoms such as emotional numbing, poor sexual functioning, and loss of intimacy can lead to separation, alienation, and divorce for many PTSD patients unless spouses and family members become part of the counseling process.

Couples Therapy

Couples therapy involves direct counseling with a therapist to address the different relationship problems the couple has been unable to resolve. While similar to sex therapy, couples therapy focuses on the whole relationship and the problems that have been undermining it. For people with PTSD and their partners, couples therapy usually begins with a formal assessment to identify particular risk factors such as potential domestic abuse and emotional issues. The couple then receives joint education in PTSD symptoms and how they can affect a relationship. Over the course of treatment, couples learn about joint coping strategies through training exercises during treatment sessions as well as homework exercises.

While dropout rates can be high, especially for people with severe PTSD, couples therapy can be an effective way of dealing with marital problems although some research has suggested that it is not as effective in relieving PTSD symptoms. For that reason, couples therapy needs to target specific symptoms such as emotional numbing and avoidance behavior to be effective.

There are therapy programs that have been specifically developed for use with couples dealing with post-traumatic issues. Two have shown particular promise in recent years.

Structured Approach Therapy

Structured approach therapy (SAT) was specifically developed for use in veterans with PTSD to help them deal with emotional numbing and other symptoms as well as improving relationships. It is conducted with individual couples and runs from twelve to fifteen hour-long sessions. SAT follows the same pattern as stress inoculation training (SIT) and focuses on developing skills to cope with stressful experiences and to learn to deal with new stress in the future. SAT extends the SIT model by training couples to handle new stressful situations that might strain their relationship.

Much like SIT, SAT comes in three phases:

1. An education phase where the therapist develops a rapport with the couple and educates them about stress, PTSD, and how to respond to stress effectively.
2. A skills training phase during which coping skills are taught to the couple and they learn how to make the skills a part of their lives.
3. An application phase during which the couple is encouraged to apply the skills they learned to deal with current and future problems they may face.

SAT has been shown to be effective in helping couples work through issues with PTSD, extreme phobias, and anger management. While following a fixed format, it can also be adapted to the specific needs of individual couples.

Emotionally Focused Therapy for Couples

Emotionally focused therapy (EFT) is a short-term structured psychotherapy approach that can be used for individuals, couples, and families. A more specialized version, emotionally focused therapy for couples (EFT-C) was developed in the 1980s by psychologists Sue Johnson and Leslie Greenberg. Developed from emotional-based psychotherapy and attachment theory, EFT-C helps couples work through attachment problems that make them unable to solve their conflicts. One of the basic principles of EFT-C is that couples adapt to attachment problems in ways that can cause distress. Since many of the symptoms that result from trauma are actually coping strategies that helped them survive, couples in treatment need to recognize this and work through their experiences during therapy. The chief goal of EFT-C is to help couples improve their relationships and to develop a better understanding of what their partners have gone through. In that way, they form a stronger partnership and are better able to cope with new stressful situations as they arise.

In EFT-C, people work through previous trauma through a series of stages during which they learn to "de-escalate" negative emotions and ways of responding and developing more positive alternatives. The couple also explores how they interact with one another and learn to be more accepting and to identify attachment needs. For couples dealing with trauma, the emotional distress can be particularly high and the therapist may need to move slower through the treatment sessions as a result. The therapist also needs to avoid passing judgment on the clients and to help the couple develop a stronger attachment to one another. One of the advantages of EFT-C is that it is highly flexible and can be adapted to the specific circumstances that each couple is facing.

Research into EFT-C has shown a strong success rate, and it can be combined with other forms of treatment as needed. Along with treating PTSD, EFT-C has also been used with depression, chronic illness, and related problems and is considered one of the best evidence-based treatments for couples available.

FACT

The International Centre for Excellence in Emotionally Focused Therapy (ICEEFT) provides a list of certified EFT therapists and treatment centers throughout the world. The site also includes a Find a Therapist link, provides information on the ICEEFT community, and sells training resources including books, workshops, and audiotapes. For more information, go to *www.iceeft.com*.

Family Therapy

Family therapy can be known by different names, including family counseling or family systems therapy. Though the concept of family typically involves spouses, parents, or children, the definition of family has grown in recent years to include people who may not be related by blood or marriage but who still have strong long-term relationships. Families in therapy may have problems due to undergoing a crisis or because one or more members have developed problems that are best treated by including the entire family in therapy. Family therapy often includes many of the same techniques used in individual and couples therapy adapted for use with entire families. Mental health professionals practicing family therapy are typically licensed by formal governing bodies and have completed specialized training before offering services to the public.

There are different types of family therapy that can be used depending on the specific nature of the problems faced by the family and the age range of the family members involved, including children. For family therapy around PTSD issues, the therapist begins with a formal assessment to identify the treatment needs and whether there are added problems such as domestic violence or substance abuse. For family therapy with PTSD families, there are usually three basic stages that need to be worked through:

- **Psychoeducation**—Teaching family members about PTSD symptoms and about the traumatic event that caused them. Family members are also taught how those symptoms may be affecting the PTSD patient's interactions with the people around him or her. This education can involve teaching about PTSD during treatment sessions, presenting videos, or through educational handouts and reading assignments. Issues such as blame, shame, and stigma are also addressed. During the early stage of treatment, the therapist also gathers more information about how the family members interact to identify problems to be faced.

- **Disclosure**—The reality of the trauma is dealt with by having trauma victims discuss their experience to give the other family members an idea of what they went through. How much detail they provide is usually based on what they are comfortable telling their family and how ready the family members are to hear about what happened. Disclosure is a delicate process and can take a lifetime in some cases.

- **Learning to interact**—Coming to terms with what they learn about the traumatic experience often leaves family members with the problem of how to go on with their family life without being overwhelmed by their own reaction. Families can become divided with some members being better able to handle what they learned than others. The therapist needs to bring the family members together so they can discuss how what they learned is affecting them and develop more effective relationships. It also lets the trauma survivor know that their experiences are being validated by family members instead of feeling isolated.

Recognizing the importance of family therapy, the Veterans Administration has developed a multifamily group program titled REACH (*R*eaching Out to *E*ducate and *A*ssist *C*aring, *H*ealthy Families). Designed as a nine-month program, REACH involves weekly fifty-minute sessions that four to six patients attend with a family member (or any trusted adult). During the sessions, patients and their family members learn how to strengthen social support networks. They also learn about anger management, communication skills, how to cope with stress and depression, and how to improve the quality of their relationships. Most important, REACH also focuses on the emotional needs of the family member and addresses issues such as burnout and how to avoid damaging family relationships. Early results looking at REACH suggest that the veterans and family members who participate learn how to improve their relationships and avoid many of the difficulties faced by families after a long deployment.

ESSENTIAL

More information about REACH including course materials are available online at *www.ouhsc.edu/REACHProgram*. Along with the provider manual and student handbook, the REACH site also includes toolkits on veteran parenting, links to other VA family support programs, and copies of research articles on the effectiveness of REACH.

Families are an important part of the recovery process, but trauma survivors need to be aware that family interactions work both ways and that they and their family members are both affected by how they cope with their symptoms. Maintaining good communication is the key to remaining flexible and being able to handle new problems as they occur.

CHAPTER 15

Handling the Symptoms

While being in treatment can help people with PTSD and their families learn to cope with all the symptoms linked to traumatic stress, managing those symptoms will seem easier at some times than others. There will always be days when nothing seems to go right, anniversaries that bring back the traumatic memories, certain situations that trigger flashbacks, or simply a case of being in a bad mood. At times like these, there are certain techniques that can help make the symptoms a little less troubling.

Learning to Cope

Please note that the best way to learn coping strategies is in treatment while under the supervision of a qualified therapist. Although you can learn some helpful tips from books such as this one, that does not take the place of proper treatment. Medication can also help control some symptoms and simply talking to a family member can help as well. Still, it is also important not to try to do too much, too fast. Though you might feel impatient because you are not improving as quickly as you would like, you must realize that the process of recovering from trauma takes time.

That also means coming to terms with your own emotions, including feelings like anger and anxiety, which you may be afraid of expressing. Many people coping with trauma may try shutting down their emotions completely, at least temporarily. Telling yourself not to feel may seem like a good idea, especially if you are afraid of becoming angry, but it can also lead to cutting yourself off from the people around you. Ultimately, it is your feelings that make you human and you will not be able to function long without them. Though negative emotions such as sadness and anger are never pleasant, shutting down your emotions makes you unable to experience positive ones like joy and love. Until you learn to recognize the emotions you are experiencing and let them come out naturally, you will not be able to handle your normal day-to-day existence.

ALERT

Research has shown that emotional numbing symptoms, especially detachment or being estranged from others, are strongly linked to suicidal thoughts. Even when depression and all other PTSD symptoms are taken into account, PTSD survivors experiencing emotional numbing show a strong suicide risk. If you or a family member is experiencing emotional numbing symptoms, they should *not* be ignored and treatment is strongly recommended.

Along with working through your emotions in therapy, you also need to recognize the different feelings that you experience throughout the day. Feelings of rage, irritation, frustration, insecurity, and anxiety are going to strike at times depending on where you are and what is happening around you.

These feelings can range in intensity from very mild to severe depending on the kind of stress you are experiencing, and you should just let them subside without reacting. Some feelings can be completely appropriate to the situation; they are the kind of feelings that anyone might have. Don't be afraid of your emotions and don't pass judgment on yourself for feeling them.

Controlling Stress

In PTSD, much of the stress you are going to experience comes from dealing with feeling "on alert" at all times. If you remember the chapter on PTSD and the brain, most PTSD symptoms are caused by your brain and nervous system being in a constant fight-or-flight mode and the difficulty you face in desensitizing yourself to get that stressful sensation under control.

Anxiety attacks can come on all at once and can seem overwhelming to the people experiencing them. These anxiety attacks can be relatively brief or can last for hours depending on what triggered them and how people respond to them. As one example, people experiencing panic attacks can actually find themselves gasping for breath because they feel they are not getting enough air into their lungs. Though panic attacks typically last no more than a few minutes, they can seem much longer because of the altered sense of time that goes with the acute state of alarm that triggers the attack.

Coping with Panic Attacks

According to Claire Weekes, a medical doctor and authority on stress and anxiety, problems with panic and anxiety are usually due to an overly sensitized nervous system and relying on *avoiding* the situational triggers that can lead to anxiety attacks rather than learning to *master* the symptoms instead. While her many self-help books and seminars on handling sensitized nerves were mainly intended for people with panic disorder and anxiety, they can be just as valuable for people suffering from PTSD as well.

The four principles that Dr. Weekes gave for coping with sensitized nerves are:

1. Face the symptoms. The only way to cope successfully with anxiety is to confront the symptoms until they no longer matter. No matter how

aroused your nervous system is, your body will eventually adapt. In fact, a certain amount of arousal is necessary to stay alert.

2. Accept the symptoms you are experiencing. Learn to handle what you are feeling. Don't react in a way that might make the symptoms worse. Just relax and don't withdraw. Many of the symptoms linked to stress and anxiety subside as the body realizes that it is not under attack and things return to normal.

3. Just float. Use meditation or deep breathing to stabilize yourself. Stop tensing your muscles and let the body unwind. Many activities such as pacing, clenching your teeth, rapid breathing, or not being able to sit still will just make the symptoms worse. If you are sitting and doing work, just try to keep on doing what you were doing while controlling your breathing. Most therapy programs will include relaxation training exercises that you can use to control stress and anxiety. You can also try simple meditation or simply relaxing while listening to soft music.

4. Give it time. An overly sensitized nervous system is not going to reset itself overnight. Your body's chemistry will need time to become stable and you are going to need to learn not to overreact to stressful situations.

FACT

There are also lifestyle changes that can help you learn to cope with stress. This includes cutting back on caffeine, nicotine, and other anxiety-producing chemicals in what you eat or drink. That means coffee, tea, cigarettes, certain soft drinks (check the label), chocolate, and even weight-control medications. If you are having trouble sleeping at night, make certain you don't take in any caffeine for up to ten hours before bedtime. Proper nutrition, regular exercise, and getting enough sleep can also help keep stress under control.

For people getting treatment for panic attacks, it is often helpful to simulate a panic attack while in therapy. That involves breathing rapidly to build up the oxygen in the bloodstream and then learning to control the symptoms as they occur. Once people learn that panic attacks are relatively harmless and easy to control, they are better able to handle the attacks when they occur. For people with PTSD, learning to control anxiety symptoms can work in the same way by confronting the symptoms and floating until those symptoms subside.

Dealing with Flashbacks

Intrusive memories are one of the key symptoms of PTSD and can be the hardest thing for a trauma survivor to control. In a previous chapter, you were introduced to grounding as a way to help trauma survivors bring themselves back to the present. Grounding can also work as a way of controlling intrusive thoughts. Grounding techniques include:

- Grounding in your body by noting all the sensations you are feeling. Are your muscles clenched? Are you aware of your breathing or the fabric of the chair in which you are sitting? Try focusing on these things or else try wiggling your toes and fingers. Stamp your feet on the floor or clench your teeth. Blink your eyes or tense the muscles in your face.
- Grounding in your surroundings by describing five objects you can see in the room. Then describe five sounds that you hear. Then handle and describe five objects. Check if the intrusive memories are reduced. If not, repeat the exercise but with four instead of five objects, and so on, working yourself down to a final grounding.
- Grounding in symbols of the present. Do you have a newspaper handy with today's date? Or you can try using recent photographs, birthday cards, or other reminders of your life as it is now. By grounding yourself in how your life is now, the memories of the past should trouble you less.
- Ground yourself verbally by saying things such as "I am safe now" and "This is just a memory of the past. That was then, this is now." Even focusing on the present with self-statements such as "Today is (today's date) and the time is (current time)" can help with grounding.
- Grounding in your posture by taking note of how intrusive memories are affecting you at that moment. Are you slouching, tensing up your muscles, crouching in fear? Standing in an upright position and having a confident expression on your face can relieve some of the fear

you are feeling. Behaving as if you are in control can ease the feelings of dread and relieve some of those intrusive memories.

- Distract yourself with simple tasks such as counting the coins in your pocket or the number of books on your shelves. Make it a verbal counting task to ground yourself in the present.

Grounding basically involves rooting yourself in the here and now to break the hold that past memories have on you. Splash water in your face, exercise, do chores around the house, or spend time with pets or children.

Coping with Reminders

There will always be reminders of what you have experienced, whether it be a similar situation, an anniversary date, or a story in the news that brings back unpleasant memories. During therapy sessions, you will be asked to describe what you experienced and learn ways to defuse the feelings it arouses, but reminders can occur anywhere and at times that you least expect them.

While traumatic memories can be overwhelming, you should not try confronting those memories on your own. Most therapists dealing with PTSD patients encourage them to confront these memories but only in therapy where they can learn to control the feelings that come with them. This is known as "memory work" and can be dangerous for anyone trying to work through extremely traumatic memories without professional help. Along with learning different ways of coping, therapists can also provide emotional support and the sense of safety that people with PTSD need to begin healing.

In addition to grounding exercises and stress management techniques, you can deal with reminders by creating a "safe place" image in your mind that can be used as a sanctuary to keep from being overwhelmed by unwanted memories. This can a real place where you felt safe in the past or somewhere completely in your imagination. It can be a place where you are alone or there can be someone you love and trust there with you. When you are thinking of that place, also think of all the sights, sounds, and smells you associate with that place. Think up a mental image that reminds you of that place and learn to bring that image up whenever you are feeling stressed or bothered by memories.

Many therapists encourage patients with PTSD to develop their own safe places as part of their treatment sessions and teach them to think of that place whenever the memories become too strong. If the safe place is someplace you've been before, having a physical reminder such as a photograph or a memento from that place with you at all times can help as well. Just look at the photograph or touch the memento while you are picturing the safe place in your mind.

Mindfulness

There are also mindfulness exercises you can try to reduce the feelings that come with painful memories. As you learned in the chapter on treatment, mindfulness means being completely open and aware of yourself and the world around you in a way that is accepting and noncritical. Though you are aware of the memories and feelings they bring, you are also aware of your environment, your other memories, and how they make up the total package of your existence.

There are five underlying principles to how mindfulness exercises work:

1. With PTSD, it is not the memories that are the problem, but rather what people do to try to escape them. Avoidance is one of the major features of PTSD, and it is the refusal to face traumatic memories that causes much of the distress in trauma survivors.
2. You can never change what happened. People try suppressing their memories of traumatic events but the *fact* of what happened can never change. Despite the appeal of movies such as *Eternal Sunshine of the Spotless Mind* with science-fiction memory erasing, traumatic memories will always be a part of the lives of people with PTSD.
3. Though you cannot change the memories, you can change how you respond to them. People need to come to terms with traumatic memories and make them a part of their lives. As people learn to cope with the

memories instead of reacting to them, the memories become less likely to disrupt their lives.

4. Suffering can be a way of learning how to be more human. While thinking of suffering as a learning experience seems hard to accept, you can learn to embrace pain and get in touch with your inner feelings. Much of the distress you face with PTSD comes from trying to escape the pain rather than simply coming to terms with it.

5. Mindfulness means making the traumatic memories a part of your life rather than running away from them. It may take time and effort, but the traumatic memories can be something you learn to live with.

FACT

While mindfulness-based exercises are best learned and practiced under the guidance of a qualified therapist, practicing mindful breathing and other kinds of meditation can give people with PTSD a break from the racing thoughts that come with intrusive memories. Again, the focus of mindfulness-based exercises is not to escape the trauma symptoms, but to keep them from overwhelming your life.

Mindful Breathing

Practice the following steps for ten minutes each day:

1. Sit comfortably with feet flat on the floor and hands resting in your lap. Close your eyes gently or else focus them on a spot in front of you.

2. Release the tension in your body. That includes the shoulders, mouth, abdomen, and any other part of your body where you are feeling tension.

3. Breathe *abdominally* (with your abdomen rising and falling, not your chest). Keep the breathing slow, with a steady rhythm. Feel your body taking in breaths and letting them out again. Though you breathe every day, how often do you simply relax and notice how it feels to breathe?

4. Be aware of the thoughts that enter your mind, but don't react to them. Simply let the thoughts float in and out of your consciousness. Notice these thoughts, but don't interrupt the breathing exercise and don't give in to the distress you might be feeling.

The point of this exercise is to realize that having the thoughts doesn't mean giving in to the distress you usually associate with them. It is not a way of escaping or avoiding having to think about your memories. Those will always be a part of you, but practicing this exercise can help you learn how to reduce the anxiety and depression.

Just about any physical activity can be turned into a mindfulness-based exercise. That can include eating while slowly savoring each bite of food and being aware of all the tastes and smells that go with it, walking while being aware of the feeling as you place each step on the ground, or aerobic exercise with you being aware of the sensations of breathing and tensing your muscles as you work out.

Along with learning about different ways of coping with intrusive thoughts is recognizing what *not* to do to get these symptoms under control. When faced with memories that seem impossible to forget, it is easy to give in to despair or to try more harmful ways of coping including substance abuse or self-destructive behavior. Some people may begin self-medicating with prescription drugs gained through doctor-shopping or purchased on the street. Though medications can relieve some of the symptoms, they are potentially dangerous unless prescribed by a qualified professional.

ESSENTIAL

It is also important to realize that medication is a short-term solution and that you are better off in the long run learning to control those symptoms yourself. Make sure you are working with your doctor to monitor how well your medication is working and do not try to mix medications or "doctor-shop" even if you are in distress.

Confronting Triggers

Part of learning to deal with the various triggers that can bring on intrusive memories or the negative emotions linked to them is recognizing what those triggers are. This is not always easy since triggers have a way of being completely unexpected, especially if you are in an unfamiliar setting or situation. Though many people with PTSD try to protect themselves by limiting their activities as much as possible (some even become completely housebound), learning different strategies to handle the feelings aroused by different triggers is a better way of coping.

Remember that these triggers lead to your body responding as if you were in immediate danger. This is the familiar fight-or-flight response that has already been covered in a previous chapter. Even if you know perfectly well that you are safe, your body may be telling you something completely different because of the feelings brought on by the trigger.

Basically, triggers are learned cues that have been linked to a specific traumatic event. While harmless in themselves, these learned triggers bring about unwanted memories and emotions that can be overwhelming for many survivors. There can be different kinds of triggers including:

1. **Visual triggers**—Seeing blood or roadkill on a highway can bring back memories of death and violence for some veterans. Television news stories about a natural disaster can trigger memories of a similar disaster in survivors.

2. **Auditory triggers**—Hearing certain sounds such as a scream or an ambulance siren can trigger traumatic memories in survivors. An engine backfiring can sound like gunfire.

3. **Olfactory triggers**—Certain smells can remind survivors of traumatic experiences. Olfactory triggers have long been linked to recall of traumatic memory and can lead to intense flashbacks.

4. **Somatic triggers**—Feeling pain or being touched in a certain way can trigger flashbacks associated with past trauma. Being touched is often a trigger for survivors of sexual assault and can lead to flashbacks even when they are feeling safe.

5. **Taste triggers**—The senses of taste and smell are highly linked and certain tastes can trigger flashbacks.

6. **Anniversary triggers**—Anniversary dates, especially in the early stages of recovery, can be powerful reminders of traumatic experiences. Certain seasons of the year can have multiple reminders depending on how significant they are to the survivors.

7. **Feeling stressed or emotional**—Any time your body comes under pressure, whether you are in actual danger or not, you are going to be reminded of previous times you have faced something similar.

8. **Any combination of different triggers**—Some situations can lead to multiple triggers at once. A crowded room or a minor traffic accident can lead to survivors being overwhelmed by multiple reminders of previous trauma.

Over time, you will become aware of the different triggers that can bring on the negative thoughts and, one hopes, learn to deal with triggers during treatment. You will also learn to stop and reflect whether the trigger is actually signaling danger instead of responding to it automatically. That means easing the sense of distress and evaluating the situation you are in to judge how best to react.

According to psychologist Anna Baranowsky, people with PTSD can learn to counter triggers that lead to intrusive memories by developing a "safety and support club" technique to surround themselves with the various people who can help to overcome those memories. This technique, which she and her colleagues use with PTSD patients, involves:

1. Taking a comfortable position, relaxing and closing your eyes, and imagining your safe place. Recall all the things that make that place seem so safe to you.
2. Think of all the different people who would make good members of your "safety and support club." These can be people you know and trust, whether they are living or dead, and can even include imaginary characters. Call each one of them by name, think of what they look like, and imagine they are in your safe place making you feel safe without judging you.
3. Always remember that these are people in your club who can provide you with comfort and support. Know that you are the one in control and that you can ask anyone who doesn't make you feel comfortable to leave the club.
4. With your club fixed firmly in your mind, bring yourself back to where you are at present. If you can, write down the names of all the people in your club or repeat their names in your mind. Think about how the exercise made you feel.

You can also try different soothing exercises such as mindful breathing (see previous section), grounding, or containment exercises to ease the distress you are feeling and learn to evaluate your surroundings more objectively.

The point of these kinds of exercises is to gain control of those feelings that are overwhelming you and to learn how to bring yourself back to a state of relative calm at any time. Practice the exercises on a regular basis to improve your confidence. They may seem awkward at first, but rehearsing them can make them part of your regular routine.

ALERT

Practicing exercises you learned from books should not take the place of formal treatment under the supervision of a qualified professional. Techniques should be learned and practiced while in therapy sessions since they can be adapted to your specific symptoms. You and your therapist should decide together whether the techniques are working or if you should try something else.

Containment

Containment means learning to contain the distress you might be feeling as a result of a traumatic memory or different triggers. Containment exercises help survivors keep intrusive memories under control and separate past from present. These exercises need to be rehearsed on a regular basis to ensure that they can be used whenever they are needed. Since there is no one technique that can work best for everyone, a certain amount of experimenting is needed to decide what is best for you.

One containment technique involves imagining that there is a "split TV screen" in your mind with the intrusive memories on one screen and the present day on the other. Mentally picture yourself using a remote control to shrink the distressing memory or lowering the volume to make it less intrusive. You can also picture yourself saving the traumatic memory to a video recording so that you can look at it later. As an alternative, you can try "freezing" the image, knowing you can unfreeze it at any time. The point of containment is not to delete unpleasant memories but to recognize that you can control them as needed to keep them from taking over your life.

Learning Hope

Hope is the greatest weapon any trauma survivor has in learning to deal with PTSD symptoms. Though it is easy to be pessimistic at times when survivors are not recovering as quickly as they would like, staying hopeful can often be the key to getting better. There are different definitions of what hope means, but it is usually defined as "a feeling of expectation and desire for a particular thing to happen." As part of his own research, psychologist Charles R. Snyder proposed that hope has three necessary ingredients: (1) having a conscious goal (one that is both attainable and challenging); (2) pathway thoughts (coming up with ways of *achieving* that goal); and (3) agency thoughts (*believing* that you can attain that goal). While hope is usually thought of as an emotion, it can also be described as a form of goal-directed thinking that people engage in to reach their goals, whatever they may be. People with a high level of hope are usually able to form strong plans for achieving the goal for which they are hoping, whether that goal is to win a game or recover from a serious injury.

Health researchers have consistently shown that hope is an important factor in developing symptoms of depression and anxiety or whether people will get better after an illness. In a previous chapter, you were introduced to "learned helplessness" and the negative consequences of people believing they are unable to control their own lives. That belief that you are helpless to make things better for yourself often leads to total despair and refusing to participate in treatment as a result.

For people who have experienced a traumatic event, the feeling of hopelessness can seem overwhelming. According to Kerrie Glass and her colleagues at the University of South Carolina, loss of hope is a major factor in psychological distress and coping in survivors. Many traumatized veterans waiting for treatment report a profound sense of hopelessness that can persist for months or even years. Not surprisingly, hope can also determine whether or not someone remains in treatment or drops out after a few sessions.

While hope is an essential part of the recovery process, it is also important to be realistic about what is achievable and what isn't. For people with PTSD, recovery takes time and effort, and expecting symptoms to go away after only a few weeks of therapy or even no therapy at all will simply lead to despair and a sense of failure when the hoped-for outcome doesn't happen. Make certain that you discuss your hopes for recovery with a therapist or other trusted figure and develop a workable plan to put into effect. Most of all, don't let a few setbacks along the way make you lose sight of your ultimate goal. Stay hopeful.

CHAPTER 16

What Is Resilience?

Not every disaster or traumatic event is going to affect people in the same way. Often defined as "the psychological processes that permit individuals to maintain or return to previous levels of well-being and functioning in response to adversity," psychological resilience (or simply resilience, for short) has become a major focus for research into trauma and child development over the past four decades.

Research on Resilience

Beginning in the 1970s, research looking at how well children adjusted to growing up in abusive households found that many of these children seemed relatively unharmed by what was happening around them. Though studies showed that as many as 60–70 percent of abused and neglected children developed behavioral and psychiatric problems later in life, a large minority of these children showed remarkable emotional maturity that protected them and allowed for a fairly normal development despite their upbringing. One researcher, Emmy Werner, coined the term "resilience" to describe what she was finding with these children.

Along with at-risk children, researchers have also looked at resilience in soldiers, people surviving catastrophic life events, physical and sexual abuse, urban poverty, and refugees. Along with reduced risk of PTSD, high resilience has been linked to lower risk of suicide, reduced risk of substance abuse, depression, and other psychiatric symptoms. Resilient people are also less likely to have health complaints and function better in stressful situations.

There can be different ways of measuring resilience, including whether people cope well with stress, have good outcomes despite being exposed to high levels of stress, recover well from trauma, and are able to learn from their previous traumatic experiences to protect themselves in future. Though resilience is often linked to cultural differences in survivors, it also appears to involve different types of protective factors that can limit the impact of traumatic events on survivors. These can include:

- Personality factors and attitudes about their own abilities and the world in general
- The presence of one or more emotionally caring family members able to provide support
- Being part of a supportive community

Resilience can also be linked to self-confidence, intelligence, stress tolerance, sense of personal control, being able to accept change, and having a spiritual outlook on life. There will be more on the different factors underlying resilience in the next section.

QUESTION

What is psychological hardiness?
Psychological hardiness is a personality trait first suggested by psychologist Suzanne Kobassa. It is considered a major factor in psychological resilience and usually defined as the inner strength needed to turn stressful circumstances from potential calamities into opportunities for personal growth. Researchers suggest that hardiness has three main dimensions: commitment to the activities of life, belief in the power to control life events through personal effort, and recognizing that change is an essential part of life.

Why Are Some People More Resilient?

What predicts resilience after a traumatic event? Though we can make guesses over why some people will bounce back after being exposed to traumatic stress while others will not, there seems to be a range of different factors that can make a difference in how well people cope with a major crisis. Though some of these factors can be internal, including things such as personality traits and outlook on life, other factors depend on the type of emotional and physical support they receive before, during, and after the trauma occurs. There is no one pathway to resilience and people can achieve it in a number of different ways.

Individual Differences in Resilience

In any wide-scale traumatic event involving large groups of people, there are always going to be individual differences in how these different people respond to what happened. These individual differences can be due to personality traits, attitudes, how they see themselves, and the methods of coping they use.

Two particular factors linked to resilience following trauma have been proposed by psychologists Anthony Mancini and George Bonanno. The first of the factors, *pragmatic coping*, involves a "whatever it takes" attitude toward whatever is required to cope after a traumatic event. This means being willing to do whatever is needed to get through the event and being realistic about the need to make sacrifices in order to survive. The second factor, *flexible adaptation*, involves the ability to be flexible in adapting to adverse situations. Flexibility is linked to people having a positive mindset, a good self-image, and strong pre-existing beliefs about themselves and the world. Having a strong sense of control can help as well although the sense of being in control may not always be realistic.

Having a strong set of beliefs about the world around them also seems to help protect people from traumatic events. Though those beliefs might be strongly tested by whatever they are experiencing, having confidence that life is ultimately fair and just and that the world will become predictable again in time can help people survive whatever they are experiencing.

Many people dealing with trauma can often find themselves floundering for a sense of "why did this happen?" and trying to find meaning in what they have experienced. While desperately searching for a meaning in what happened can make PTSD symptoms worse in some cases, many survivors can find mental peace by concluding that what they endured had an ultimate purpose.

FACT

In his book, *Man's Search for Meaning*, psychiatrist Viktor Frankl discussed his own traumatic experiences as a Holocaust survivor and stated that "in some ways suffering ceases to be suffering at the moment it finds a meaning, such as the meaning of a sacrifice." Finding meaning is the end-stage of the process of coming to terms with trauma.

Self-confidence is another factor that can make a difference in how well people adapt to a traumatic event. While this confidence can be strongly tested following a major disaster, the people who cope best appear to be the ones who are most confident that they can handle what is happening to them. Whether that confidence is due to prior experiences with similar events or training in emergency preparedness, it can be an important component in preventing later trauma issues.

Finally, being able to retain positive emotions and an optimistic outlook can also be crucial in adapting to a traumatic event. Having a good sense of humor, compassion for fellow survivors, and a willingness to trust others and care about the well-being of survivors can also help prevent later problems.

Demographics of Resilience

Research into resilience suggests that demographic differences such as age, gender, and level of education can predict who will respond better in a traumatic event. Though age appears to be important, with older people tending to be more resilient than younger people, this relationship is not entirely clear. Children are more likely to be traumatized than adults, but older adults can also be vulnerable due to medical problems that can make coping more difficult. Males also appear to be more resilient than females, although this may be a function of cultural and upbringing factors encouraging men in many cultures to be more independent than women.

ALERT

Education can also be an important factor though previous training may not necessarily prepare survivors to deal with a wide-scale disaster completely outside their previous experience. Emergency preparation, including first-aid training and learning basic survival skills, can be an important tool to help ensure effective coping with any traumatic event.

Previous Experience and Level of Exposure

Though some disasters are completely unprecedented, such as the 2004 tsunami, other disasters including hurricanes and tornadoes occur often enough for people living in some areas to make advance preparations and form emergency preparedness plans. Depending on the intensity of the disaster, having emergency plans in place can help protect survivors from the most traumatic effects of many disasters they experience. These plans may not provide complete protection, however, especially if the disaster is much more severe than anticipated. Hurricane Katrina is one example of a disaster that caused enormous damage and trauma even though climate authorities had been warning about the possibility of "the Big One" for decades. While prior experience and training may help make people more resilient to some extent, it may still not be enough when a major disaster strikes.

Another thing to consider is the fact that not every disaster is going to affect people in the same way. Some people will be more hard-hit by a traumatic event than others. Whether this is due to trauma over the loss of a loved one, total destruction of property, or economic circumstances, the risk of trauma is going to vary depending on what people experience and the level of support they receive afterward.

Can Resilience Be Learned?

While counseling programs designed to promote resilience have been developed to help prepare people who are felt to be at risk for later PTSD, including military personnel being deployed to high-risk settings and emergency response workers, most resilience-training programs target people who have already experienced a traumatic event. This can include children and adolescents dealing with a traumatic loss, disaster survivors, or other at-risk populations.

FACT

One example of resilience training is the UK Resilience Programme (UKRP). Developed for use with school-age children, the UKRP is an eighteen-hour cognitive-behavioral treatment program developed to reduce depression in mainstream schools across the United Kingdom. Though early research has shown that it is effective in reducing depression, how helpful the program is in helping children become more resilient is still being studied.

As you saw in a previous chapter, psychological first aid and short-term counseling for people exposed to trauma can help build resilience as a way of learning to cope with trauma. Resilience building in adults usually focuses on education about resilience, learning coping strategies such as problem-solving and stress management, and how to deal with emotional issues as they arise.

Resilience-building programs often focus on developing a sense of trust in other people (and yourself), learning to become more independent, and learning to solve problems as they arise. Resilience building can occur before, during, or after adversity happens. Though many of the factors underlying resilience depend on the level of support people receive, there are still some suggestions you can follow to make yourself better prepared to handle major crises as they occur.

Problem-Solving Therapy

To help combat the feeling of helplessness that many trauma survivors experience, therapists can often teach problem-solving techniques to help them develop greater self-confidence and resilience. This involves applying four basic problem-solving skills to find the "best" solution to any specific problem.

1. **Defining the problem**—This step involves gathering as much information as possible about the problem including setting realistic goals and recognizing the barriers that can prevent success.
2. **Generating alternative solutions**—There is never going to be just one answer to any problem. Ideally, a problem-solver should come up with a number of possible answers by being as creative as possible. Just generate potential solutions, though. Evaluating them to see which is the most practical one comes later.
3. **Decision-making**—Now, the problem-solver needs to evaluate each solution to decide which one to put into effect. This involves weighing the relative costs and benefits and coming up with a practical plan to solve the problem.
4. **Applying the solution and measuring its success**—This involves carrying out the solution, evaluating how well it worked, deciding if the problem has worked, and repeating the entire problem-solving process if that solution failed to solve the problem.

Getting Ready for Adversity

Not every disaster will strike out of the blue. It is possible to prepare ahead of time so that you can respond effectively when the time comes. That includes:

- **Building a support network**—Who can you trust when something bad happens? There are people you have regular contact with and you should make a real effort to keep your relationship with them as strong as possible. Are these people inside or outside your immediate family? Perhaps as important, are you prepared to help them if they are in trouble? A trusting relationship works in both directions.

- **Developing your own sense of independence**—How much help do you think you might need in a crisis situation? Many people are likely more dependent on other people than they are willing to admit. You cannot assume that help will always be available when you need it. Being more independent often means learning to do many things for yourself.

- **Having good role models**—Who do you admire most and would like to imitate when things get tough? Is this someone you know in real life or someone you've read about or seen on screen? If you know how other people responded in similar crisis situations, it might help guide your own behavior.

- **Knowing how to get the help you need**—In an emergency situation, do you know how to contact help? Not just in terms of dialing 911 but knowing how to access other support services whenever you might need them. Knowing about available resources ahead of time can make otherwise overwhelming situations a little easier to bear.

- **Having a stable family and/or community**—Being active in your family and community and paying attention to problems as they arise makes things more stable. Many community agencies depend on volunteers to keep things running smoothly and to provide help for people in need. Helping others can be a good way of ensuring that help is available for you when it's needed.

- **Hoping for the best and planning for the worst**—Make emergency preparations, especially if you are living in a community that is at risk for natural disasters. Take an emergency first-aid course, lay in emergency supplies, get your amateur radio license and buy an emergency radio, etc. Make sure you have enough insurance coverage and have an emergency evacuation plan in place.

- **Being calm and good-natured in your regular life**—Try not to overreact to problems as they arise and learn to handle stress in your daily life. There will always be hassles and inconveniences and learning to take them in stride will help you deal with major hurdles as they come along.

Handling the Unexpected

Every crisis is going to be different and an important part of resilience is handling the unexpected. When disaster strikes, whether it be a personal disaster affecting you alone, or a wide-scale disaster affecting an entire community, there are important steps to help control the sense of panic that likely goes with it:

- In the immortal words of Douglas Adams, "Don't panic!" Take a deep breath, remind yourself that you can handle whatever is happening, and start evaluating the situation and the resources you have at hand.
- Get as much information as possible. Listen to the news and follow the instructions in emergency broadcasts. Unless you are specifically told to evacuate, remaining in your own home and preparing to ride out the disaster is likely your best strategy. Assuming you laid in emergency supplies for at least the seventy-two hours it usually takes for a wide-scale emergency response to get underway, you should be able to cope.
- Reassure family members who might be having difficulty coping with the emergency. Acting as a source of strength for others can provide you with the added motivation to get yourself and others to safety.
- Evaluate your options. Have there been any changes that might put your survival plans in jeopardy? Do you need to take action or are you better off just sitting and waiting? While many people dealing with a crisis feel the need to take action, waiting consumes less energy, which you may need later.
- Draw on your resources as you need them. Don't be hesitant about asking for help if you need it. Though community resources are usually strained during a disaster, people in critical need still get priority (remember the previous section on triage). There is also the help you can get from family members or friends though their own resources

may be limited during the disaster. Many people are afraid of asking for help due to the fear of seeming weak or demanding.

Resiliency after the Emergency

Another key factor in resiliency is learning to think of emergencies as learning situations. We learn from adversity and learning what we did right (or wrong) in one emergency can better prepare us for a similar emergency in future. Accept the fact that you will make mistakes and don't waste time brooding over them. Just make the needed changes to keep from making the same mistake again. So long as you realize that the experience has made you stronger, you will have done all right for yourself and your loved ones.

As part of your process of evaluating how resilient you were during the emergency, it helps to ask yourself the following questions:

- What did you learn about yourself? Were there any problems that you couldn't handle on your own?
- What did you learn about your friends and family? Did they ask for your help and were they willing to help you?
- Did you get the help you needed from community agencies and other support organizations in your area? Would you be willing to go to them again in future?
- Is there anything about yourself that you would need to change to improve your chances in a future emergency? That can include taking training courses, becoming more physically fit or losing weight, or just realizing that you need to be more confident in your own ability to respond.

Is Resilience Enough?

People showing resilience are not necessarily immune to the symptoms of PTSD. Many survivors are able to function at work just fine but may still have difficulty getting to sleep at night because of nightmares of previous traumas. While resilience is often described as being all-or-nothing (either you have it or you don't), more recent research suggests that there are different degrees of resilience in survivors.

Virtually anyone dealing with PTSD will show resilience to some extent, and it is perfectly possible for survivors to experience emotional distress while having the resilience to keep it from completely disrupting their lives. Part of the value of treatment comes from building on this resilience and helping people learn the skills to increase their ability to cope with all the different symptoms that are causing distress. There is also a practical danger in how resilience research can be applied in real life. Therapists need to avoid telling PTSD patients that "increasing resilience" is a goal of treatment since that often leads to feelings of guilt because they are "not resilient enough."

Being resilient is not necessarily about being a rugged action-hero type who can survive anything. It just means not letting your own fears get in the way of doing what needs to be done. Though some survivors are better able to cope than others, that may be due to a combination of different factors including simply being luckier or having better emotional support than other survivors who may have experienced greater loss.

There is still much to learn about resilience and how different protective factors can help people cope with risk over time. There may also be a trade-off between successful resilience in some areas of life and not in others. As one example, the emotional detachment that can damage the relationships that survivors have with loved ones can also make them better able to survive future traumatic events.

ALERT

Research looking at successful aging in older adults (average age of seventy-seven years) found that resilience was a significant predictor of whether older people considered themselves to be aging successfully. Along with reducing depression, increasing resilience in older people can be important in helping them remain mentally and physically active even in their declining years.

It is also important to note that resilience is not the same thing as post-traumatic growth. Used to describe the positive psychological changes that can occur after experiencing trauma, post-traumatic growth (PTG) can lead to increased self-confidence, a greater appreciation of life, changes in personal priorities, increased respect for other people, and a general sense of being stronger for what was experienced. Ironically, resilient people are less likely to report the same feeling of personal growth or search for meaning that many survivors report following a major life event. Like resilience, however, PTG does not necessarily occur in all areas of life and it may not lead to major life changes. How people grow and develop after experiencing a traumatic event often depends on the treatment they receive and the emotional support provided by the important people in their lives.

Though programs have been designed to encourage resilience and post-traumatic growth, many researchers recommend against pushing survivors into treatment for which they may not be ready. The best treatment programs encourage building on skills that trauma survivors already demonstrate and helping them develop further skills over time. The process of developing greater resilience or improved post-traumatic growth can take months or even years.

Incorporating Resilience Into Everyday Life

There are different ways of enhancing resilience in your life. Building up resilience in yourself is not necessarily enough to ensure that you and the people you care about are going to be safe. For parents, encouraging children to be more independent and self-confident can be an important part of resilience, and there are even resilience-building programs that have been developed for use in schools.

Building Resilience in Children

Many of these resilience-building programs are specifically designed for older or younger children, depending on how well developed their cognitive skills are. Perhaps as important, building resilience in children depends on how well developed their interpersonal skills are. Children who have difficulty learning to trust people might not have the confidence or the social skills needed to handle a serious crisis, especially if it involves problems with other children or adults. Resilience-building can often take time and effort, especially with children who are at risk for experiencing trauma, whether because of family problems or economic hardship.

The American Psychological Association has published a *Resilience Guide for Parents and Teachers* describing different ways to build resilience in children and adolescents. These include:

1. Teach children to make connections. This can mean making friends and learning to feel empathy for others. Children need to learn that being a friend is a good way of making friends. For teachers, this means ensuring that some children are not being isolated and encouraging them to connect with others to build resilience.

2. Teach children to help others. By learning to help others, children can learn that they are capable of making a difference. Parents and teachers can encourage this process by asking for the child's help on a task that the child is able to carry out. Children can also be encouraged to brainstorm for ideas on how to help others.

3. Maintain a daily routine. Children need structure in their lives and can often be made uncomfortable by unexpected changes. Young children are especially vulnerable to unpleasant surprises in their lives and need reassurance. Encourage children to develop their own routines.

4. Take breaks. If children are disturbed by something in their regular routine, such as seeing something upsetting on television, they should be encouraged to take a brief break so they can focus on something else instead. Doing something completely different can be an excellent tension reliever.

5. Teach children self-care. Children should be encouraged to develop healthy eating habits, regular exercise, and know how to relax. Learning to stay balanced makes stressful situations easier to deal with, both for children and adults.

6. Teach children to set goals. While younger children may have difficulty making long-term plans, learning to set and meet short-term goals can be a good confidence-builder. Parents and teachers should also provide verbal praise to children who meet their goals to reinforce their goal-setting behavior. That also encourages them to set larger goals for themselves.

7. Encourage children to have a positive self-view. Children need to be reminded of how they handled previous problems. Along with building up their self-confidence, they can also learn that past challenges can make them better able to handle future challenges. Encouraging them to develop a sense of humor can be important as well.

8. Teach children to be more optimistic. Although children may have difficulty developing a long-term perspective, they can learn that there is a future beyond whatever short-term problem they are facing. For teachers, using examples from history can help children learn that life always goes on.

9. Have children recognize that crises can also be learning situations. Encourage them to learn from whatever painful situation they are encountering so they can be better prepared for the future.

10. Teach children that change is part of living. Goals are going to change with time as new goals come along to take their place. Though change can be scary, it can be challenging as well.

Parents and teachers should watch for signs of extreme stress in children, including regression, separation anxiety, and general anxiety. Children need a safe place where they can escape from the stresses of daily living, especially during times when they are experiencing more stress than usual. This can include bullying, teasing, and other social pressures from peers. During times of extreme stress, such as after the death of a loved one, adults need to share their own feelings with children to show them that grief is a normal part of life.

Adolescents occupy a particularly gray area when it comes to maturity. Though relatively mature physically, they still lack the emotional balance of adulthood and are prone to emotional highs and lows due to hormonal changes. Encourage teens to do their best and to use the skills they have already learned to handle high-stress situations as they arise. Even for children who have handled traumatic events in the past, dealing with new traumatic events as they arise can be a major challenge. Resilience will grow and change over time as life circumstances change.

Making Families More Resilient

As part of her practice dealing with families in crisis, Duke University Medical Center psychologist Robin Gurwitch, PhD stresses the importance of teaching good parenting skills to improve family resilience. Using parent-child interaction therapy, Gurwitch and her colleagues combine personal coaching, practice exercises, and supportive counseling to help parents learn positive parenting skills and unlearn other parenting practices that might interfere with the normal emotional development of their children.

With funding from the Substance Abuse and Mental Health Services Administration (SAMHSA) and in cooperation with military bases, parent-child interaction therapy programs are being increasingly used to help military families. Though still in the early stages, military family therapy has already helped reduce reported stress levels in parents while their children are showing few behavior problems. Given the special stress issues faced by military families dealing with deployment and frequent moving, families involved in the treatment sessions are finding them enjoyable as well as useful.

The treatment program begins by observing how parents interact with their children under different control situations to see how they handle stress issues. The counselors then coach the parents on improving their relationship with their children and managing behavioral problems as they occur. The parents practice the skills at home in brief homework assignments (usually just a few minutes each day).

Examples of Family Resilience Training

Another treatment program that has been developed for promoting resilience in families is known as FOCUS (Families Overcoming Under Stress). Designed for military families with children ranging from three to eighteen years of age, FOCUS is currently being used on twenty-two U.S. military bases and has helped thousands of patients. The program includes psychoeducation about PTSD and other mental health problems, as well as resilience training in how to regulate emotions, set goals, manage trauma, and communicate more effectively. Couples counseling and marital therapy can also be included for families dealing with potential breakup. Given that many families needing treatment are separated by long-term deployments, video counseling and mobile applications are also available.

A second treatment program, titled HomeFront Strong, was developed by University of Michigan psychologist Michelle Kees and social worker

Kate Bullard, specifically for military partners dealing with deployment. Along with providing counseling and support services, HomeFront Strong can also help families deal with feeling isolated from other military families when they are not living on military bases. Though still in the pilot stage, the HomeFront Strong program is already showing great promise as a way of improving family resilience.

For parents and families unable to participate in direct programming, the Department of Veterans Affairs and the Department of Defense National Center for Telehealth and Technology has developed a web-based parenting course for military families. Titled "Parenting for Service Members and Veterans," the course can be taken online at *www.veteranparenting.org*. The six modules of the course include:

- Reconnecting with your family
- Promoting positive parent-child interactions
- Helping your child with difficult emotions and behaviors
- Positive approach to discipline
- Managing stress and emotions as a parent
- Parenting with emotional and physical challenges

The course site also includes a useful resources page with links to local treatment programs, help for veterans, and online parenting resources. Some of those resources are also listed in Appendix C.

Resilience in the Workplace

For most people, the greatest amount of stress they will encounter in their daily lives will be on the job. Most surveys looking at working Americans suggest that at least one in four workers report major job stress. Sources of stress include feeling powerless, unreasonable work demands, financial strain, and lack of support from employers and fellow workers. The trauma of losing a job can be as devastating as any other emotional loss and prolonged unemployment (or underemployment) can be a major drain on available resources.

Not surprisingly, workplace stress can lead to a variety of medical problems including cardiovascular disease, depression, and job burnout. Other common problems linked to workplace stress can include suicide, cancer, and many of the same medical issues associated with chronic PTSD.

FACT

Psychological capital (PsyCap) is a term that has become increasingly popular in the positive psychology community. Referring to the total resources available for each individual, PsyCap is made up of the psychological resources of hope, efficacy, resilience, and optimism. Research into workplace psychology suggests that workers with strong psychological capital tend to have better attitudes, are more well-behaved, and perform better than workers who have reduced PsyCap and higher stress.

In recent years, research into occupational health has suggested that career resilience can be an important factor in preventing many of the problems associated with workplace stress. Usually defined as the process of adapting to adversity in the workplace and using life experiences to guide the career choices people make, career resilience can help protect workers from burnout and other health problems.

Developing career resilience typically involves (1) doing a self-evaluation to determine personal skills, interests, and type of job for which people are best suited; (2) acquiring new skills to become more competitive; and (3) keeping track of new job openings to find a position that is more suitable. The workplace is always changing and being as flexible as possible while upgrading job skills can help protect against sudden unemployment and workplace stress.

Resilience and Aging

While people are living longer than their parents (and certainly their grandparents), there is no guarantee that the retirement years will be free from stress. Even assuming that your financial needs are met (and for many people, they won't be), growing older will mean new challenges and a greater need for resilience. Even though new health problems will develop over time, making healthy choices such as sensible dieting and regular exercise can keep you healthier longer. It is also important to stay mentally active, whether through life-long learning, volunteer work, part-time work, or forming new interests.

Many of the suggested ways for building resilience still apply for older adults. They include finding positive role models who have aged successfully, letting go of old grudges and painful memories that might be interfering with living, renewing old relationships or changing ones that are not bringing you the satisfaction you used to enjoy, or taking up new causes.

One good strategy for many older adults is to act as a mentor for younger people in need of guidance. These can be members of your own family or people you meet along the way. Offering your own experience to help them deal with their own problems can be a great source of satisfaction as well as providing you with a new support network.

Three basic steps for maintaining resilience and high functioning for older adults include:

1. **Selection**—Be more selective about the activities you engage in to avoid wasting time and energy on things that provide little benefit. One of the advantages of retirement is being able to choose your own interests and not getting bogged down by what doesn't matter.
2. **Optimization**—With fewer activities, older adults can devote more of their time and attention to the things that interest them. Arthur Rubinstein gave piano recitals for over eight decades by concentrating on those pieces he could still do despite problems of old age.
3. **Compensation**—As people decline, mentally and physically, they are often able to compensate by using workarounds to avoid problems. Using modern computer technology, older adults can use online resources and day planners to keep track of important information and to stay mentally active longer.

Resilience can also be useful in avoiding the emotional problems that develop in old age, including depression resulting from feeling useless or unappreciated. As we develop resilience, the skills we learn will become automatic with time and can be used at any point in life when they are needed most.

CHAPTER 17

When PTSD Goes Untreated: How Not to Cope

As you have already seen in previous chapters, most people will experience at least one potentially traumatic event in their lifetimes though only a minority will develop PTSD symptoms. But what happens when people fail to get the treatment they need? Many people who experience trauma may never receive treatment, whether it is because they do not feel that they need it or because treatment is simply not available. According to World Health Organization studies looking at PTSD, most people never receive treatment that would help them recover and live normal lives. Of those that are able to access some sort of treatment, the amount of help they receive is often limited by the stigma that people with mental illness often face.

PTSD Does Not Just Go Away

Though most people dealing with traumatic stress will not develop PTSD, a sizable minority will, due to various risk factors making them more vulnerable. Many of those risk factors have been covered in previous chapters but can include previous exposure to trauma, lack of proper emotional support, and exposure to additional stress that makes survivors unable to cope.

The consequences of not receiving treatment are harder to predict since people can vary depending on their inner resources and the support they receive from friends and family. Many people developing post-traumatic symptoms shortly after experiencing a life-changing event may well find those symptoms subsiding with time even if they never seek treatment. That does not mean that the trauma has been forgotten, however. While post-traumatic symptoms may subside with time, later exposure to a similar traumatic event or even something that reminds them of the event may be enough for post-traumatic symptoms to re-emerge worse than ever. For survivors who have not received treatment or have not been educated about the potential problems posed by trauma exposure, dealing with these new symptoms can be overwhelming. Some therapists have even suggested that cases of untreated PTSD can be thought of as "psychological time bombs" ready to be cued unexpectedly at any point in their lives as a result of different trigger events.

Does Time Heal All Wounds?

Do traumatic symptoms simply go away over time? Studies of assault victims, including victims of sexual assault, suggest that while the majority of victims meet diagnostic criteria for PTSD shortly after the event (one or two weeks post-assault), this can decline sharply after three months. With normal processing of the trauma, people coming to terms with what they experienced can help reduce symptom distress significantly over the first six months. Once that initial period is over, however, many trauma survivors reach a plateau where very little further recovery takes place without proper treatment. The symptoms are often still there and can re-emerge for a variety of reasons. So time does *not* heal all wounds.

It is important that even survivors who choose not to seek treatment or who feel that treatment is unnecessary educate themselves about potential short- and long-term consequences of trauma. Recognizing possible risks may help them avoid the development of additional problems and cope more successfully. The book list in Appendix D is a good place to start.

Self-Medication

Following any sort of trauma, the temptation to relieve pain through alcohol, street drugs, misused prescription medications, or some combination of the three can be overwhelming for many people. A survey conducted five years after Hurricane Agnes found that half of all flood survivors reported drinking as a way of relieving stress compared to only 16 percent of people from neighboring regions that were less affected. Following the eruption of Mount St. Helens in Washington, there was a sharp rise in alcohol-related convictions. Along with increased alcohol use, survivors may also report greater use of tobacco, sleeping pills, and tranquilizers as much as three years after the traumatic event occurred.

In a meta-analysis of fifty-two research studies looking at disaster victims, about 35 percent showed increased alcohol use after a disaster while 23 percent showed increased drug use. Though many survivors justify their substance use as an effective way of coping with short-term stress, the problem does not necessarily go away.

Though exposure to trauma does not necessarily lead to increased drug or alcohol use, the high rates of PTSD symptoms among people seeking treatment for drug or alcohol abuse has been consistently demonstrated across different research studies. Not only is the risk of abuse greater, but people with combined PTSD/substance abuse problems also have a poorer outcome than people having either problem alone. Using self-medication with drugs or alcohol to deal with PTSD symptoms does not just affect the trauma survivors directly, but also spouses and children who are at risk for developing drug and alcohol problems later in life.

Emotional Numbing

Since many survivors of serious trauma find themselves losing control of their emotions, suppressing those emotions can seem like a reasonable way of coping. This is especially true for survivors who are afraid of harming themselves or the people around them. Except, these same emotions are also necessary for interacting with other people and maintaining intimate relationships. Experiencing emotions is also needed for good mental health and for being able to handle stress effectively. Ultimately, feelings make us more human and survivors suppressing their emotions can become detached from the world around them.

But these emotions never really go away. They are still there below the surface and can come boiling out at the worst possible time. Anger is the emotion most likely to emerge during stressful episodes when self-control is strained. Angry outbursts can often be the only way some survivors can interact with the world, and these outbursts typically lead to survivors becoming even more isolated by driving family or friends away.

FACT

There is usually a protective purpose to different emotions. Even negative emotions such as anger and fear play a role in protecting you from external threats or avoiding harm. Both positive and negative emotions are needed and learning to express them comfortably is an important part of the recovery process.

Avoiding Unpleasant Reminders

While a certain amount of avoidance of unpleasant reminders is always going to occur and can even be healthy to some degree, many survivors take avoidance behavior to extremes. This behavior can take different forms, depending on what survivors are trying to avoid. As you have already seen in the section on triggers, certain sights, sounds, and odors can all trigger traumatic memories and survivors can go to extreme lengths to avoid being reminded of what happened. This can lead to survivors isolating themselves from most social situations and even refusing to leave their homes to avoid being reminded. While this may work as a coping strategy in the short term as they come to terms with trauma, treatments such as exposure therapy can help survivors learn to confront their anxiety and become more comfortable dealing with reminders.

Short-Term Consequences

Though post-traumatic symptoms can drop sharply in the months immediately following a traumatic event, the emotional turmoil many survivors experience can still prevent them from returning to a normal life. Along with symptoms such as avoidance and emotional numbing, survivors can also experience:

Sleep Disorders

Even as other post-traumatic stress symptoms are successfully dealt with through treatment, post-traumatic sleep problems including chronic insomnia, nightmares, and disrupted sleep can still persist. While sleep medication can be used as a short-term solution, people experiencing trauma-induced sleep problems need to learn how to sleep naturally, without becoming dependent on sleep aids.

Nightmares can be especially distressing for people dealing with severe trauma since the dreams can involve "reliving" the traumatic memory. These vivid nightmares can be accompanied by violent thrashing and other body movements that can cause injury. Though vivid nightmares usually fade with time, they can be particularly distressing in the early months while survivors are still coming to terms with their memories.

Sleep problems such as insomnia and nightmares can lead to additional problems such as depression, mood shifts, delayed recovery, and even hallucinations in severe cases. Lack of sleep can also lead to reduced coping resources for dealing with the stress most survivors experience as they attempt to put their lives back together following a life-changing event.

Treatment for sleep problems usually focuses on sleep and nightmare management (training in sleep hygiene and education about trauma-induced sleep problems). For people not receiving formal treatment, drug treatment with benzodiazepines may also be helpful in controlling nightmares but not necessarily improving sleep quality.

Sleep Apnea

A related condition that may also contribute to sleep problems is sleep apnea. Due to disrupted breathing at night, sleep apnea patients may experience episodes of shallow or infrequent breathing while sleeping. Many sleep apnea patients have no idea of what is happening, but they may be prone to vivid nightmares, disturbed sleep, and extreme fatigue during the day. Sleep apnea may occur due to lack of proper respiration (central sleep apnea) or because of physical obstruction in the breathing tube (obstructive sleep apnea). People with untreated sleep apnea can develop psychiatric symptoms including panic attacks, insomnia, and depression. Sleep apnea is also a risk factor for heart disease, strokes, and high blood pressure.

Symptoms of sleep apnea may also be similar to sleep problems linked to PTSD. Some apnea patients may even become afraid to sleep at night. While sleep apnea is typically diagnosed by a formal sleep study conducted in a sleep laboratory, family members may notice loud snoring, nightmares, and violent thrashing at night. Treatments for sleep apnea can include corrective surgery in the windpipe and use of a specialized breathing machine known as a CPAP (continuous pathway airway pressure) device. A sleep specialist can make the best recommendation for treatment. Sleep medication is not recommended for sleep apnea patients, but weight loss and proper nutrition can help control symptoms.

Emotional Detachment

Dissociation refers to the psychological state of being disconnected from reality. As was mentioned in previous chapters, dissociation is often used by trauma survivors as a defense mechanism to help cope with extremely traumatic experiences. Dissociative symptoms can fall along a continuum from mild dissociation to far more severe psychiatric problems. Research looking into dissociative symptoms in trauma survivors has shown that the symptoms are most likely to occur immediately following a traumatic event with the symptoms gradually declining over time. Cases of dissociation have also been seen in trauma survivors occurring years after the initial trauma, although they are relatively rare.

FACT

Just remember that dissociation can be a perfectly normal reaction to an extremely traumatic situation. All it takes is a single traumatic event severe enough for a survivor to try to block out the memory as a way of avoiding pain. In some cases, dissociation can be severe enough to lead to psychogenic amnesia (in which traumatic memories are completely blocked out) or dissociative identity disorder (forming a new identity to avoid dealing with the survivor's former life).

Secondary Gains

The longer your recovery is delayed, the easier it will become to identify yourself as an "invalid" who is unable to take charge of your life. Remember back in grade school when you were sick with the flu for a week or so and how hard it was to return to school afterward? Think of how hard it would have been if you had been out sick for weeks or months. For people who are recovering from any kind of illness, there is often a payoff in terms of being able to delay having to make important life decisions. There can also be financial and social payoffs such as receiving disability benefits or having family members act as full-time caregivers.

People who have had PTSD symptoms for a long time can find those symptoms becoming part of their sense of identity. For some survivors, overcoming their PTSD symptoms can seem like losing a part of themselves because they are unable to see themselves as more than their symptoms. Other survivors can see their symptoms as a way of justifying the lack of progress they made in meeting their life plans.

Whatever the reason for the secondary gain, it can become a major barrier preventing people from moving on with their lives.

Self-Destructive Behavior

Though the increased risk of suicide in trauma survivors was already covered in a previous chapter, there are other kinds of self-destructive behavior as well. Research studies looking at active-duty military service personnel before and after they were deployed overseas as well as in civilian life found that people with psychiatric problems, including PTSD, were more likely to take part in risky recreational activities including unprotected sex, illegal drug use, "thrill-seeking," aggressive behavior, suicide attempts, and nonsuicidal self-injuries. They were also more likely to own firearms and to have problems with aggressive driving. These risk behaviors were more common during civilian life than when they were deployed and were strongly linked to problems with coping.

ESSENTIAL

People with a history of childhood sexual abuse or violence are also more likely to engage in self-harm behavior such as wrist-cutting, which also appears linked to PTSD symptoms as well as long-term personality problems. Not surprisingly, people with PTSD symptoms were also found to be more prone to problems with impulsive and antisocial behavior.

Long-Term Consequences

The potential role of untreated trauma can be especially strong in victims of physical and sexual abuse. A classic 1984 study looking at psychiatric inpatients found that as many as half had a history of abuse, mostly by family members. Abuse victims often showed difficulty coping with anger and aggression, low self-esteem, and being unable to trust others. In many cases, the traumatic abuse had gone unreported and untreated for years, leading to later psychiatric problems. Based on this research, psychiatrist Elaine Carmen and her colleagues have referred to this as the *victim-to-patient process*.

For many trauma victims, there can be seven major categories of long-term reactions:

1. Post-traumatic reactions (whether short- or long-term)
2. Emotional reactions (such as survivor guilt, depression, self-blame)
3. Poor self-perceptions and beliefs (feeling "dirty," contaminated, shamed)
4. Physical and somatic symptoms (chronic pain, headaches, hyperarousal)
5. Sexual reactions (sexual aversion, impotence)
6. Interpersonal problems (inability to trust, fear of relationships, parenting problems, fear of intimacy)
7. Social problems (isolation or fear of being alone)

Many of these symptoms can be linked to a history of childhood trauma and can become diagnosed in different ways, depending on how the trauma was dealt with at the time.

And the symptoms can persist for decades afterward. A 2005 research study of political detainees in Romania found that PTSD symptoms could persist as long as four decades in a third of the survivors. Along with the PTSD symptoms, former detainees reported problems with major depression, substance abuse, and somatic problems that persisted well into old age. Not only does unresolved PTSD increase the likelihood of developing later mental illness, the clinical outcome tends to be worse than in mental patients without a history of trauma.

FACT

A 1990 study looking at survivors of the *Alexander L. Kielland* oil-rig platform accident in 1980 that killed 123 people over a nine-year period found significant differences between survivors and nonsurvivors in terms of number of sick leaves from work and the length of these sick leaves. Survivors were eight times more likely than nonsurvivors to have psychiatric diagnoses. They were also far more accident-prone than nonpatients, suggesting they were a greater danger to themselves and the people around them.

Along with the damage that untreated PTSD symptoms can have on survivors and their families, there is also the damage that comes from survivors unable to work or being dependent on family members for support. The economic damage from lack of treatment for PTSD can be considerable as well.

An Australian study published in 2003 found that cases of PTSD resulting from automobile accidents led to substantially higher economic and health-care costs than cases in which PTSD was successfully treated.

Negative Attitude Toward Mental Health

Though researchers have found that having a negative attitude toward mental health professionals can keep many people from asking for help in dealing with their PTSD symptoms, a new research study suggests that cynicism may play a role as well. According to Minneapolis Veterans Affairs Health Care researchers, veterans scoring high on measures of cynicism (i.e., having a general negative worldview and pessimism) are far less likely to accept referrals to mental health workers because they refuse to believe that treatment can work. The study focused on National Guard veterans who had served in Iraq and were later diagnosed with traumatic stress symptoms. Compared to a control group, scoring high in cynicism before being deployed significantly predicted refusal to attend treatment long after the veterans returned. For many people reluctant to seek treatment, helping to change their attitudes about mental health care and their general outlook on the world may be an important first step in getting them the help they need.

CHAPTER 18

Where to Go from Here

So, assuming you've worked hard to attend treatment and try to get your symptoms under control, what is the next step? While trauma survivors often dwell on how their lives have changed as a result of their experience and typically express the hope of "getting their old life back," that hope is usually not realistic. For better or worse, your life has changed. Obsessing about returning to a time that is already past is only going to add to the stress of coming to terms with PTSD symptoms.

It might be better to recognize that your traumatic experiences are now a part of you and that the things you have learned as a result can make you better able to handle new crises in the future. Whether by sharing your experiences or acting as a mentor for other people going through similar crises, you can move on with your life and make valuable contributions to the world as well.

As you continue to heal, you will learn that surviving a traumatic event can open the door to a range of new possibilities in your life. People who have endured horrifying experiences can find their lives becoming better in unexpected ways. These can include:

- New opportunities to develop other life interests, to explore a new life path, or to find meaning in your life.
- Learning more about how much inner strength you have and recognizing that every experience, whether good or bad, can contribute to learning about yourself. That can mean greater confidence and a more practical way of looking at the world.
- Growing spiritually and developing a greater appreciation for life. Often, it is only after a life-changing experience that we realize how wondrous life can be. That can mean learning to put daily hassles into perspective and not getting worried about petty concerns.
- Learning to relate better with others. It is often through personal experience with adversity that we can learn how to have compassion for others and to develop greater patience and understanding.

FACT

After surviving the Bataan Death March in 1942 as well as years of being a Japanese prisoner of war, Bert Bank returned home and retired from the military. He became a radio pioneer and founded two radio stations as well as the Alabama Football Radio Network. Major Bank also served terms in the Alabama House of Representatives and Senate and narrowly lost the election for lieutenant governor in 1978. His book, *Back from the Living Dead: The Infamous Death March and 33 Months in a Japanese Prison,* was self-published in 1945 and is still one of the most gripping stories of survival ever written.

Ultimately, whether you will be able to grow and adapt after surviving a traumatic event is something you will need to discover for yourself.

Living Life with PTSD

Though healing can take a lifetime, the coping skills learned in therapy can make each day a little easier to bear as the symptoms of trauma slowly come under control. Some of the signs that healing is taking place can include:

1. Being able to recall and dismiss the traumatic memory at will. The intrusive flashbacks, nightmares, triggers, and distressing reminders are, if not completely gone, as least more infrequent. That means working through problems with dissociation by integrating traumatic memories and putting them into a proper perspective.
2. When you recall the traumatic event, you can experience normal emotion, and do not feel detached or overwhelmed. By coming to terms with the traumatic memories, you can confront the avoidant symptoms and develop healthier ways of coping.
3. The symptoms of depression, anxiety, and other negative emotions are more under control than before. By developing a greater sense of balance and controlling automatic thoughts contributing to feelings of hopelessness and pessimism, the negative emotions will seem less overwhelming.
4. The sense of isolation is no longer there and you have regained your ability to form emotional attachments with other people. That includes normal relationships with friends and family as well as being capable of intimacy. The old fears about letting people into your life will no longer make you build emotional barriers.
5. You have regained your feeling of self-confidence and moved beyond the feelings of self-blame. That also means no longer obsessing about the past and what you should have done differently. By grounding yourself in the present, you will be able to move on with your future plans.
6. You have resumed a normal sex life, including resuming your old intimate relationship or forming new ones.

7. You are more comfortable with your feelings without having to rely on emotional detachment. You will be able to confront those feelings and calm yourself down whenever they start to overwhelm you.

8. You are making realistic plans for the future and taking responsibility for moving ahead with your life. That also means giving up the secondary gains that might be preventing you from moving ahead with recovery (e.g., refusing to help yourself because you are "sick").

ESSENTIAL

For many survivors, learning to thrive means more than simply finding the strength to keep going. It means making the conscious decision to live well despite the memories of traumatic events faced in the past. It also means learning to have optimism about the future, not in terms of assuming that everything will be wonderful, but in resolving to find something to enjoy no matter what happens.

There is no one road to recovery for every trauma survivor. Some will recover quickly while others will take years to move past their experiences. There will be setbacks and delays along the way but the confidence you develop over time will help you stay on track. It also means recognizing that life is never perfect, but it can still be good.

Moving On

In recent years, research has shown that trauma cannot only be overcome but can make survivors stronger as well. Post-traumatic growth can take many forms and survivors often report viewing what they have experienced as a source of strength and inspiration. The Mexican painter Frida Kahlo survived polio, a serious traffic accident, and multiple miscarriages to become one of the greatest painters of her generation. Adversity can be a source of emotional and spiritual growth, and many famous people have attributed their success to what they learned about themselves during the dark periods in their lives.

According to positive psychology research, traumatic experiences can lead to survivors discovering new possibilities in their lives and finding new directions to take. In many ways, dealing with disaster often means rediscovering the joy of life, though this may seem impossible at first for many survivors. They can also have a greater appreciation of the people around them and learn not to take these important relationships for granted.

Although it is important not to minimize the suffering that trauma survivors experience, it is also important to recognize that traumatic experiences do not mark the end of the world, but are often the beginning of a new life for many survivors. Coming to terms with trauma often means relearning how to deal with the world around you and how to interact with the important people in your life.

Research into post-traumatic growth suggests that optimism and mental flexibility can play an important role in helping survivors move on with their lives after adversity. Though not every traumatic event is going to have a positive outcome, survivors can recover and thrive if they accept that future growth and happiness is possible despite what has happened to them.

What is event centrality?
Defined as the degree to which an individual believes a negative event has become a core part of his or her identity, event centrality occurs when survivors come to view a traumatic event as a part of their personal identity. Rather than moving on and placing the event in perspective, some survivors begin to think of themselves in part, or perhaps exclusively, as someone who has been victimized. Research into event centrality suggests that it may be strongly linked to post-traumatic distress and development of later mental health problems.

Gaining Control

Even though feeling helpless is one of the diagnostic features of PTSD, part of the recovery process involves learning that survivors can take control of their own lives. Participating in treatment and developing coping skills can help survivors regain that sense of control in their daily lives. Being in control means learning how to cope with symptoms at work, home, school, or any other setting where problems can arise.

For many survivors, regaining a sense of control that was lost due to a traumatic experience can take years of testing themselves in new situations and applying the skills they learned. It also means taking a series of small steps and not being discouraged by the inevitable setbacks that will occur along the way. Simply paying attention to those inner feelings that serve to warn about doing things you are not ready for can help build that sense of self-control. But it is also necessary to take risks and learn from any mistakes you make. And, yes, you will make mistakes. That is simply part of the process when it comes to recovering from trauma.

While there are things in life over which you have no direct control, you can still control how you choose to react to new crises that come along, especially if you choose to identify them as threats or challenges. It's also important to recognize that self-control is something that can be learned and practiced like any other skill.

With greater self-control comes the opportunity to regain a sense of joy in your life. According to research conducted by psychologists David Myers and Michael Fordyce, happiness is often associated with:

- Self-esteem, peace of mind, and spiritual commitment
- Healthy habits such as good nutrition, regular exercise, and getting enough sleep
- Rewarding social interactions in life, including developing high-quality, supportive relationships with family and friends
- Active involvement with meaningful and satisfying activities, including volunteer work, spending time with loved ones, pursuing educational or vocational goals, or anything else that can make you feel more energetic
- Learning mastery and control by developing an active coping style, including effective problem-solving, setting realistic goals, and planning ahead to achieve those goals

Not all of these things are going to be accomplished overnight, but forming short-term goals will provide you with the confidence to realize that the long-term goals are achievable as well.

Just take it one day at a time.

ESSENTIAL

Try to write down those goals you'd like to see yourself achieve. Picture how you would like to see yourself in a) a month, b) three months, c) six months, d) one year, e) five years. Make your goals realistic and achievable and begin planning out your strategy for achieving each goal. Always remember to discuss these goals and your coping strategies with your therapist to ensure that you will be able to do things slowly and effectively.

Easing the Destructive Impact

Recovering from trauma means learning to accept your fears and recognizing that they are natural consequences of surviving a traumatic event. That means learning not to judge yourself for what you are experiencing rather than feeling ashamed because you can't "just get over it." Through treatment and by interacting with other survivors, you can learn that their life stories are not so different from yours and that the symptoms you are experiencing can help make you stronger in future.

That also means letting go of the various assumptions and ideas that might get in the way of your recovery. These same assumptions may also be interfering with the relationship you have with family and friends. Ideas such as "I can't be a burden to others" and "Nobody can possibly know how I feel" are common in trauma survivors who are afraid of becoming too dependent on others or who are terrified of being abandoned. Learning to let other people into your life is also a natural part of recovering.

Learning to recognize the emotions you are feeling and how to handle them is another crucial step in recovery. That means being able to defuse anger and deal with stress naturally and effectively. Part of the training you receive in therapy involves learning about relaxation training, stress management, and anger management, which are all vital coping skills. Review any course materials you have on a regular basis to ensure that the skills you learn stay fresh in your memory. Once they become automatic, problems with anger and stress will become easier to handle.

ALERT

Part of the treatment process, especially for people in family or couples therapy, is learning about communication problems that might be damaging your relationships. Recognize how you might be alienating other people and learn better ways to express affection, resolve problems as they arise, and set appropriate boundaries in personal relationships. Communication is especially important for intimate relationships in preventing misunderstandings and resentments that might sabotage them.

Finally, you need to take a step back and try to learn from any mistakes you might make along the way. Don't become discouraged or decide that things are hopeless. Giving in to pessimism will make your recovery much harder than it needs to be. Ask the people around you about their own impression of how well you are doing and take their suggestions seriously.

Dealing with stress also means identifying high-risk situations and recognizing those triggers that can lead to problems arising. Develop a strong coping plan for each high-risk situation that you are likely to encounter. With some advance planning, you can anticipate many of these high-risk situations and have specific coping strategies in place to deal with the negative symptoms as they occur. As you move through therapy and gain more confidence in yourself, learning and applying those coping strategies will become easier with time.

While many survivors think that avoiding these situations is the best strategy, that isn't always going to be practical or safe. There will always be unpleasant people and situations out there and avoidance can't work forever. Better to recognize how to handle things as they arise. That includes using preplanned self-talk statements to replace the negative thinking that often accompanies feelings of panic. These statements can be used before, during, and after the stressful situation occurs to reinforce your self-confidence.

Here are some of the self-talk statements you can use:

Before:
What is the worst thing that can happen?
I know I am capable of doing this.
I have the skills I need.
Situations like this are just part of life.

During:
This isn't so bad.
I'm doing fine.
Just a little while longer.
Just relax and breathe calmly.

After:
I did pretty well.
It will be even easier next time
What have I learned from this?
Some symptoms don't mean a total relapse.

Once you have your coping plan in place, don't forget to practice it a few times to make certain you know what to do. A brief practice session visualizing the situation as it unfolds can help you mentally prepare yourself. Don't let setbacks get you down. Treat them as learning experiences instead.

Learning to Cope in the Future

In 1942, Viktor Frankl and his entire family were transferred to Theresienstadt Ghetto where he used his skills as a psychiatrist to help fellow internees cope with the shock and grief of being imprisoned by the Nazis. These skills helped keep him alive after he and his wife were transferred to Auschwitz, where his wife later died. Following his liberation by American troops, Frankl wrote extensively about his experiences and the deaths of most of his family in the Holocaust. His book, *Man's Search for Meaning*, became an international classic and introduced the world to his new school of psychotherapy that he named logotherapy.

In his book, Frankl wrote that those prisoners who had strong goals and a clear reason for living were more likely to survive traumatic experiences. In his own case, he was able to keep himself alive by picturing himself years later giving lectures about his experiences and how he was able to use what he learned to keep others alive. Even in a death camp, it was still possible to take pleasure in seeing the sunrise through barbed wire and by sharing jokes with fellow prisoners.

Frankl also wrote about the importance of love as a means of surviving any hardship. In describing one of the harshest episodes he experienced in the camp, he also wrote:

> A thought transfixed me: for the first time in my life I saw the truth as it is set into song by so many poets, proclaimed as the final wisdom by so many thinkers. The truth: that love is the ultimate and the highest goal to which Man can aspire. Then I grasped the meaning of the greatest secret that human poetry and human thought and belief have to impart: The salvation of Man is through love and in love. I understood how a man who has nothing left in this world still may know bliss, be it only for a brief moment, in the contemplation of his beloved. In a position of utter desolation, when Man cannot express himself in positive action, when his only achievement may consist in enduring his sufferings in the right way—an honorable way—in such a position Man can, through loving contemplation of the image he carries of his beloved, achieve fulfillment. For the first time in my life I was able to understand the meaning of the words, "The angels are lost in perpetual contemplation of an infinite glory."
>
> —Man's Search for Meaning

As Frankl pointed out, being in prison only meant that the body was no longer free. No prison could take away the freedom to choose how to handle suffering. It is always possible to find meaning in any traumatic event and, with that sense of meaning, to make plans for the future and to set new goals in life.

Following any trauma or hardship, ask yourself what it is that makes life worth living and what your hopes and dreams are for the future. Once you regain that sense of meaning and learn to trust your ability to achieve the new goals you set for yourself, you can truly move on to what comes next.

DSM-5 Criteria for PTSD Diagnosis

Criteria for PTSD in Adults, Adolescents, and Children over the Age of Six

The criteria provided here should **not** be used for self-diagnosis or diagnosing someone close to you. A formal diagnosis should only be carried out by a trained professional. These are only provided for your reference.

For adults, adolescents, or children over the age of six, a diagnosis of PTSD is given if the following occur:

A. Exposure to actual or threatened death, serious injury, or sexual violence in one or more of the following ways:

1. Directly experiencing the traumatic event.
2. Witnessing, in person, the event(s) as it occurred to others.
3. Learning that the traumatic event(s) occurred to a close family member or close friend. In cases of actual or threatened death of a family member or friend, the event(s) must have been violent or accidental.
4. Experiencing repeated or extreme exposure to aversive details of the traumatic event(s) (e.g., first responder collecting human remains; police officers repeatedly exposed to details of child abuse).

NOTE: This criterion does not apply to exposure through electronic media, television, or pictures unless the exposure is work-related.

B. Presence of one (or more) of the following intrusive symptoms associated with the traumatic event(s), beginning after the traumatic event(s) occurred:

1. Recurring, involuntary, and intrusive distressing memories of the traumatic event. For children older than six years, this can involve repetitive play featuring elements of the traumatic event(s).
2. Recurrent distressing dreams in which the content and/or effect of the dreams are related to the traumatic event(s). For children, these can be frightening dreams, which do not necessarily have any recognizable dream content.

3. Dissociative reactions (e.g., flashbacks) in which the individual feels or acts as if the traumatic event(s) were recurring. These reactions can vary from being relatively mild to extreme reactions in which the PTSD patient completely forgets his/her present surroundings. In children with PTSD, this re-enactment can occur while they are playing.
4. Intense or prolonged psychological distress at exposure to internal or external cues that symbolize or resemble an aspect of the traumatic event(s).
5. Marked physiological reactions to internal or external cues that symbolize or resemble an aspect of the traumatic event(s).

C. Persistent avoidance of stimuli associated with the traumatic event(s), beginning after the traumatic event(s) occurred or with one or both of the following:

1. Avoidance of or efforts to avoid distressing memories, thoughts, or feelings about or closely associated with the traumatic event(s).
2. Avoidance of or efforts to avoid external reminders (whether people, places, activities, objects, etc.) that arouse distressing memories, thoughts, or feelings about or closely associated with the traumatic event(s).

D. Negative alterations in cognitions and mood associated with the traumatic event(s), beginning or worsening after the traumatic event(s) occurred. This includes two or more of:

1. Being unable to remember an important aspect of the traumatic event(s) (usually due to dissociative amnesia rather than other factors such as head injury or drugs).
2. Persistent and exaggerated negative beliefs about others or him- or herself ("This world is bad," "Nobody can be trusted," etc.).
3. Persistent beliefs about the cause or consequences of the traumatic event(s) leading sufferers to blame themselves or others.
4. Persistent fear, horror, anger, guilt, or other strong emotion.
5. Feeling detached or estranged from others.

6. Persistent inability to feel positive emotions such as happiness, pleasure, or love.

E. Marked change in arousal or reactions related to the traumatic event(s) including two or more of:

1. Irritable behavior and angry outbursts (with little provocation) whether in the form of verbal or physical lashing out at people or objects.
2. Reckless or self-destructive behavior.
3. Hypervigilance (enhanced sensitivity to possible threats around them).
4. Exaggerated startle response.
5. Problems with concentration.
6. Disturbed sleep (either insomnia or restless sleep).

Along with these criteria, being diagnosed with PTSD requires a person to be experiencing symptoms for at least one month, and for the symptoms to be causing a significant disruption in the person's life (whether at work, at school, socially, or in another important area of that person's life). Also, the symptoms cannot be related to another medical condition or being under the influence of drugs or alcohol.

In diagnosing PTSD, mental health professionals also need to specify whether the PTSD is accompanied by persistent or recurring *dissociative symptoms* including:

1. **Depersonalization**—Persistent or recurring experiences of feeling detached from, and as if one were an outside observer of, one's mental processes or body (e.g., feeling as if one were in a dream; feeling a sense of unreality of self or body or of time moving slowly).
2. **Derealization**—Persistent or recurring experiences of unreality of surroundings (such as feeling as if the world around one feels unreal, dreamlike, distant, or distorted).

Since PTSD can often be linked to traumatic brain injury, substance use, depression, or other problems, isolating which symptoms are due to PTSD alone is something best left to trained professionals.

DSM-5 Diagnostic Criteria for PTSD in Children under the Age of Six

For children under the age of six, a diagnosis of PTSD is given if the following occur:

A. Exposure to actual or threatened death, serious injury, or sexual violence in one or more of the following ways:

1. Directly experiencing the traumatic event.
2. Witnessing, in person, the event(s) as it occurred to others, especially primary caregivers.
3. Learning that the traumatic event(s) occurred to a close family member or close friend. In cases of actual or threatened death of a family member or friend, the event(s) must have been violent or accidental.

Note: This criterion does not apply to exposure through electronic media, television, movies, or pictures.

B. Presence of one (or more) of the following intrusive symptoms associated with the traumatic event(s), beginning after the traumatic event(s) occurred:

1. Recurring, involuntary, and intrusive distressing memories of the traumatic event. For children younger than six years, this can involve repetitive play featuring elements of the traumatic event(s) and may not appear distressing to the child.
2. Recurrent distressing dreams in which the content and/or effort of the dream are related to the traumatic event(s). For children, these can be frightening dreams, which do not necessarily have any recognizable dream content.

3. Dissociative reactions (e.g., flashbacks) in which the individual feels or acts as if the traumatic event(s) were recurring. These reactions can vary from being relatively mild to extreme reactions in which the PTSD patient completely forgets his/her present surroundings. In children with PTSD, this re-enactment can occur while they are playing.
4. Intense or prolonged psychological distress at exposure to internal or external cues that symbolize or resemble an aspect of the traumatic event(s).
5. Marked physiological reactions to internal or external cues that symbolize or resemble an aspect of the traumatic event(s).

C. One or more of the following responses representing persistent avoidance of stimuli associated with the traumatic event(s), beginning after the traumatic event(s) occurred or with one or both of the following:

1. Avoidance of or efforts to avoid distressing memories, thoughts, or feelings about or closely associated with the traumatic event(s).
2. Avoidance of or efforts to avoid external reminders (whether people, places, activities, objects, etc.) that arouse distressing memories, thoughts, or feelings about or closely associated with the traumatic event(s).
3. Substantially increasing frequency of negative emotional states (e.g., fear, guilt, sadness, shame, confusion).
4. Markedly diminished interest or participation in significant activities, including constriction of play.
5. Socially withdrawn behavior.
6. Persistent reduction in expressing positive emotions.

D. Alterations in arousal associated with the traumatic event(s), beginning or worsening after the traumatic event(s) occurred. This includes two or more of:

1. Irritable behavior and angry outbursts (with little or no provocation) typically expressed as verbal or physical aggression toward people or objects (including extreme temper tantrums).
2. Hypervigilance.

3. Exaggerated startle response.
4. Problems with concentration.
5. Sleep disturbance (including disturbed or restless sleep).

E. The duration of the disturbance is more than one month.

F. The disturbance causes clinically significant distress or impairment in relationships with parents, siblings, peers, or other caregivers or with school behavior.

G. The disturbance is not attributable to the physiological effects of another medical condition. In diagnosing PTSD in children younger than six years, mental health professionals also need to specify whether the PTSD is accompanied by persistent or recurring *dissociative symptoms* including:

1. **Depersonalization**—Persistent or recurring experiences of feeling detached from, and as if one were an outside observer of, one's mental processes or body (e.g., feeling as if one were in a dream; feeling a sense of unreality of self or body or of time moving slowly).
2. **Derealization**—Persistent or recurring experiences of unreality of surroundings (such as feeling as if the world around one feels unreal, dreamlike, distant, or distorted).

PTSD in younger children can also be diagnosed as having *delayed expression* if the full range of diagnostic symptoms do not occur until at least six months after the traumatic event (though some symptoms may be immediate). Though children with behavior problems or other psychiatric conditions may show some PTSD symptoms, diagnosis should only be carried out by a trained professional.

APPENDIX B

PTSD Checklist (PCL)

The PCL is a standardized self-report rating scale for PTSD comprising seventeen items that correspond to the key symptoms of PTSD. Two versions of the PCL exist: (1) PCL-M is specific to PTSD caused by military experiences; and (2) PCL-C is applied generally to any traumatic event. The PCL can be easily modified to fit specific time frames or events. For example, instead of asking about "the past month," questions may ask about "the past week" or be modified to focus on events specific to a deployment.

How Is the PCL Completed?

The PCL is self-administered. Respondents indicate how much they have been bothered by a symptom over the past month using a 5-point (1–5) scale, choosing their responses. Responses range from 1, Not at All, to 5, Extremely.

Instructions

Following is a list of problems and complaints that people sometimes have in response to stressful experiences. Please read each one carefully. Circle the response that indicates how much you have been bothered by that problem in the past month.

1. Repeated, disturbing memories, thoughts, or images of a stressful experience?

   A. Not at all
   B. A little bit
   C. Moderately
   D. Quite a bit
   E. Extremely

2. Repeated, disturbing dreams of a stressful experience?

   A. Not at all
   B. A little bit
   C. Moderately
   D. Quite a bit
   E. Extremely

3. Suddenly acting or feeling as if a stressful experience were happening again (as if you were reliving it)?

   A. Not at all
   B. A little bit
   C. Moderately
   D. Quite a bit
   E. Extremely

4. Feeling very upset when something reminded you of a stressful experience?

   A. Not at all
   B. A little bit
   C. Moderately
   D. Quite a bit
   E. Extremely

5. Having physical reactions (e.g., heart pounding, trouble breathing, sweating) when something reminded you of a stressful experience?

   A. Not at all
   B. A little bit
   C. Moderately
   D. Quite a bit
   E. Extremely

6. Avoiding thinking about or talking about a stressful experience or avoiding having feelings related to it?

   A. Not at all
   B. A little bit
   C. Moderately
   D. Quite a bit
   E. Extremely

7. Avoiding activities or situations because they reminded you of a stressful experience?

   A. Not at all
   B. A little bit
   C. Moderately
   D. Quite a bit
   E. Extremely

8. Trouble remembering important parts of a stressful experience?

   A. Not at all
   B. A little bit
   C. Moderately
   D. Quite a bit
   E. Extremely

9. Loss of interest in activities that you used to enjoy?

   A. Not at all
   B. A little bit
   C. Moderately
   D. Quite a bit
   E. Extremely

10. Feeling distant or cut off from other people?

   A. Not at all
   B. A little bit
   C. Moderately
   D. Quite a bit
   E. Extremely

11. Feeling emotionally numb or being unable to have loving feelings for those close to you?

   A. Not at all
   B. A little bit
   C. Moderately
   D. Quite a bit
   E. Extremely

12. Feeling as if your future will somehow be cut short?

   A. Not at all
   B. A little bit
   C. Moderately
   D. Quite a bit
   E. Extremely

13. Trouble falling or staying asleep?

   A. Not at all
   B. A little bit
   C. Moderately
   D. Quite a bit
   E. Extremely

14. Feeling irritable or having angry outbursts?

   A. Not at all
   B. A little bit
   C. Moderately
   D. Quite a bit
   E. Extremely

15. Having difficulty concentrating?

    A. Not at all
    B. A little bit
    C. Moderately
    D. Quite a bit
    E. Extremely

16. Being "super-alert" or watchful or on guard?

    A. Not at all
    B. A little bit
    C. Moderately
    D. Quite a bit
    E. Extremely

17. Feeling jumpy or easily startled?

    A. Not at all
    B. A little bit
    C. Moderately
    D. Quite a bit
    E. Extremely

Note: Created by Weathers, Litz, Huska, and Keane (1994); National Center for PTSD–Behavioral Science Division. This is a government document in the public domain. Modified with permission from authors.

APPENDIX C

Useful PTSD Resources

General Mental Health Resources

- Mental Health America—Provides a nationwide referral service to support programs and treatment professionals across the United States. (*www.mentalhealthamerica.net*)
- Canadian Mental Health Association—Provides referrals to trauma support services and treatment professionals across Canada. (*www.cmha.ca*)
- SupportLine—Offers confidential help and treatment referrals to children, adolescents, and adults across the United Kingdom. (*www.patient.co.uk/support/supportline*)
- For other countries, contact the International Society for Traumatic Stress Studies for information on local support programs and treatment professionals. (*www.istss.org*)

PTSD Resources for Children and Adolescents

- National Child Traumatic Stress Network—Provides resources for traumatized children and adolescents as well as parents and caregivers. (*www.nctsn.org*)
- Child Trauma Toolkit for Educators—Teachers and staff can help reduce trauma in children following tragic events. (*www.nctsn.org/resources/audiences/school-personnel/trauma-toolkit*)

PTSD Resources for Victims of Crime

- National Center for Victims of Crime—Dedicated to helping victims of crime rebuild their lives. (*www.victimsofcrime.org*)

PTSD Resources for United States Veterans

- National Center for PTSD—The principal resource site operated by the Veterans Administration for veterans, their family members, and professionals looking for resources to deal with PTSD in veterans. Also includes resources for VA services and additional community resources. The site also includes links for finding a therapist in your local community. (*www.ptsd.va.gov/public/index.asp*)

- Courage to Care—Center for the Study of Traumatic Stress. One of the nation's oldest and most highly regarded, academic-based organizations dedicated to advancing trauma-informed knowledge, leadership, and research. Provides resources for military veterans, children and families, and people dealing with disaster issues. (*www.cstsonline.org*)
- Veterans and Military Crisis Line—Available anywhere in the United States at 1-800-273-8255 (Press 1). (*www.veteranscrisisline.net*)

PTSD Resources for Veterans in Other Countries

- Canada—The Operational Stress Injury Social Support (OSISS) is a joint-partnership program between the Department of National Defence and Veterans Affairs Canada. The program site offers a range of resources in both French and English. (*www.osiss.ca*)
- United Kingdom—Combat Stress works with veterans of British Armed Forces providing treatment services and support resources. (*www.combatstress.org.uk/veterans*)
- Australia—Veterans and Veterans Families Counseling Services (VVCS) provides treatment and support services for Australian veterans and their families. (*www.dva.gov.au/health_and_wellbeing/ health_programs/vvcs/Pages/index.aspx*)

PTSD Fact Sheets

- Finding a Therapist: *www.brainline.org/content/2008/07/ptsd-fact-sheet-finding-therapist.html*
- How Crime Victims React to Trauma: *http://victimsofcrime.org/help-for-crime-victims/get-help-bulletins-for-crime-victims/how-crime-victims-react-to-trauma*

APPENDIX D

Suggested Reading

Baranowsky, Anna, and Teresa Lauer. *What is PTSD? Three Steps to Healing Trauma.* Toronto: Traumatology Institute, 2012.

Frankl, Viktor. *Man's Search for Meaning.* New York: Pocket Books, 1963.

Kubany, Edward, Mari McCaig, and Janet Laconsay. *Healing the Trauma of Domestic Violence: A Workbook for Women.* Oakland: New Harbinger Publications, 2003.

Kushner, Harold. *When Bad Things Happen to Good People.* New York: Schocken Books, 1981.

Schiraldi, Glenn. *The Post-Traumatic Stress Disorder Sourcebook: A Guide to Healing, Recovery, and Growth,* 2nd ed. New York: McGraw-Hill, 2009.

Index

Acceptance and commitment therapy (ACT), 206

Acute post-traumatic interventions, 193–94

Acute stress disorder, 69, 76–77, 139, 151, 196

Adams, Douglas, 245

Adaptation, flexible, 240

Adaptation syndrome, 42–43, 138–39

Adolescents. *See also* Children
coping skills for, 107–8, 188–90
diagnosing, 276–79
with PTSD, 107–11
resilience in, 242, 248–50
self-harm in, 166
substance abuse in, 25
treatment for, 188–90

Adrenaline, 42–43

Adrenocorticotropic hormone (ACTH), 42–43

Afghanistan War, 11, 102–4, 120, 141

Aggression, 50, 106, 118–21, 149, 208, 212

Agoraphobia, 137

Alexithymia, 83. *See also* Emotional detachment

Allostatic load, 45–46, 138–39

Alzheimer's disease, 114, 139

Ambiguous loss, 119

American Journal of Psychiatry, 198

American Psychological Association, 180, 249

Amnesia, psychogenic, 64, 168, 261

Amnesia, traumatic, 82, 83

Andreasen, Nancy, 38

Anger issues, 62, 68, 120

Anger management therapy, 208–9, 219, 222, 271–72

Anxiety Association of America, 180

Anxiety attacks
breathing difficulties with, 171, 178–79, 225
in children, 109
conversion disorder and, 85
coping with, 225–27
heart attack and, 64, 78
medication for, 78, 196

Anxiety disorders, 77–78, 137

Attention-Deficit Hyperactivity Disorder (ADHD), 109

Auditory triggers, 232. *See also* Triggers

Back From The Living Dead, 266

Bank, Bert, 266

Baranowsky, Anna, 233

Battered spouse syndrome, 88

Beetle Bailey, 11

Betrayal trauma, 113

"Big Five" personality dimensions, 53–54

The Body Remembers, 132

Bonanno, George, 239

Boston Marathon bombings, 153–54

Bowlby, John, 122

Brain
child abuse and, 106–8
PTSD and, 41–57
stress and, 41–42
trauma and, 46–50
traumatic brain injury, 11, 31, 82–83, 113–15

Brewin, Chris, 46

Bullard, Kate, 251

Canadian Mental Health Association, 180

Cannon, Walter, 42, 76

Cardiac neurosis, 28

Cardiovascular disease, 140–41

Career stress, 252–53

Caring Letters Project (CLP), 215

Carmen, Elaine, 262

Catecholamines, 42, 47–48

Chemical dependence
beginning of, 134
chronic pain and, 143–44

medications and, 196–97, 259
understanding, 165–67
in veterans, 134, 143–44

Child abuse, 105–11

Children. *See also* Adolescents
abuse of, 105–11
coping skills for, 107–8, 188–90
counseling for, 195
diagnosing, 16, 276–81
emotional attachment for, 122
impact of PTSD on, 19, 29, 105–11
insomnia in, 105
nightmares in, 105, 107, 138, 173
nurturing, 122
positive attitudes in, 250–54
psychoeducation for, 188–90
psychological first aid for, 154
with PTSD, 16, 105–11, 173–74
resilience in, 242, 248–50
risk factors in, 110–11
separation anxiety in, 138
sexual abuse and, 105–6, 109, 111, 136, 173, 262
symptoms in, 16, 105–11, 173–74
treatment for, 188–90
vulnerability of, 19, 29

Chronic pain, 132–33, 139–44, 197–98

Civil War, 27, 30

Cognitive appraisal, 95

Cognitive-behavioral therapy (CBT), 186–87, 189, 199–202. *See also* Therapy options; Treatment

Cognitive processing therapy (CPT), 202

Cognitive restructuring (CR), 203

Cohen, Judith, 189

Combat fatigue, 34–36

Communication skills, 125, 128, 222, 272

Complex PTSD (C-PTSD), 70–71

Concentration camp syndrome, 36, 68, 92

Concerns, expressing, 167–73

Containment exercises, 234–35

Continuous traumatic stress (CTS), 71–72
Control, gaining, 269–71
Conversion disorder, 84–85
Coping
  in future, 273–74
  pragmatic coping, 239–40
  problems with, 21–22
  in relationships, 128–29, 163–74, 218–22
  strategies for, 96–97, 186–88, 192–93, 200, 224–30, 271–72
Cortisol levels, 43, 47–50, 55–57, 111
Counseling. *See also* Therapy options
  for children, 195
  finding counselors, 150–51, 180–83
  grief counseling, 194–95
  psychotherapy and, 192, 204–9
  trauma counseling, 150, 194–95
Couples therapy, 218–22. *See also* Therapy options
Crawford, Kermit, 154
Crimean War, 91
Crisis intervention, 193–94
Critical incident stress debriefing (CISM), 151–52
Cullberg, Johan, 147

Da Costa, Jacob Mendes, 28–29
Da Costa's Syndrome, 28–30
Dallaire, Romeo, 93–94
"Dead zone," 95
Debriefing sessions, 151–52
Defense Centers of Excellence (DCoE), 215
Defusing sessions, 151
Dehydroepiandrosterone (DHEA), 50, 55
Dementia, 114
Denial, dealing with, 63–64, 95, 168
Depersonalization, 68–69, 76, 96
Depression
  conversion disorder and, 85

diagnosing, 80
disasters and, 68
genetic traits and, 55
heart disease and, 140
immune system and, 139–40
learned helpless and, 68–69
negativity and, 61–62
treating, 80–81
Diagnostic and Statistical Manual of Mental Disorders (DSM-5), 13, 36, 275–81. *See also* DSM-5 criteria
Dialectical behavior therapy (DBT), 206–7
Disasters
  depression and, 68
  earthquakes, 38, 67, 71, 88, 90–91
  effects of, 17, 38, 51, 67–68, 88–89, 91, 108, 154, 257
  fires, 17, 18, 53–54
  floods, 17, 257
  hurricanes, 17, 38, 51, 88, 91, 97, 108, 154, 159–60, 241, 257
  psychological first aid for, 153–59
  PTSD and, 17, 38, 65–68
  responding to, 65–67
  school shootings, 97, 108
  surviving, 17
  tsunami, 17, 38, 51, 67, 88, 91, 123, 141
  types of, 88–90
  workplace shootings, 126
Dissociation, 95, 168, 260–61, 267
Dissociative identity disorder, 168, 261
DNA sequences, 55–56
Domestic violence
  battered spouse syndrome, 88
  help for, 179, 221
  impact of, 12, 99–100, 124–26
  learned helplessness and, 68
  resulting in death, 126
  victims of, 18–24, 68, 99–100, 212
Drug therapy. *See also* Medications
  anesthetic procedure, 197–98

anti-anxiety medications, 197
antidepressant medications, 197
antipsychotic drugs, 196–99
anxiety medications, 196–97
mood stabilizers, 197
options for, 195–99
DSM-5 criteria, 13–15, 76–77, 80–84, 102, 135, 177, 275–81
DSM-I, 36
DSM-II, 36
DSM-III, 36–37, 107–8
DSM-IV, 81, 108, 132

Earthquakes
  continuous threats of, 71
  depression and, 90
  effects of, 38, 67, 88, 91
Eisenhower, Dwight D., 35
EMDR, 203
Emergency workers, 125–27, 145–46, 152
Emotional detachment
  alexithymia, 83
  dissociation and, 95, 260–61
  in emergency workers, 127
  emotional numbing and, 95–96, 118–19, 123, 224
  resilience and, 247
  sexual intimacy and, 25
  trauma and, 118–23
Emotionally focused therapy (EFT), 219–20
Emotional numbing
  emotional detachment and, 95–96, 118–19, 123, 224
  expressing emotions and, 258–59
  in parents, 123
  PTSD and, 14, 63–64
  shock and, 148–49
  suicidal thoughts and, 224
  therapy for, 218
Emotional responses, 61, 65, 77, 83, 94–95, 190
Emotional withdrawal, 125, 164

Eternal Sunshine of the Spotless Mind, 229
Event centrality, 269
Evidence-based therapy, 199
Exercise programs, 171, 226
Exhaustion, 28–31, 43–45
Exposure therapy, 201
Eye movement desensitization and reprocessing (EMDR), 203–4

Faison, Forrest, 198
Family
    characteristics of, 213–14
    coping with PTSD, 217–18
    couples therapy, 218–22
    defusing stress in, 216–17
    disclosure within, 221
    interactions within, 221–22
    psychoeducation for, 221, 251
    PTSD and, 211–22
    resilience in, 250–52
    support network for, 214–16
    symptoms in, 212–13
    therapy options for, 218–22
Fight-or-flight response
    acute stress disorder and, 76–77
    norepinephrine and, 42, 46–50
    stress and, 42–48, 76–77, 106, 225
    triggers and, 232
Fires, 17–18, 53–54
First aid, 153–59
Flashbacks
    anger issues and, 120
    dealing with, 212–13, 227–28, 267
    insomnia and, 61
    intrusive memories and, 15–16, 46–48, 60–63, 165, 227–34, 267
    reducing, 60
    therapy options for, 156
    traumatic brain injury and, 83–84
    triggering, 60–63, 112, 119–22, 150, 217, 231–34
    of violent experiences, 212–13

vivid memories and, 46
Flexible adaptation, 240
Floods, 17, 257
Foa, Edna, 201
Folkman, Susan, 96
Fordyce, Michael, 270
Frankl, Viktor, 97, 240, 273–74
Freud, Sigmund, 34–35, 84, 186
Freyd, Jennifer, 113, 125
Fukushima Daiichi nuclear crisis, 38

Gamma-aminobutyric acid (GABA), 55
General adaptation syndrome, 42–43, 138–39
Genetic traits, 55–57
Gill, Susan, 95
Glass, Kerrie, 235
Goals, achieving, 183–84, 235–36, 270–71
Goals, setting, 243, 249–51, 273–74
Greenberg, Leslie, 219
Grief counseling, 194–95. *See also* Counseling
Grounding techniques, 165–66, 217, 227–28, 267
Group support, 184–87
Group therapy, 184–88, 192, 200. *See also* Therapy options
Guilt, 61, 68, 92, 118, 126
Gulf War, 38
Gurwitch, Robin, 250–51

Happiness, regaining, 269–71
Hartshorne, Henry, 28
Harvey, Allison, 142
Hayes, Stephen, 206
Healing rituals, 172
Health care costs, 132–33, 264
Health care needs, 18, 132, 199, 263–64
Heart attack, 64, 78
Heart disease, 140

Herman, Judith, 70
Hickey, Anita, 198
High-risk behaviors
    re-victimization, 24, 112
    self-harm, 21–24, 69, 109, 156, 166, 262
    substance abuse, 25–26, 69, 132–35, 143
    suicide, 22–23, 68, 166, 206, 238, 262
    transmission of trauma, 24–25
Hitler, Adolf, 34
Holocaust survivors, 24–25, 36, 92, 121, 240, 273–74
Hope, learning, 235–36, 274
Hurricanes
    children and, 108
    effects of, 17, 51, 88, 108, 154, 257
    preparedness for, 241
    support networks for, 159–60
Hypothalamic-pituitary-adrenal (HPA) axis, 43, 50, 57, 139
Hysteria, 31, 71, 83, 84

Identity disorder, 168, 261
Immune system, 45, 138–40
Infection resistance, 138–40
Insomnia
    in children, 105
    as distress response, 64–65, 149
    medication for, 196
    sleep apnea and, 63
    sleep hygiene for, 165, 167
    treatment for, 259–60
    triggering flashbacks, 61
International Centre for Excellence in Emotionally Focused Therapy (ICEEFT), 220
International Society for Traumatic Stress Studies, 180
International Statistical Classification of Diseases and Related Health Problems (ICD-10), 14–15, 83

Intervention, 165–66, 193–94
Intrusive memories. *See also*
  Memories
    in children, 108, 123
    flashbacks and, 15–16, 46–48,
      60–63, 165, 227–34, 267
    help with, 182
    in parents, 123
    "safe place" image for, 228–29,
      233
Intrusive thoughts
    in children, 108
    coping with, 230–31
    flashbacks and, 112, 227
    obsessive-compulsive disorder
      and, 78–79
Iraq War, 11, 102–4, 120, 141, 264
"Irritable heart syndrome," 28–30

Johnson, Sue, 219
Joseph I, King, 91
Journal of Psychiatry, 133
Journal of Traumatic Stress, 104
Joy, regaining, 269–71
Jung, Carl, 84

Kabat-Zinn, Jon, 207
Kahlo, Frida, 268
Kardiner, Abram, 34–35
Kaufman, Fritz, 32
"Kaufman Cure," 32
Kees, Michelle, 251
Kobassa, Suzanne, 239

Lazarus, Richard, 96
Learned helplessness, 68–69, 72,
  235
Levi, Primo, 92
Linehan, Marsha, 206
Lipov, Eugene, 198
Logotherapy, 273–74

MacKenzie, James, 30
Mancini, Anthony, 239
Man's Search for Meaning, 240,
  273–74
Martin-Baro, Ignacio, 72
McEwen, Bruce, 44–45, 138
Medications. *See also* Drug therapy
    anti-anxiety medications, 197
    antidepressant medications,
      48–50, 78, 197
    antipsychotic drugs, 196–99
    anxiety medications, 196–97
    mood stabilizers, 197
    opioids, 143
    pain relievers, 132, 143
Meditation, 207–8, 226, 230
Memories. *See also* Traumatic
  memories
    flashbacks and, 15–16, 46–48
    intrusive memories, 15–16,
      48, 60–63, 108, 123, 165, 182,
      227–34, 267
    of trauma, 45–46, 64, 168, 187–89,
      201–6, 228–35, 259–61, 267
    vivid memories, 46
Mental Health America, 180
Milligan, Spike, 93
Mindfulness-based cognitive
  therapy (MBCT), 205–7
Mindfulness-based stress
  reduction (MBSR), 205, 207
Mindfulness exercises, 205–7,
  229–31
Mindfulness explanation, 208
Mindfulness therapy, 205–7
Mitchell, Jeffrey, 151
Mood disorders, 133, 135–36
Motivation, 95–96
Multi-modality trauma treatment
  (MMTT), 188–89. *See also*
  Treatment
Munchausen syndrome, 132
Murphy, Audie, 92
Myers, Charles, 31
Myers, David, 270

National Center for Telehealth and
  Technology (T2), 215
Natural disasters, 17, 37–38. *See
  also* Disasters
Negative attitudes, 61–62, 264–65
Negative emotions
    coping with, 94, 220, 224, 231–32,
      267
    purpose of, 258
    toward mental health
      professionals, 264
    triggering, 205–6, 231–32
Neurasthenia, 31
Neuroticism, 53
New York Times, 37
Nightingale, Florence, 91–92
Nightmares
    causes of, 62–63
    in children, 105, 107, 138, 173
    dealing with, 267
    treatment for, 259–60
Norepinephrine, 42, 46–50, 55, 111
Nuclear crisis, 38
Numbing, 63–64, 258–59
Nutritional needs, 171, 226

Obsessive-compulsive disorder
  (OCD), 78–79
Oil-rig accident, 263
Olfactory triggers, 232. *See also*
  Triggers
Online resources, 160–61, 203,
  289–91
Opioids, 143
Optimism, 216, 240–41, 250–53,
  268–69

Pain relievers, 132, 143, 197–98
Panic attacks
    breathing difficulties with, 171,
      178–79, 225
    in children, 109
    conversion disorder and, 85
    coping with, 225–27

heart attack and, 64, 78
medication for, 78, 196
Parents. *See also* Children
authoritarian parents, 122
emotional numbing in, 123
intrusive memories in, 123
with PTSD, 20, 121–24
therapy options for, 218–22
trauma in, 123–24
Patton, George S., 35
Persistent depressive disorder
(PDD), 80
Personality dimensions, 53–54
Personality disorders, 81
Personal trauma, 99–100. *See also*
Trauma
Pessimism, 19–20, 25, 69, 107, 136,
264
Phobias, 77–78, 137
Positive attitudes
in children, 250–54
developing, 204, 220
encouraging, 250–54
expressing, 224, 258
retaining, 240–41
sharing, 169
Post-concussive syndrome, 83
Post-traumatic amnesia, 82
Post-traumatic growth (PTG),
247–48
Post-Traumatic Stress Disorder
(PTSD)
basics of, 13–26
behaviors of, 68–69
brain and, 41–57
checklist for, 283–88
in children, 16, 105–11, 173–74
complex PTSD, 70–71
continuous traumatic stress,
71–72
coping with, 10
counseling for, 150–51, 180–83,
194–95
definition of, 14–16
diagnosis of, 14–16, 164, 195,
275–81

differences in, 94–96
in everyday life, 248–54
facts about, 19–21
family and, 211–22
famous people with, 91–93
forms of, 22–26
help for, 12, 146–61, 177–80
history of, 27–39
impact of, 118–20, 132, 271–73
living life with, 267–71
in parents, 20, 121–24
predictors of, 52–54, 102, 133
prevalence of, 12, 17–19
prevention of, 19–20, 145–46
psychological first aid for,
153–59
recognition of, 36–37
relationships and, 117–29
research on, 37–38
resources for, 160–61, 203,
289–91
responding to, 19, 94–95
in special populations, 101–15,
121–24
stress debriefing, 151–52
symptoms of, 14–16, 60–73,
212–13
therapy options for, 191–209
traumatic events, 88–90
treatment for, 128, 142–43,
175–90
untreated PTSD, 12, 255–64
vulnerability to, 19–20, 51–54
Professional help, finding, 180–83
Professional relationships, 125–26.
See also Relationships
Psychiatric Annals, 198
Psychiatrists, finding, 180–83
Psychic numbing, 94, 95
Psychodynamic group therapy, 186.
See also Therapy options
Psychoeducation, 186, 188–90, 221,
251
Psychogenic amnesia, 64, 168, 261
Psychological capital (PsyCap),
253

Psychological first aid (PFA),
153–59, 193
Psychological hardiness, 239
Psychological resilience, 237–39.
See also Resilience
Psychological shock, 148–50. *See
also* Shock
Psychological withdrawal, 76
Psychologists, finding, 180–83
Psychology Today, 180
Psychoneuroimmunology, 138, 139
Psychotherapy, 192, 204–9. *See also*
Therapy options

REACH program, 222
Refugees, 98–99
Regehr, Cheryl, 126
Relationships
communication in, 125, 128, 222,
272
concerns about, 128–29
coping with, 128–29, 163–74
family relationships, 122–24,
211–22
professional relationships,
125–26
PTSD and, 117–29
romantic relationships, 127–28
social relationships, 124
Relaxation techniques
breathing exercises, 158
meditation, 207–8, 226, 230
mindfulness technique, 207–8
stress inoculation therapy, 200
trauma treatments, 188–90
Resilience
ability for, 239–46
aging and, 247, 253–54
benefits of, 239–43, 246–47
building, 242–46, 248–54
in children, 248–50
differences in, 239–42
emotional detachment and, 247
in everyday life, 248–54
experience with, 241–42

explanation of, 237–39
facing adversity, 243–46
in family, 250–52
learning, 242–46
maintaining, 254
predictors of, 239–40
psychological resilience, 237–39
research on, 238–39
self-confidence and, 238–40, 243, 247–50
in workplace, 252–53
Resilience Guide for Parents and Teachers, 249
Resources, 160–61, 203, 289–91
"Reversion under stress," 65, 69
Re-victimization, 24, 112. *See also* Victimization
Romantic relationships, 127–28. *See also* Relationships
Rosenheck, Robert, 121
Rothschild, Babette, 132

"Safe place" image, 228–29, 233, 250
Sandy Hook school shooting, 97
School shootings, 97, 108
Secombe, Harry, 93
Secondary gain, 166, 261, 268
Secondary trauma, 17, 25, 61, 98, 126–27, 212. *See also* Trauma
Secondary victimization, 20–21, 111–12. *See also* Victimization
Second-generation syndrome, 24–25, 121
Seeking Safety program, 189–90
Self-confidence
developing, 209, 267, 272–73
encouraging, 247–48, 250
regaining, 267, 272–73
resilience and, 238–40, 243, 247–50
Self-diagnosis concerns, 14, 75, 276
Self-harm, 21–24, 69, 109, 156, 166, 262
Self-medication concerns, 25–26, 134, 165, 177, 257–58

Self-medication hypothesis, 25–26
Self-talk statements, 272–73
Seligman, Martin, 68
Sellers, Peter, 93
Selye, Hans, 42, 138
Separation anxiety, 78, 138
Serotonin, 49–50
Service dogs, 205
Sexual abuse
children and, 105–6, 109, 111, 136, 173, 262
PTSD and, 12, 19–25, 100, 128
resilience and, 238
therapy for, 189, 207
Sexual problems, 25, 128
Shake Hands with the Devil, 93
Shalev, Arieh, 152
Shapiro, Francine, 203–4
Sharp, Timothy, 142
Shatan, Chaim, 37
Shell shock, 30–34, 113. *See also* Shock
Shephard, Ben, 32
Shock
coping with, 168, 193, 273
emotional numbing and, 148–49
psychological shock, 148–50
shell shock, 30–34, 113
state of, 148–51, 155–56, 168
Sleep disorders
insomnia, 61–65, 105, 149, 165, 167, 196, 259–60
medication for, 196
nightmares, 62–63, 105, 107, 173, 259–60, 267
sleep apnea, 260
treating, 196, 259–60
Sleep hygiene, 165, 167, 187, 260
Snyder, Charles R., 235
Social anxiety, 78
Social relationships, 124–26. *See also* Relationships
Social workers, finding, 180–83
"Soldier's heart," 28–30

Somatic triggers, 232. *See also* Triggers
Somatization, 65, 132, 232, 263
Spitzer, Robert, 37
Stanford cue-centered therapy (SCCT), 189. *See also* Treatment
"Startle response," 15, 51, 63, 173
Stellate ganglion block (SGB), 197–98
Stille, Alfred, 28
Stress. *See also* Post-Traumatic Stress Disorder
allostatic load and, 45–46, 138–39
controlling, 225–26
dealing with, 42–45
debriefing sessions for, 151–52
definition of, 14
defusing, 216–17
immune system and, 45, 138–40
impact of, 41–42
reduction of, 19–20, 152, 188, 207
reversion under, 65, 69
stages of, 42–45
in workplace, 126, 252–53
Stress debriefing, 151–52
"Stress hormone," 48
Stress inoculation therapy (SIT), 200
Stressor event types, 88–90
Structured approach therapy (SAT), 218–19
Substance abuse, 25–26, 69, 132–35, 143
Substance Abuse and Mental Health Services Administration (SAMHSA), 251
Suicide
risk of, 68, 166, 206, 238, 262
suicidal attempts, 206
suicidal thoughts, 80, 135, 191, 194, 216, 224
warning signs of, 23, 183
Support
from family/friends, 20, 124–27
group support, 184–87

providing, 124–27, 164–73
support networks, 20, 159–60,
214–16
Support and Family Education
(SAFE) Center, 212
Supportive group therapy, 185. *See
also* Therapy options
"Survivor guilt," 61, 68, 92, 118, 126
Symptoms
coping with, 224–30
in family, 212–13
handling, 223–36
of PTSD, 14–16, 60–73, 212–13
Systematic desensitization (SD),
201

"Talk" therapy, 192. *See also*
Psychotherapy
Tanielian, Terri, 103
Taste triggers, 232. *See also* Triggers
Teicher, Martin, 106
Television, 105–6, 232, 249
Temperament factors, 53–54
Terr, Lenore, 107
Terrorist attacks, 68, 104–6, 153–54,
172
Therapy options. *See also*
Treatment
acceptance and commitment
therapy, 206
acute post-traumatic
interventions, 193–94
anger management therapy,
208–9, 219, 222, 271–72
cognitive-behavioral therapy,
186-87, 189, 199–202
cognitive processing therapy,
202
cognitive restructuring, 203
counseling options, 150–51,
180-83, 194–95, 204–9
couples therapy, 218–22
dialectical behavior therapy,
206-7
drug therapy, 195–99

EMDR, 203–4
emotionally focused therapy,
219–20
evidence-based therapy, 199
exposure therapy, 201
family therapy, 218–22
group therapy, 184–88, 192, 200
mindfulness therapy, 205–7
psychotherapy, 192, 204–9
service dogs, 205
stress inoculation therapy, 200
structured approach therapy,
218–19
Thomson, Jane, 121
Trauma. *See also* Post-Traumatic
Stress Disorder
counseling for, 150–51, 180–83,
194–95
definition of, 14
effect on brain, 46–50
impact of, 118–20, 132
memories of, 45–46, 64, 168, 187–
89, 201–6, 228–35, 259–61, 267
in parents, 123–24
personal trauma, 99–100
processing, 149–50
reactions to, 65–68, 148–49
responding to, 19
secondary trauma, 17, 25, 61, 98,
126–27, 212
shock and, 148–50
stages of, 146–51
vulnerability to, 19–20, 51–54
wartime trauma, 98, 102–4
Trauma Affect Regulation: A
Guide for Education and
Therapy (TARGET), 190. *See also*
Treatment
Trauma-focused cognitive
behavioral therapy (TF-CBT), 189,
190. *See also* Treatment
Traumatic amnesia, 82, 83
Traumatic brain injury (TBI), 11, 31,
82–83, 113–15
Traumatic memories
blocking out, 261

dealing with, 168, 187–89, 228–
35, 267
emotional numbing and, 64
explanation of, 45–46
therapy for, 201–6
triggering, 232, 259–60
Traumatic stressor events, 88–90
"Traumatic symptomatology," 107
Treatment
basics of, 176
for children, 188–90
finding, 179–83
group therapy, 184–88, 192, 200
importance of, 177–79
information on, 180–83
lack of, 12, 21, 255–64
necessity of, 177–78
refusal of, 176–77
results of, 183–84
self-medication concerns,
257–58
therapy options, 191–209
Triage, 146–47, 150, 153, 157, 193
Triggers
confronting, 231–34
containment exercises for,
234–35
countering, 233–35
recognizing, 190, 231–34, 272
types of, 232–34
Tsunami, effects of, 17, 38, 51, 67, 88,
91, 123

VetChange, 203
Veterans
Caring Letters Project for, 215
depression in, 133, 135–36
isolation of, 60, 205, 215, 221–22,
252
with PTSD, 56, 102–4, 127–28,
133–36
substance abuse in, 132–35
treatment for, 128, 142–43
Veterans Treatment Courts (VTCs),
103

Victimization
    prior victimization, 19–20, 102
    re-victimization, 24, 112
    secondary victimization, 20–21,
        111–12
    sexual victimization, 112–13
Victim-to-patient process, 262–63
Video games, 60
Vietnam War, 36–38, 52, 102, 133
Vincent, Clovis, 32
Violence
    battered spouse syndrome, 88
    domestic violence, 12, 18–24, 68,
        99–100, 179, 212, 221
    exposure to, 105–6
    in families, 212, 221
    help for victims, 179
    predictors of, 120
    in social relationships, 124–26
    victims of, 111–16
Visual triggers, 232. *See also*
    Triggers

Walker, Mort, 11
War neurosis, 31, 34–36
*War of Nerves: Soldiers and
    Psychiatrists, 1914–1994*, 32·
Wartime trauma, 98, 102–4
Weekes, Claire, 225
Wiesel, Elie, 92
Withdrawal, 76, 125, 164
Wolpe, Joseph, 201
Workplace resilience, 252–53
Workplace shootings, 126
Workplace stress, 126, 252–53
World Health Organization, 11,
    38–39, 81, 255
World War I, 30–34
World War II, 30, 34–36, 68, 92–93,
    122

We Have
EVERYTHING®
on Anything!

The Everything® list spans a wide range of subjects, with more than 500 titles covering 25 different categories:

Business	History	Reference
Careers	Home Improvement	Religion
Children's Storybooks	Everything Kids	Self-Help
Computers	Languages	Sports & Fitness
Cooking	Music	Travel
Crafts and Hobbies	New Age	Wedding
Education/Schools	Parenting	Writing
Games and Puzzles	Personal Finance	
Health	Pets	